WIRR

Plea
last
re

The Real Falstaff

The Real Falstaff

Sir John Fastolf and The Hundred Years' War

Stephen Cooper

Sir John Fastolf was one whose memory ought to be vindicated from that
inimitable scoundrel character given him by Shakespeare.
John Anstis, Garter King of Arms, 1721

Pen & Sword
MILITARY

For my Grandfather, Arthur Cooper (1886–1918),
who lies in some corner of a Flanders field

First published in Great Britain in 2010 by
Pen & Sword Military
an imprint of
Pen & Sword Books Ltd
47 Church Street
Barnsley
South Yorkshire
S70 2AS

Copyright © Stephen Cooper, 2010

ISBN 978 1 84884 123 9

Printed and bound in the UK by
CPI UK

Pen & Sword Books Ltd incorporates the imprints of
Pen & Sword Aviation, Pen & Sword Maritime, Pen & Sword Military,
Wharncliffe Local History, Pen and Sword Select, Pen and Sword Military Classics,
Leo Cooper, Remember When, Seaforth Publishing and Frontline Publishing.

For a complete list of Pen & Sword titles please contact
PEN & SWORD BOOKS LIMITED
47 Church Street, Barnsley, South Yorkshire, S70 2AS, England
E-mail: enquiries@pen-and-sword.co.uk
Website: www.pen-and-sword.co.uk

Contents

List of Boxed Text

List of Maps and Illustrations

Maps

Plates

Glossary

achievements	a heraldic term for items on a coat of arms
apannage	hereditary landed estate, carved out of the French kingdom, for the benefit of a prince of the royal blood
appâtis	see *pâtis*
arbalest	a type of heavy crossbow
bailli	a French official
banneret	a knight entitled to carry a banner
bascinet	a type of helmet
bastard feudalism	a term coined in the nineteenth century, to describe late medieval society (supposedly characterized by the grant of money fiefs rather than grants of land)
bastille	a fortress (sometimes *bastide*)
bill	a long spear-like weapon
bombard	an artillery weapon of the largest size, below which were *veuglaires* or fowlers, serpentines and culverins
bourgeois	citizen of a town
brigandine	a padded jacket
carrack	multi-masted sailing ship first developed in the fifteenth century
chantry	a chapel where masses are sung for the souls of the dead
chevauchée	a mounted raid into enemy territory
coat armour	coat of arms
cog	a traditional type of ship, with a single mast and square-rigged sail
culverin	see bombard
entail	an estate in land, granted on the basis that it will descend to the males of the direct line
feoffees	trustees
fleur-de-lys	the lily flower, symbol of the Valois dynasty
fowler	see bombard
galain	whalebone
gens de trait	artillerymen (whether archers or cannoneers)
gorget	a piece of armour for the neck

guet et garde	the system of providing a watch in French towns: what would be known in England as 'watch and ward'
guisearme	a long curved weapon with a spear-like point
habergeon	a (sleeveless) coat of mail
Hanse	a late medieval league of German ports and towns
indenture	a kind of medieval document, often a contract
jurades	the municipal authorities in Bordeaux
lance	a small unit of men, whether mounted or infantry
mortmain	ownership in perpetuity by the Church
oyer and terminer	a judicial commission appointed to look into disorders in a particular locality in England
pâtis	a local agreement as to the amount of tribute payable to soldiers occupying the area
pays de conquête	that part of France, outside the Duchy of Normandy, which the English won by right of conquest after 1417
pipe	a quantity of wine, beer, cider etc.
poursuivant	a junior herald (who in theory progressed to being a full herald after seven years)
provost	an officer in charge of supplies or discipline
pyx	a box for keeping items required for the celebration of the Mass
regard	a bonus, payable in addition to basic rates of pay
rosary	a chain of beads for counting prayers
sallet	a type of helmet which replaced the bascinet
serpentine	see bombard
trebuchet	a siege-engine: essentially a large catapult
veuglaire	see bombard
white armour	a type of plate armour

Acknowledgements

I am very grateful to Rupert Harding for suggesting the idea of this book; to Maurice Keen and Tony Pollard for pointing the way forward, and particularly to Dr Anthony Smith for reading the text several times and making so many helpful comments. (It was his PhD thesis and subsequent articles which first explained the relationship between Fastolf's investments and East Anglian politics, and he was kind enough to discuss this and other matters Fastolfian with me.) I would also like to thank Dr Jeremy Catto for sending me a typescript of Basset's Chronicle; Bill Alexander for commenting on the first chapter; and Mlle Amélie Limoes for the conducted tour of Sillé-le-Guillaume in June 2009. Dr Tim Pestell, Curator of Archaeology at Norwich Castle Museum and Art Gallery, provided information about the Fastolf Sword. Dr Robin Darwall-Smith, Archivist at Magdalen College, Oxford, kindly allowed me to inspect the Fastolf Papers: my thanks also go to the President and Fellows of the College in that respect. I am grateful to the National Trust for allowing me to take photographs of Sir John's coat of arms in the Brown Drawing Room at Blickling Hall and to John Bradley for his comments. Madeleine Arnold Tetard helped me with the history of Meulan, Jean-Marie Levesque, *conservateur-en-chef* at the Museum of Caen, with the history of that city. Timothy Duke, Chester Herald at the College of Arms, supplied me with information about Fastolf's coat of arms. My friend Captain Graham Jeffs helped answer my questions about the geography of Normandy. Martin Kaufman, Roy Stephenson and John Clark of the Museum of London provided information relating to recent excavations at Southwark. Last, but by no means least, my wife Gaye was endlessly patient during visits to Fastolfian sites in England and France and made many invaluable suggestions as to style.

Stephen Cooper
Thorpe Hesley
September 2009

Introduction

There was no Hans Holbein or Anthony Van Dyck at the court of Henry V, Henry VI or the Duke of Bedford to paint the portraits of the men and women who frequented them; and there was no contemporary portrait of Sir John Fastolf of Caister (1380–1459) – indeed, there was not even a tomb effigy. The only print of him which was ever made is that in the National Portrait Gallery, but that dates from the 1790s and the artist, James Parker, did not even take the trouble to depict his coat of arms correctly. Yet, despite the absence of reliable portraiture, we know more about Fastolf than we do about most of his contemporaries. He wrote numerous memoranda relating to the war in France and dozens of letters to the Paston family, and his literary circle produced several books. He was the owner of a large territorial estate and had a propensity for litigation, so that there is a vast collection of accounts, deeds, pleadings and other documents, which now survive as the Fastolf Papers. There is no shortage of materials for a biography.

Surprisingly, no full-length treatment of Fastolf appears to have been published before, though there have been several short 'lives' and many learned articles about him. Where he has been written about, he has generally had a bad press, principally because of the way he is portrayed in Shakespeare's history plays, 130 years after his death. Shakespeare portrays him as a fat rogue and coward, following the Tudor historians Hall and Holinshed, who tell us how Fastolf 'fled the field' at the Battle of Patay in 1429, abandoning his comrades and, in particular, his fellow Garter Knight Sir John Talbot. This is not an account which stands up to scrutiny when one reads the eyewitness report of the Burgundian chronicler Jean de Waurin, but it is the version of events which was generally accepted in England, particularly because Talbot died a hero's death in the last great battle of the Hundred Years' War.

There were other sources which fed the black legend. Some of the correspondents in the Paston Letters give a highly unfavourable view of Fastolf's character. In particular Henry Windsor, who served Sir John for many years, wrote that his master was always 'cruel and vengible'. Windsor's comment was the source of many subsequent judgements, but this is very unfair, because he was only one of many servants, some of whom were clearly devoted to Fastolf. Likewise, the view taken by his stepson Stephen Scrope, that Fastolf was a cruel and heartless man who was prepared to sacrifice the boy on the altar of financial expediency, has to be set alongside an almost universal acceptance, at the time, of the benefits of wardship and of the practice of sending young boys away to complete their education.

Why was no biography written? Fastolf's secretary William Worcester did begin to write a life of his master, but it is thought that this was never completed, and what was written was subsequently lost. John Anstis, in his book on the Order of the Garter (1724), the editor of *Biographia Britannica* (1793), Dawson Turner (1842), Sir George Poulett Scrope (1852) and the Reverend Duthie (1907) all wrote *Lives*, and all took the view that Sir John was not the coward portrayed by Shakespeare; but these scholarly accounts were very short and did not have much effect on the popular imagination. K B McFarlane (1903–66), the great Oxford don who revolutionized the way in which we look at late medieval English history, thought that it was 'folly and even fraud' to attempt a biography of anyone who lived before 1500. I have chosen to ignore that advice. Whether I have been rash in so doing (and in relocating the Battle of Rouvray) remains to be seen.

Chapter 1

The Real Falstaff

Everyone has heard of Sir John Falstaff, but hardly anyone has heard of Sir John Fastolf of Southwark and Caister (1380–1459). Shakespeare's fat rogue was immediately popular with his Elizabethan audience when he appeared in *Henry IV* in 1597–8 and was resurrected in the farcical *Merry Wives of Windsor* of 1602. Though he was a fictional character, Falstaff quickly took on a life of his own and has remained a favourite with audiences, in addition to inspiring Verdi, Elgar, Vaughan Williams and Orson Welles. By contrast, Fastolf is known only to scholars of the Late Middle Ages. Yet Shakespeare wrote about both men.

Shakespeare's Fastolf

Shakespeare wrote for the stage, and at high speed. He was interested in telling a good story and creating great drama, less interested in getting his facts right. *Henry VI* was a dramatic counterblast to Marlowe's *Tamburlaine*, which celebrated overweening ambition, but it is full of anachronism. The rebel Jack Cade condemns printing, years before Caxton printed his first book in England, and the Duke of York refers to Machiavelli, years before the Italian was born. Shakespeare regularly telescopes many years into a single scene: Sir John Talbot is killed at the Battle of Castillon some twenty years before it was fought. Joan of Arc sweeps all before her in Normandy and Aquitaine, whereas she actually fought on the Loire, in Champagne and the Île de France.

    Almost everything about Shakespeare is controversial, not least the dating of his plays, but it seems to be generally agreed that he wrote all three parts of *Henry VI* some years before he wrote *Henry IV*, so that the former counts, paradoxically, as an early play. *Henry VI* was a commercial success, but the drama is crude. Sir John Talbot is shown as a paragon of English knighthood and he dies a heroic death; on the other hand, Sir John Fastolfe is the personification of evil. We are told early on that he has 'played the coward' at the Battle of Patay in 1429 and he is never given a chance to refute the allegation. Even before he appears on stage, a messenger announces:

> Here had the conquest fully been seal'd up,
> If Sir John Fastolfe had not play'd the coward.

He being in the vanward, placed behind
With purpose to relieve and follow them,
Cowardly fled, not having struck one stroke,
Hence grew the general wreck and massacre.

The story is taken up in a scene outside the walls of the city of Orléans, where Talbot inveighs against his rival:

But O! The treacherous Fastolfe wounds my heart:
Whom with my bare fists I would execute
If I now had him brought into my power.

This account of what happened at Patay, in the plains of the Beauce, has some foundation in history, though the chronology is wrong at several points; but, a few scenes later, Shakespeare presents a scene which has no evidential basis at all. Fastolfe appears outside Rouen and is approached by a captain, who asks him what he is doing:

CAPTAIN: Whither away, Sir John Fastolfe, in such haste?
FASTOLFE: Whither away! To save myself by flight:
          We are like to have the overthrow again.
CAPTAIN: What! will you fly, and leave Lord Talbot?
FASTOLFE: Ay. All the Talbots in the world, to save my life.
CAPTAIN: Cowardly knight! Ill fortune follow thee!

At the beginning of Act IV, when Henry VI is crowned King of France, Fastolfe appears again, and is immediately taken to task by Talbot. He is accused of having abandoned a fellow Garter Knight, of being unfit to be a member of the brotherhood. This is pure fiction, since Talbot was a prisoner at the time, but it is highly effective drama:

FASTOLFE: My gracious sovereign, as I rode from Calais,
    To haste unto your coronation,
    A letter was deliver'd to my hands,
    Writ to your grace from the Duke of Burgundy.
TALBOT: Shame to the Duke of Burgundy and thee!
    I vow'd, base knight, when I did meet thee next,
    To tear the garter from thy craven's leg,
    [Plucking the garter off Fastolfe's leg]
    Which I have done, because unworthily
    Thou wast installed in that high degree.
    Pardon me, princely Henry, and the rest

This dastard, at the battle of Patay,
When but in all I was six thousand strong
And that the French were almost ten to one,
Before we met or that a stroke was given,
Like to a trusty squire did run away.

Shakespeare based his history plays on the chronicles of Edward Hall and Raphael Holinshed. Hall gives Fastolf credit for being the Duke of Exeter's lieutenant at Harfleur in 1415–16, for capturing Passy-en-Valois in 1424 and for being the Regent's deputy; but, like Holinshed, his account of what happened at Patay was a travesty of the truth, and very damaging to Fastolf's posthumous reputation:

From this battle departed without any stroke stricken Sir John Fastole [sic], the same year for his valiantness elected into the Order of the Garter. But for doubt of misdealing at this brunt the Duke of Bedford took from him the image of St George, and his garter, though afterwards by means of friends, and apparent causes of good excuse, the same were to him again delivered, against the mind of the lord Talbot.

Though it was a crude and inaccurate summary, the account given by the early Tudor historians was adopted wholesale by Shakespeare, but it is fair to say that he had good reason for doing so. Whereas Fastolf had been a member of the gentry and had died without issue, Talbot had been a nobleman and had founded a powerful dynasty. He left a son who succeeded him as Earl of Shrewsbury, and the earldom descended to Gilbert Talbot, the 7th Earl (1562–1616), who was a contemporary of Shakespeare's. Gilbert Talbot was a highly influential figure at the court of Queen Elizabeth and the playwright could not afford to offend him. Moreover, Talbot was still popular with the audience. Another Elizabethan wordsmith wrote enthusiastically about the commercial success of Shakespeare's *Henry VI*: 'How it would have joyed brave Talbot to think that after he had lain two hundred years in his Tomb, he should triumph again on the stage.' There is little doubt that Talbot's triumph was Fastolf's nemesis.

Shakespeare's Falstaff

In the original version of *Henry IV*, the character who became Falstaff was called Sir John Oldcastle (*c*.1378–1417). In his day, this man was one of the 'Lollard knights', a rebel who plotted against his old friend Henry V and was eventually executed for heresy. Yet, from the earliest days of the English Reformation, Oldcastle's reputation was transformed. Instead of being regarded as a traitor and a heretic, he became one of the heroes of Protestantism. John Foxe devoted eighty pages to him in his bestselling *Book of Martyrs*. Shakespeare's portrayal of him as a fat rogue therefore attracted a good deal of criticism from the staunchly Protestant audience, and not least from Oldcastle's descendant, William Brook, 7th Lord Cobham. As a result, the playwright changed the name of his fat knight to 'Falstaff'.

Falstaff was immediately popular with audiences. Accordingly, at the end of *Henry IV*, we are promised more of him, though we are also reminded that the character was only loosely based on Oldcastle in the first place:

> Our humble author will continue the story, with Sir John in it … Falstaff shall die of a sweat, unless already be a' killed with your hard opinions, Oldcastle died a martyr and *this is not the man*. (My italics)

Why did Shakespeare substitute 'Falstaff', rather than any other name? The link with the historical Fastolf must always be controversial, since the latter had already appeared in *Henry VI*. Moreover, Sir John Fastolf was clearly not the only source for the character, which is a mix of human characteristics and dramatic convention: the drunkard, the braggart soldier (of Roman and Renaissance comedy), the Lord of Misrule of medieval morality plays. The fact remains that, faced with the objections of Lord Cobham, Shakespeare had to come up with a new name, and the name he chose was a variant of Fastolf. It should not surprise us that he altered 'Fastolf' to 'Falstaff'. The Elizabethans were relaxed about spelling and Shakespeare also changed 'Hamnet' (the name of his son) to 'Hamlet'.

This is not accepted by everyone. Some say that 'Falstaff' – or 'false-staff' is a play on Shakespeare's own name. Yet it seems unlikely that the name was merely invented, when the playwright was already aware of Fastolf's existence and both versions of it can be shown to have been used by the same family. Studies of the rare Shakespearean manuscripts which pre-date the First Folio of the 1620s show that, when he made the alteration, Shakespeare sometimes used the abbreviated prefix 'Fast' rather than 'Falst' or 'Fal'. Moreover, we find many variants in fifteenth-century documents: Fastolf and Fastolfe, Falstoff and Falstolfe. Everything points to its being the same name, though the spelling varied wildly. As to pronunciation, we can never be sure of this, but late fifteenth-century court records refer to property in Norwich which was called 'Fastolf's, late of Sir John Fastolf or Forstaff'.[1]

The similarity between the historical Fastolf and the Shakespearean Falstaff does not end with the name: they were clearly different men, but they had much in common. They were both captains in the king's wars, much involved in recruiting and mustering soldiers, including drunken soldiers. They were both associated with a Boar's Head tavern (though Falstaff's was at Eastcheap, Fastolf's in Southwark). They may both have been pages to Thomas Mowbray, Earl (and later Duke) of Norfolk. Each man used forceful and colourful language (Fastolf in writing, Falstaff in speech); and each attracted devoted servants. Most importantly in terms of reputation, Shakespeare portrays both men as cowards. We shall see that, in the case of Fastolf, this was most unjust; but Falstaff does not for a moment hide his cowardice. On the contrary, in *Henry IV* he makes a famous speech, criticizing honour:

> What is that word honour? Air. A trim reckoning! Who hath it? He that died o' Wednesday. Doth he feel it? No. Doth he hear it? No. Is it insensible then? Yea, to the dead ... Therefore I'll none of it. Honour is a mere scutcheon; and so ends my catechism.

A little later comes the line which no speaker of the English language is likely to be ignorant of:

> The better part of valour is discretion ...

Falstaff dies at the beginning of *Henry V*, but he had already taken on a life of his own, and Shakespeare brought him back in *The Merry Wives of Windsor*, a farce in which he has a central role. This is knockabout comedy and the fat knight is a figure of fun who at one point appears in disguise, at another in women's clothing. Nothing remains of the historical Fastolf; and indeed the play is entirely set in the late sixteenth century, not in the fifteenth at all. The New World has now been discovered and the characters talk about the riches of Guiana, and potatoes.

For more than two and a half centuries after Shakespeare lived and died, it was always assumed that the character of Falstaff was based on Sir John Fastolf. In his best-selling *Worthies of England*, Thomas Fuller (1608–61) even affected to be angry with the playwright, for making the knight into a 'Thrasonical Puff and emblem of mock valour'. In 1789 the antiquarian Drake regretted that Fastolf had become 'an object of national contempt and detestation'.[2] In the mid-nineteenth century Sir George Poulett Scrope (a descendant of Fastolf's wife) shared the same assumption. However, by 1907 the link had become controversial, so that the Rector of Caister in Norfolk felt moved to write a tract in support of the traditional view, entitled *The Case of Sir John Fastolf*. Nowadays, the debate is much less heated. Most students of the subject, while recognizing the link with Oldcastle, also accept a link between Fastolf of Caister and Falstaff of Eastcheap, though no one would nowadays argue that the characters were identical.

It is time to return to the real Fastolf, while acknowledging the difficulty of setting the record straight. Shakespeare damned Fastolf in *Henry VI* and double-damned him when he created the character of Falstaff. Whatever doubts there may be in the minds of scholars, the public will always associate both men with cowardice, however unjust that may be to Fastolf. When Anstis was searching for material relating to past Knights of the Garter in 1721, he wrote to Sir Hans Soane to ask for the loan of some documents:

> You will very much oblige me by the loan of the *Phisicall Collections* in
> manuscript of William Wyrcester alias Botaner, for I suppose he may
> mention somewhat of his patron Sir John Fastolf ... the Knights of the
> Garter having enjoined me to lay before them some notices of the lives of
> their predecessors (whereof Sir John Fastolf was one whose memory ought
> to be vindicated from that inimitable scoundrell character given him by
> Shakespeare).

It is very doubtful if Anstis's own attempt to vindicate Fastolf was successful,
even with a select readership like the current Knights of the Garter. As the travel
writer Turner wrote a hundred years later: 'Not one individual troubles himself
about history, whilst a thousand read the drama, and the stains which
Shakespeare's pen has affixed to the name of Fastolf are of a nature never to be
taken away.'[3]

Yet it is surely worth trying to rescue Fastolf. The real person was a man who
had more in common with the 'perfect gentle knight' of Chaucer and the chivalric
ideals of Froissart's *Chronicles* than with the cowardly rogue who still treads the
boards. He was a soldier and a Christian (albeit of the medieval variety) and he
lived a long life, packed with extraordinary events and adventures. There are
numerous traces of him still to be found, in Norfolk and in Wiltshire, in Oxford
and in London, in Paris, Maine and Normandy and all along the central section of
the River Loire.

Chapter 2

Early Travels and Campaigns, 1380–1413

Jerusalem

Fastolf was born around 1380 at Caister Hall in Norfolk, a house he later rebuilt on the grand scale. Nearby Great Yarmouth was a thriving port and East Anglia the most prosperous region in England, with a long and deep connection with the North Sea. The surname Fastolf is thought to be of Viking origin and there is a tomb in the Church of St Nicholas in Yarmouth which commemorates another John Fastolf, who was a mariner. The maritime connection was to remain important to Fastolf all his life: when he wanted a house in London in the 1440s, he bought land next to the Thames in Southwark. He owned two wharves there, as well as a barge-house at Caister Castle.

Between 1280 and 1391 ten Fastolfs served as bailiffs of Yarmouth, and various of them were Members of Parliament for the area. There was a Hugh Fastolf who transported the expedition of Sir Robert Knolles to France before the *chevauchée* of 1370, as well as shipping a quarter of all the sacks of wool exported from Yarmouth that year. The Fastolfs invested the profits of trade in land, as well as benefiting from the lucrative business of holding office, and became members of the rising gentry. Fastolf's father married the daughter of a local landowner and was squire to the Earl of Warwick, before entering the royal household. There is no reason why our John Fastolf should have lacked an appropriate education.

John Fastolf was a 'man of single allegiance'. He served the Lancastrian dynasty from the moment it took power in 1399, and he remained loyal to it throughout the reigns of Henry IV (1399–1413), Henry V (1413–22) and Henry VI (1422–61), holding high office under the Regent, John, Duke of Bedford (1422–35). He fought for the Lancastrians in Ireland and France, though never in Wales or Scotland. Although he sympathized with the demands made by Richard, Duke of York in the 1450s, he died before York claimed the throne in 1460, and he never became a 'Yorkist'. He was an old man by the time the first battle of the 'Wars of the Roses' was fought in 1455 and his interest in the conflict was limited.

The most surprising episode in Fastolf's youth took place when he travelled to Königsberg in Prussia (now Kaliningrad in Russia), then overland to Venice and finally by sea to Jaffa and Jerusalem, between September 1392 and June 1393. The expedition was led by Henry Bolingbroke (later Henry IV). It was fitted out in King's Lynn in Norfolk, where it took on stores and where three ships were hired. One of the Norfolk men who accompanied Bolingbroke was Sir Thomas Erpingham, who became Steward of the King's Household in 1404, fought along with his son at Agincourt eleven years later and appears prominently in Shakespeare's *Henry V*; but Fastolf probably went as a page attached to the retinue of the Earl of Norfolk (Shakespeare's Mowbray).

The journey to Jerusalem started as a crusade but ended as a pilgrimage. Bolingbroke set out with the intention of joining the Teutonic Knights in one of their regular expeditions against the heathen, but diverted to the Holy Land when the Knights unexpectedly made peace with the Lithuanians. Pilgrimages like this were not uncommon. Mowbray himself made a similar journey in 1399, the Earl of Warwick in 1408. In very different circumstances the mystic Margery Kempe was a pilgrim in 1414, as was Cardinal Henry Beaufort in 1418–19, while the Lollard knight John Cheyne spent several years in the Middle East. Nevertheless, Fastolf was doing something quite extraordinary when he participated in an abortive crusade and then travelled on to Jerusalem in the company of a future king, at the age of twelve or thirteen.

This remarkable journey has been largely overlooked, because the evidence for it lay hidden in court records in France, which were only printed in England in 1982, but we have Fastolf's own testimony, given in 1435, in the course of proceedings in Paris (Overton v Fastolf). Fastolf was by now a knight, and Grand Master of the Regent's household, but he was still required to prove his credibility. To do so, he rehearsed the main events of his career, claiming that 'from his earliest years he had applied himself in the service of the king and in arms, in the countries of England and of Ireland and on the journey to Jerusalem' ('dès son jeune âge [il] s'est appliqué au service du roy et en armes en pais d'Angleterre et Yrlande et en voyage de Jherusalem [sic]').

Did he make this up? Is it possible that he was augmenting his curriculum vitae, to compensate for the fact that he had not been there when the great Battle of Agincourt was fought in 1415, and had been accused of cowardice at Patay fourteen years later? It is such an extraordinary story, and there seems to be nothing, either in the records of the journey itself or in those relating to the Mowbray affinity, to corroborate it:

> Old men forget; yet all shall be forgot,
> But he'll remember, with advantages
> What feats he did that day. (*Henry V*, Act IV, scene iii)

However, by 1435 Fastolf had nothing to apologize for. He had an excellent war record (notably during the two sieges of Harfleur in 1415–16 and at the Battle of

Verneuil in 1424) and the best of reasons for missing Agincourt. Moreover, the story of his journey to Jerusalem fits precisely the known facts about Bolingbroke's pilgrimage of 1393.

Bolingbroke's household accounts, which were published in 1894, show that he travelled with a sizeable company (about 300 when he set off for Prussia, though the number reduced to forty or fifty on the final part of the journey to the Holy Land). Fastolf's name does not appear individually in the surviving pay-lists, but this does not disprove his story, since it was only those who were in Henry's own 'chamber' whose names were recorded, and there were many 'supernumeraries' who remained anonymous. Young Fastolf would have been a very junior member of the expedition indeed, perhaps in Mowbray's household, and would not have merited a mention. Mowbray Herald was certainly present – he was paid at regular intervals for producing 'tables', displaying the coats of arms of the most distinguished knights and men-at-arms who were present.

We should therefore give Fastolf the benefit of the doubt. It is very likely that the claim to have visited Jerusalem in his youth was true. Perhaps the most surprising thing is that he did not boast more often of his great adventure, and the sights he had seen along the way. Christopher Tyerman has suggested that his 'voyage' may have been no more than a journey to the Levant, undertaken in the company of the French hero Marshal Boucicault, who is known to have gone to the East in 1403, but stopped short of the Holy Land. However, this seems most unlikely. Apart from anything else, Fastolf was probably in Ireland in 1403, and he was perfectly capable of distinguishing the Levant from Jerusalem. The most telling point is that the claim to have visited the Holy City was not made in the course of telling some traveller's tale, in the manner of Sir John Mandeville, but in the context of the court-room, where Fastolf's opponent had every reason for wanting to discredit him and could have disproved what he said, if it had been manifestly untrue.[1]

Ireland

We have no idea of Fastolf's whereabouts during the Revolution of 1399, when Henry Bolingbroke seized the Crown from Richard II. At the same time, it would not have been surprising if he welcomed the advent of Henry IV and even fought for him, in what little fighting there was. Unlike the man he overthrew, Henry IV was popular with the military class, being a Crusader as well as an internationally famous jouster.

The great feats of arms performed by the English during the first phase of the Hundred Years' War between 1337 and 1360 were a thing of the past by 1400, though they were still widely celebrated by the chronicler Jean Froissart and other writers. Yet England and France were still at war. The French never recognized Henry IV as a legitimate sovereign and they were more than ready to fish in troubled waters. They sent armed assistance to the Scots in 1402; they attacked the march of Calais in 1404–6; they encouraged acts of piracy against English shipping; and they recognized the rebel Owen Glendower as Prince of Wales. In 1406 they besieged the town of Bourg near Bordeaux, in English Aquitaine. For his part, Henry IV was too weak to embark on foreign adventures, but he never renounced his predecessors' claims to the Crown of France. He also had an inheritance to defend in Ireland.

Ireland was a school of hard knocks. Overrun by Anglo–Norman barons in the twelfth century, it had never been entirely conquered and Gaelic culture was now resurgent. In the 1390s Froissart described it as a place where the fighting was more difficult than in France. There were several reasons for this. Firstly, the Gaelic annalists portray a society that was continually at war with itself. The English are not even central to the action: when they do appear, they are referred to, almost in passing, as 'the Foreigners'; and the main stories revolve around the endless feuds between the Gaelic clans. Secondly, Ireland was a poor country and the English could not live off the land and take the profits of war, as they could in France. Their strategy had to be defensive, especially given the resistance they constantly encountered. Paradoxically, it was the un-warlike Richard II who had led two major expeditions to Ireland: neither Henry IV nor Henry V ever crossed the Irish Sea. Nor did they attempt to conquer Ireland, or expand the 'pale' of English settlement centred on Dublin.

Henry IV had four sons, Henry of Monmouth, who was Shakespeare's Prince Hal and later Henry V, Thomas of Lancaster (later Duke of Clarence), John (also of Lancaster, later Duke of Bedford) and Humphrey (also of Lancaster, later Duke of Gloucester); and all four were soldiers. In the first decade of the fifteenth century, Henry of Monmouth fought the Welsh, while John of Lancaster spent much of his time on the Scottish Borders. It was Thomas who was sent to Ireland at the age of fourteen, and it was here that Fastolf first saw action. It is impossible to pinpoint his movements there, because most of the contents of the Public Record Office of Ireland were destroyed by the IRA in 1922. Moreover, Fastolf is not referred to by name in the Anglo-Irish Annals, or in their Gaelic equivalent. Nevertheless, we know that he served there for several years, fighting to defend the Pale around Dublin. He was in his early twenties and not yet a knight: Fastolf's secretary William Worcester wrote that he was 'at that time [still] an esquire' ('ad tunc armiger'). His commanding officer was Sir Stephen Scrope, son of Richard Scrope, 1st Lord Bolton, who had built Castle Bolton in Wensleydale, and sailed for Ireland in 1401.[2]

Fastolf served Prince Thomas for fourteen years between 1401 and 1415, but he was not with him continuously. In fact, he probably travelled between England and Ireland at regular intervals, as his commanders did. In the Annals traditionally attributed to William Worcester, there is a memorandum that the Prince was made lieutenant for the whole of Ireland in 1401 and again in 1405–6; and that John Fastolf Esquire was with him in Ireland throughout that time, which implies that the two men were not always together at other times. As for Scrope, he had other responsibilities. He owned land in several counties of England and was warden of the castle of Roxburgh, which was an English enclave in the south of Scotland. There is an intriguing entry concerning Scrope's movements in the Patent Rolls in October 1404, which may also indicate a route which Fastolf took on his early travels:

> Commission ... to take ships, barges, ballingers and other vessels in the port of Chester and Liverpole [sic] and masters and mariners for them for the passage to Ireland of Stephen Lescrope, deputy of the king's son Thomas of Lancaster, lieutenant in Ireland, and his men and servants with 300 horses in his company.[3]

Ireland was not Scrope's only concern, but he was not unsuccessful there, from the military point of view. The Anglo-Irish annals portray him as an English Joshua, and even the Gaelic Annals of Loch Cé record 'a great victory by the Foreigners and by Scrope' under 1407. This took place when Walter Burke and the O'Carroll of Ely raided County Kilkenny and Scrope routed them near Callan. The Irish writer tells us that Taig O'Carroll and 800 others were killed, Taig being highly thought of by the Gaels as 'general protector to the poets of Ireland and Scotland'.

Nonetheless, English rule in Ireland was in deep trouble during these years. In the 1420s the governments in Dublin and London were to receive numerous complaints of rapine, arson, destruction and devastation, committed by the Gaels across a swathe of territory in and around the Pale, while the Anglo-Irish were causing difficulties of their own. The result was a statute, enacted in the Irish Parliament of 1429. This provided that a grant of £10 be paid to every man in the Pale who wished to build a castle within ten years. The minimum requirement was that these should be 20 feet by 16 feet and 40 feet in height, and the archaeological evidence shows that literally hundreds of tower-houses were built. The army of which Fastolf was a member cannot have achieved very much in the way of pacification, if the government found it necessary to encourage the building of castles on this scale immediately afterwards.[4]

What did Fastolf learn in Ireland? The Lancastrian kings aimed to hold down the resurgent Gaels, militarily and with apartheid-style legislation, to make the English colonists obey the legislation which prohibited absenteeism and, as the opportunity allowed, to bring over more settlers from England. All these policies were to be tried in the territories which Henry V and his brother Bedford later conquered from the Valois kings in France.

Unpleasant as they sound to us, it was Fastolf's job to help his masters implement them. From 1435, the English were to find themselves on the defensive in France too, as they had long been in Ireland; and the problems faced by the armies of occupation in Ireland and in France were in many ways not dissimilar. The settlers in Normandy and Maine, like the English in Ireland, proved unable to protect themselves by their own efforts alone. English garrisons became a necessary part of the solution, but they were also part of the problem. In each country, the occupying forces needed repeated injections of men and money, which the government was unwilling to provide indefinitely.

Fastolf served with many other Englishmen in Ireland. It was there that he met Philip Branch, later a member of his retinue in France; but by far the most important person he met there was his wife, Millicent. Under 1408 the Gaelic Annals of Loch Cé recorded the death of the deputy-lieutenant of Ireland, Sir Stephen Scrope:

> Thomas, son of the king of the Saxons [Clarence], came to Erinn [Ireland] in this year, and the Earl of Cill-dara [Kildare] was taken prisoner by him. A hosting by the king's son afterwards into Laighen; and Hitsin Tuit was slain on this hosting; and that was a great loss. There was a great plague in Meath this year and Scrope, a very valiant knight, and deputy to the king of the Saxons in Erinn, died of this plague.

Only a few months later, on 13 January 1409, John Fastolf married Millicent Scrope, widow of Sir Stephen, a marriage which brought him great wealth and prestige.[5]

Aquitaine

The Duchy of Aquitaine had been joined to the kingdom of England when Henry Plantagenet had married Eleanor of Aquitaine and become Henry II of England (1154–89), as well as Duke of Aquitaine. By the Treaty of Brétigny of 1360, Edward III had secured a large principality there, which his son the Black Prince ruled over for a few years. By 1399 the area subject to the English Crown had been reduced to a shadow of its former self, consisting of little more than Bordeaux, the inland wine-growing area, and a coastal strip running down to Bayonne. Nevertheless, the province was very important to the English: Bordeaux was almost as big as London, and Bordeaux and Bayonne were each significant ports. The Gascons were different from their neighbours in language and customs; they still recognized the English king as their duke, and this loyalty was transferred to the new Lancastrian dynasty.

Edward III had intervened in various parts of France, and on various pretexts, but the new factor, working in England's favour in the early fifteenth century, was the long insanity of Charles VI (1380–1422). In 1407 the retainers of John the Fearless, Duke of Burgundy murdered the King's younger brother, Louis of Orléans, and this turned a struggle for power into full civil war. The two sides were known as 'Burgundians' and 'Orleanists' (though the latter became better known as 'Armagnacs'). Since the Burgundian ducal house came to control a large block of territories in north-eastern France and the Low Countries, as well as in Burgundy

Castle Combe and Oxenton

As a result of his marriage to Millicent Scrope, Fastolf acquired a controlling interest in the Tiptoft and Scrope manors. His wife conveyed all her property to him during his lifetime and, as a result, he enjoyed the profits of Castle Combe between 1409 and 1459. William Worcester noted that there were 'two towns, one called Over Combe, in which reside the yeomen, who are occupied in the culture and working of the land which lies upon the hill, and the other called Nether Combe, in which dwell the men who use to make cloth'.

Fastolf regularly purchased quantities of the Castle Combe cloth for his soldiers in France, dressing them in a kind of uniform, and his investment transformed the manor back home. Worcester took great pride in this. In the late 1470s he recorded that some fifty houses had been built, rebuilt or repaired, together with two mills. There are several stone cottages by the Bybrook even today, said to have belonged to the weavers, and the names of two of the streets Worcester referred to are still in use: West Street and 'middle Market' ('medio mercato'). The timbered building known as the Court House is a reminder of a time when Sir John's word was law here.

Oxenton in Gloucestershire is more than forty miles from Castle Combe. Yet, in the Late Middle Ages, the two places were closely linked. Both were part of the Tiptoft inheritance which came to Fastolf as a result of his marriage in 1409. In March 1456 William Worcester wrote as follows to the men of Oxenton:

I have reminded [Fastolf] to give a chasuble [vestment] to your church … and trust for certain you shall have one … you, Thomas Watts … send to Castle Combe 12 good lampreys powdered at the price of 20d the piece. And they of Castle Combe shall send them to London. And forget not a couple of good lampreys for my labour in recovering the £7 that you had almost lost of my lord's money – for you know well the bailiff had spend it away; and let my lampreys come with the other lampreys. And if the propters [sic] of your church send me no lampreys for me and my fellows, ye shall the better think upon your vestment.

itself, the conflict affected large parts of France. In principle the Burgundians and the Armagnacs were equally hostile to England, but in practice they allied with her when it suited them. The English repeatedly fished in the troubled waters of French politics, while professing neutrality.

In 1411, Prince Henry formed an alliance with the Burgundians, and Thomas, Earl of Arundel, was sent to France with an expeditionary force, which entered

Paris with the Duke of Burgundy's army. By the following year there was a diplomatic volte-face. The Armagnacs promised to recognize Henry IV's claim to the Duchy of Aquitaine in return for support against Burgundy. Prince Thomas, now created Duke of Clarence, agreed to lead an expedition to France, at the head of 500 men-at-arms and 1,500 archers. He was accompanied by the Duke of York and by Thomas Beaufort, half-brother of Henry IV. Beaufort was a Knight of the Garter and an experienced soldier. He had been Constable of Ludlow (1402), Captain of Calais (1407), and an admiral. He had commanded the army sent against the northern rebels in 1405. Created Earl of Dorset in 1412, he later became Duke of Exeter. All Clarence's troops were to receive 'Aquitaine rates' of pay, which were higher than those which applied when military service was performed in what was called 'France'. The army mustered at Southampton and, on 10 August 1412, it disembarked at Saint-Vaast-la-Hougue near Cherbourg, where Edward III had landed over sixty years before.

Fastolf was a squire in this army. We know this from letters of protection, issued at Westminster, which also refer to his being in Clarence's service, and which were granted for a period of six months. The accounts kept by a bailiff in Fastolf's manor of Castle Combe at this date mention the purchase of three 'white cloths' at a cost of £7 18s 4d 'for the livery of the lord beyond the sea'.[6]

The Armagnacs deceived their opponents into thinking that Clarence's army would land in Picardy, so that when the landing actually took place in Normandy, the English had the advantage of surprise, and they soon made their way down through Maine and Anjou – areas where Fastolf would become Governor just over ten years later. They reached Blois on the Loire on 16 September, but by then French politics had undergone a further revolution: the Burgundians had occupied Berry and threatened the Bourbonnais, forcing the Armagnacs to make peace. Clarence had little choice but to come to terms with them. At Buzançais, just south of the Loire, he agreed to leave France by January 1413 and accept 40,000 crowns by way of compensation. Yet, despite the treachery of the Armagnacs, Clarence's mission was not wholly abortive. The English continued their march southwards and reached Bordeaux. Thus Fastolf reached Aquitaine – for the first and only time in his life – by marching overland, though the sea voyage to Bordeaux would have been much quicker.

Bordeaux was the political, economic and military capital of Aquitaine. The Constables of the city, sitting in their castle of Ombrière, controlled a network of fortifications throughout the Duchy. At this period they were English rather than Gascon, and Fastolf became deputy Constable under Sir William Faryngdon (1401–13), continuing to hold the office under Sir William Clifford (1413–18). Under Faryngdon, he was responsible for the garrison of Fronsac, at the mouth of the Dordogne. Nine years previously, the English Captain of Fronsac had written to the royal Council to say that he needed 120 men to defend this stronghold, for it was 'the head of all Aquitaine [Guienne] – for if all other fortresses of Aquitaine were lost, which God prevent, they could be recovered by way of the said castle of Fronsac'.

As deputy Constable of Bordeaux, Fastolf had administrative as well as military responsibilities. His superior was the chief financial officer for the Duchy, and there was both an English 'controller' and an English 'provost of the castle'. In an indenture preserved in the National Archives at Kew, Sir John is described as Clifford's 'perpetual Lieutenant'; and, on 10 April 1413, he received 765 gold crowns, being part of a sum of 1,365 crowns (£227 10s sterling) payable to Clarence under the agreement he had struck with the Armagnacs. This was an important payment, but someone seems to have been guilty of a clerical error, in that the same item was recorded twice in the accounts, once as a receipt by John Fastolf 'esquire' and the other as a receipt by 'Sir' John Fastolf, though the amount is almost identical (and Fastolf was not yet a knight). An anxious official queried this, adding a note to ask whether it was right that there were two John Fastolfs and two receipts of the same amount, because his master knew of only one man of that name, and one such payment! There are further documents in the British Library which make it clear that, while this receipt was issued in Bordeaux, the transaction also had to be approved in Paris by the French king's officers, so that it is unlikely that the error went unrectified.[7]

When Clarence left for England in July 1413, his place was taken by Thomas Beaufort, Earl of Dorset, who became Lieutenant of Aquitaine at the head of 240 men and 1,000 archers. The French had invaded the Duchy many times, most recently in 1405, and Beaufort now led a punitive expedition into the Angoumois and the Saintonge, north of the Gironde. His purpose was to damage territory belonging to the perfidious Armagnacs, and he started by heading north-east from Bordeaux, taking Riberac and Aubeterre on the Dronne. Then he headed further north, bypassing Saintes but taking Taillebourg, towards Saint-Jean-d'Angelys. He was now quite a long way from his base, but still he went north, capturing Soubise in June 1413. William Worcester tells us that this consisted of a fortress (fortalice) and a town (villa), but it was also a port, and it was here that Fastolf captured the local French lord and became captain of the place in his stead. Eighteen months later, on 22 January 1415, the following order was issued:

> To the collectors of customs and subsidies in the port of Great Yarmouth. Order, without taking custom or subsidy, to suffer John Fastolf the king's esquire to have 130 tuns of wine of Gascony now or hereafter brought to that port in certain ships to his use for the ransom of the lord of Soubise, his prisoner and not otherwise, as the said John has made oath in chancery.[8]

It was around this time that the English defeated a force sent against them from Paris by the Burgundians, which was led by Jacques de Heilly. De Heilly was taken prisoner – a satisfying conclusion, since he had previously commanded a French force in Scotland. The Percys had taken him prisoner there in 1402, but he had escaped. Beaufort (whom we shall now call Dorset, until he becomes Exeter) had therefore succeeded, not only in taking a prisoner, but in capturing a fugitive. Yet the English occupation of Saintonge only lasted a few months. In the autumn of 1413, the Duke of Bourbon came south with 1,300 men-at-arms and 800 archers and retook much of the territory which Dorset had gained, including Soubise. The town was held at the time by a force of some 500–600 English and Gascon troops, but it nonetheless fell to the French. The Jurades of Bordeaux recorded a payment, on 15 June 1414, of two nobles, to the messenger who had received the news of its fall from Dorset's trumpeter.[9]

Fastolf escaped unharmed: a truce was arranged and he returned to England, presumably by sea. Many years later, in 1455, he petitioned the Crown for a sum of £26 15s 3d:

> for divers charges and costs by him borne for the time that he occupied the office of the Constabulary of Bordeaux for the safeguard of the King's Duchy of Aquitaine, as it appeareth plainly by account made of the said office of Constabulary, remaining in the King's Exchequer at Westminster of record, whereof he has yet had neither payment nor assignment.[10]

There were other benefits to be had from service overseas, apart from pay and the recognized profits of war. On 9 July 1413 the royal justices in England issued a writ of supersedeas, which stayed proceedings upon any indictments brought against Fastolf 'until the defendant's return to England, or until further order'. This must have been a welcome bonus, but it was not the only occasion on which royal protection was afforded to the Fastolf family. In 1421 Henry V ordered Fastolf's namesake and cousin, John Fastolf of Oulton, to enquire into the circumstances in which his nephew Robert Harling (and his wife Joan) had been deprived of a property in Suffolk: 'Because the king does not wish Robert and Joan to be injured, especially because Robert is residing continuously on the king's service beyond the seas.'[11]

When the French historian Yves Renouard came to write the history of medieval Bordeaux, he made no mention of Clarence's expedition, nor of Dorset's raid into the Saintonge. Yet, at the time, the English connection was of immense importance to local people. The Jurades of the city were in regular contact with the King of England and his representatives. They voted taxes for Dorset, though they also requested that their ancient privileges be recognized and demanded compensation for damage done by English soldiers. When Henry V came to the throne in 1413, he wrote to assure the city of his gratitude for its loyalty, but reminded them that they should pay their taxes. All the time, the men of Bordeaux were busy keeping watch on their shipping, and exporting their wines to England.[12]

Chapter 3

In the King's Name of England, 1413–22

Henry V

Some French historians have taken the view that the Hundred Years' War was a struggle for the control of the wine, textiles and salt produced in Aquitaine, Flanders and Brittany, but the theory utterly fails to convince, if only because the military aristocracy, which did the fighting, had little or no interest in trade and commerce. The forceful personalities of Edward III and Henry V, men who were determined at all costs to pursue their legal rights in France and had the ability to harness the energies of that aristocracy, were much more influential.

England was in a very weak position when Fastolf was young. The south coasts were dangerously vulnerable to invasion and piracy. Ireland was quiescent, but Wales was in almost permanent revolt. Henry V transformed this situation. He led from the front, at a time when the French kings had ceased to do so. He shattered the French cavalry, and aristocracy, at Agincourt. He presided over the conquest of the rich Duchy of Normandy, which put an end to the threat of invasion for a generation. He formed alliances with the Holy Roman Emperor Sigismund and, when the Duke of Burgundy was assassinated by the Dauphin's servants in 1419, with the Burgundians. He dictated peace at Troyes in 1420. He was a hero to the English of Fastolf's generation, and to many Englishmen since. In the view of Colonel Burne, writing in 1956, he was a man who 'always acted in the most enlightened fashion'. To the Scots chronicler Walter Bower he was, on the contrary, the 'despoiler of France', who put many fine Scotsmen to death. Édouard Perroy, who nevertheless recognized his abilities, considered him an unscrupulous and ruthless empire-builder and a prince worthy of Machiavelli's praise. In Desmond Seward's view he had 'more than a little in common with Napoleon and even Hitler'. Yet few doubt his administrative as well as military abilities.[1]

When Henry came to the throne in 1413, Fastolf was already a veteran captain, with experience of fighting in Ireland and Aquitaine. Yet, there is little evidence that he knew Henry personally, as his fictional namesake Falstaff did. He was a squire, and probably a 'king's squire', when he was recruited for a further expedition to France in 1415, but there must have been dozens like him, and he had never served Henry V in Wales or the Borders of Scotland. The King relied greatly on his family, the aristocracy and the Lancastrian affinity, of which Fastolf was never a member. In May 1414, he created his two brothers John and Humphrey Dukes of Bedford and Gloucester, and confirmed his brother Thomas as Duke of Clarence and his Beaufort uncle, Thomas, as Earl of Dorset. These were the men he met on a daily basis, in council and on campaign. An untitled member of the gentry was probably of little account.[2]

Harfleur and Agincourt, 1415–16

Henry V's strategy for the invasion of France in 1415 is unknown, except by way of his actions: he kept it a closely guarded secret. Superficially, it is puzzling why he chose Normandy and specifically Harfleur, rather than Bordeaux or Calais, as the place to land. Despite Colonel Burne's criticisms of it in *The Agincourt War*, Bordeaux was in loyal hands, and it had provided Dorset and Fastolf with a convenient starting-point for their expedition only three years before. As for Calais, Edward III had expended much time and treasure in capturing the port almost eighty years before, and the English had invested an enormous amount in building forts in the *pays de Calais* to make it secure. However, if Henry's objective in 1415 was to begin the conquest of Normandy, Harfleur was an obvious place to start. In addition, it was an important naval base, from which the French had menaced the Channel.

The army mustered at Southampton was three times larger than the force led by Clarence three years before, and Fastolf joined it in June 1415. We know that he indented for ten men-at-arms and thirty archers (a ratio of 1:3 being normal at the time). Henry gave orders that he be paid 'in connection with the war service he will perform on the expedition which we will shortly make, God willing' ('pour Nous faire Service de Guerre en le Viage que Nous ferrons, Dieu devant, deinz brief'). Fastolf's rate of pay, as a squire and a man-at-arms, was 12d per day, when archers were paid half as much, knights bachelor twice as much and bannerets four times as much. Quite soon after the army arrived in France, we find him in the retinue of the great East Anglian nobleman, Michael de la Pole, 2nd Earl of Suffolk.[3]

The English landed in Normandy on 14 August 1415, near a village called Frileuse. Fortunately, the landing was unopposed. Almost twenty years later, Fastolf claimed that 'he was the first to disembark and jump into the sea up to his sword-belt, and the King gave him the first house he saw in France'.[4]

Can we accept this claim at face value? It was made when giving evidence, in the same proceedings as contain the claim that he had journeyed to Jerusalem, but in this case there is some reason to challenge Fastolf's account. According to the anonymous chaplain who wrote the chronicle known as the *Gesta Henrici Quinti*, Henry had given orders *under pain of death* that no one should land before the king, but rather that they should make ready to land early on the following morning when he did, lest, if it were done otherwise, the English in their recklessness, not foreseeing the danger and coming ashore too soon and at the wrong time, might perhaps scatter in search of plunder and leave the king's own landing too exposed.

Yet Fastolf must have performed some notable feat of arms on the day of the landing (or soon afterwards), to earn the reward which was now bestowed on him. Within a few weeks, on 29 January 1416, he was knighted and granted the lordship and manor of Frileuse for life, while the feudal service required of him in respect of this new fief – the payment of a fleur-de-lys each year – was purely nominal.[5]

The siege of Harfleur proved more difficult than expected. The town had strong walls, with no fewer than twenty-four towers, and, if Henry V had artillery, so did the garrison. The inhabitants flooded part of the land outside the walls. While this allowed the King to use boats to communicate with his brother Clarence, it also produced dysentery in the English camp. Monstrelet tells us that Henry brought up siege-engines of the old-fashioned type, while the author of the *Gesta Henrici Quinti* was impressed by the guns, with their protective screens like sliding garage doors:

These … consisting of long and thick planks, were so constructed and fitted with appliances of wood and iron that when the top was pulled down the bottom was lifted up so as to give a view of the town until, a target having been selected, the guns from immediately behind them discharged their stones by the explosive force of ignited gunpowder.

Henry was very severe with his own men and utterly ruthless towards anyone he regarded as a rebel. He relied on biblical authority to justify his actions. The so-called 'Law of Deuteronomy' was thought to require that peace be offered to an enemy town before any attack, but, if the offer was rejected, the town could be sacked and the inhabitants put to the sword.[6] The people of Harfleur knew the rules Henry operated by: they duly surrendered after a siege lasting four weeks.

Many myths about John Fastolf have circulated during the last six centuries: that he was born in France or was of French extraction; that he was a ward of the Duke of Bedford; that he was taken prisoner at Jargeau in 1429; that he captured René of Anjou at the Battle of Bulgnéville in 1431;[7] that he was an ambassador to the Council of Basle and the Congress of Arras in 1435; that his castle at Caister was erected by a French nobleman whom he had taken prisoner. Perhaps the most persistent myth is that he fought at Agincourt in 1415. Poulett Scrope exploded this as long ago as 1852, but it is still common currency today. However, the Exchequer accounts in the National Archives show that Fastolf was sent home on 4 October 1415, and could not have fought at Agincourt three weeks later. His name appears in a muster roll relating to the retinue of the Earl of Suffolk, which is headed:

> The names of the sick, belonging to the retinue of the Duke of Clarence and also those attached to other lords and Captains who were with our sovereign lord the King at the siege of the town of Harfleur.

There is also an expense account and a roll relating to the retinue of the Earl of Suffolk, which record that 'John Fastolf, esquire and man-at-arms [and another man] were invalided home' on 4 October 1415 ('revenerunt de Harfleur in Ang[liam] he hoc Regno causa infirm[itatis]').[8] In addition, the circumstantial evidence is very strong that Fastolf was not at Agincourt: if he had been, he would certainly have referred to it in later years, especially when his good character was called into question. Shakespeare's Henry V was right when he predicted the fame which would attach to any man who had fought at Agincourt:

> He that shall live this day, and see old age,
> Will yearly on the vigil feast his neighbours,
> And say 'To-morrow is Saint Crispian.'
> Then will he strip his sleeve and show his scars,
> And say 'These wounds I had on Crispian's day.'

It was only after Harfleur surrendered that the king allowed the sick to leave. Nevertheless, Fastolf recovered quickly back in England. He returned to France soon after Agincourt, as a knight under the Earl of Dorset, his old commander in Aquitaine. Dorset was now put in charge at Harfleur, where the French soon made a serious attempt to recover the town. During the winter of 1415–16, the English had to suffer an even longer siege than the one they had subjected the town to the previous autumn. Militarily, the garrison had to fend for itself, since the king and the main field army had marched away to Calais and England, after winning their great victory at Agincourt.[9]

Harfleur began to run out of food once more, quite quickly. The French had command of the sea and could prevent supplies arriving from England, and they gradually tightened their hold on the landward side of the town. In default of any relief force, the English decided to send out foragers. In the last week of November, a large party under Fastolf broke out and approached within 6 miles of Rouen, capturing 500 prisoners at Le Paulu, but found that they could not hold on to them when they were attacked. However, shortly after New Year 1416, the garrison was reinforced and on 9 March Dorset led a second raid, again with the aim of obtaining provisions.

Dorset's lieutenants this time were John Blount, Thomas Carew and John Fastolf, and they commanded around 1,000 horsemen in all. Unfortunately, the French knew the English were coming and, led by the Count of Armagnac, they caught up with them at Valmont, a few miles from the Channel coast. John Strecche, Prior of an Augustinian monastery in Warwickshire, takes up the story:

> And when, at length, the Earl had started out on the proposed journey with about a thousand cavalry, and was between Fécamp and Dieppe, more than twenty miles from Harfleur, and fully occupied in collecting provisions and spoils to stock up the town and hearten his men, there suddenly sprang out of an ambush a strong force of French and, quite apart from ambushes comprising great numbers of troops positioned between there and Harfleur, they appeared before the Earl to the number of about five thousand, drawn from the very pick of their men and led by the Count of Armagnac, the Constable of France.

The chronicler's numbers are, as usual, exaggerated; but it is clear enough that the English were both outnumbered and in serious danger. Battle-lines were drawn, but the Count of Armagnac offered terms: according to the *Gesta*, he would allow the English to return to Harfleur if they surrendered; but, though every gentleman would be released unharmed, every archer was to lose his right hand. The harshness of these terms made it inevitable that Dorset would reject them, and a battle ensued:

> The French sent forward from their positions a very large force of cavalry to attack and break our position. This force, notwithstanding our sharp arrows and the points of our spears levelled at their horses' breasts (the other end having been driven into the ground), charged through and scattered the English positions in the centre.

Unusually, the English were defeated and had to abandon their horses, stores and equipment on the battlefield; neither the author of the *Gesta* nor John Strecche attempts to conceal this, but the defeat was not total. The Battle of Valmont took place in the late afternoon and Dorset managed to regroup and withdraw by night. According to Colonel Burne, they reached the coast at Étretat – where Monet painted the cliffs 400 years later – and then marched back towards Harfleur along the shoreline, eventually reaching the mouth of the Seine at Chef-de-Caux, now Sainte-Adresse. However, the French had not finished with Dorset's force yet. They attacked him again, this time in greater numbers. The *Gesta* tells the story of this second fight in biblical terms:

> And just when they believed they had been wholly delivered from the power of their enemies, lo! suddenly, after daybreak, the French who had discovered during the night that the English had slipped away, sprang out of an ambush many thousands strong and, moving forward, took up

position facing the English, the French occupying the high ground, and the English the low ground that was between them and the river. And then the English, being so taken by surprise, lifted up their eyes to Heaven, humbled themselves before God, and besought Him in his mercy to be mindful of them, and to take compassion on them, and to deliver them by His mighty hand from the sword of vengeance.

Naturally, the Almighty, always 'gracious and merciful to the English', intervened. It was God, with just 300 English on his side, who defeated no fewer than 15,000 Frenchmen.

Again, the chronicler's figures may be unreliable, but the outcome is clear enough. The English had avenged their earlier defeat at Valmont, and they had also made good some of their losses of horses and equipment, and taken a substantial number of prisoners. Colonel Burne, who had fought in the First World War and was justifiably proud of what the British Army had achieved in the Second, was full of praise for his medieval comrades:

> The deeper I study it the more I am impressed … For pluck, endurance and sheer doggedness, for coolness, discipline, and hitting power when cornered – in short for all those military virtues that made the reputation of the English army in the Hundred Years' War – *and has [sic] kept it ever since*– this epic … stands with scarcely a rival. (My italics)

Despite this victory, Fastolf and his companions did not succeed in bringing great quantities of food back to Harfleur. In theory, the English could resupply their garrison by sea, but the French maintained an effective blockade. They had ordered new carracks from Genoa, ocean-going vessels which were superior in design to the English cogs and were able to withstand heavier seas than galleys. At the end of May, they tightened the siege. The situation became so serious that Dorset even threatened to quit if food and ammunition did not arrive soon.

The second siege of Harfleur lasted several months longer than the first, and it was now much colder. John Strecche recorded that the English were reduced to eating their horses and Fastolf long remembered the winter siege of Harfleur. William Worcester recorded some of his memories of that time in *The Boke of Noblesse*: 'A wretched cow's head was sold for 6s 8d sterling, and the tongue for 40s and [there] died of English soldiers more than 500, in default of sustenance.' It is interesting to compare this with Fastolf's recollection, recorded elsewhere, that 'a cow was at 10 marks' and that '400 died within the town for hunger'.[10] According to Worcester, he also remembered that the English had used guard-dogs to warn of French attack: 'I heard the said Sir John Fastolf say that every man keeping the scout watch had a mastiff on a leash, to bark and warn off any adverse party … coming to the dyke or approaching the town to scale it.' Not unnaturally, Fastolf seems to have embroidered the facts in old age: he told Worcester how he and the other English captains had defended the town with only 1,500 soldiers and thirty-three knights 'against the mighty power of France by the space of one year and [a] half after the said Prince Harry V departed'.[11] Fastolf exaggerated. The French siege lasted several months, but it did not last a year and a half.

Harfleur was relieved by the Duke of Bedford, who broke the French blockade in the mouth of the Seine on 15 August 1416. His victory has been called 'the most spectacular naval confrontation of the entire Hundred Years War'. At the time the author of the *Gesta* solemnly assured his readers that this was the work of the Virgin Mary, 'who as is devoutly believed, had compassion on the people of Her dower of England, so long distressed by the waves'. The hard facts were that the English fleet caught the enemy off the Normandy coast. Although Bedford had only four carracks, and the French and their Genoese allies had twice that number, he commanded more troops and two-thirds of these were archers. The French and Genoese were soundly beaten: three of their carracks were captured and a fourth was wrecked.

Bedford's victory at sea enabled Harfleur to be resupplied, but Fastolf stayed in the town for the time being. Appointed Dorset's lieutenant, he did now indeed have a 'noble retinue' of no fewer than 1,500 knights and (supposedly) thirty-five squires, including Sir Hugh Luttrell, John Standish, Thomas Lord and a man called Carew. For men like Fastolf the future seemed bright. He had survived a serious illness and was one of the first to acquire estates in Normandy. He had been made a knight and had prospects of climbing higher. More immediately, the capture and successful defence of Harfleur paved the way for Henry V to mount a second invasion of Normandy.[12]

The Conquest of Normandy, 1417–19

There is a wealth of Norman architecture in England, but no Perpendicular architecture in Normandy. The reason is not hard to find: the Norman Conquest of 1066 proved permanent and it transformed Old English society, whereas the English conquest of Normandy was transitory, lasting little more than a generation. The evidence for it cannot be found in stone or brick: it is to be found in documentary form, in the National Archives in England, where the Norman Rolls, defunct since the reign of King John, burst into new life in 1417.

Henry V's conquest was not a homecoming, since England and Normandy had developed along very different lines since 1204, when the whole of Normandy (other than the Channel Islands) was lost by John. Yet Henry subdued the Duchy in just two years and with only 15,000 men, though it was a war of sieges and he had to take it town by town. This could have been an immensely long and difficult task, since the citadels and town walls had in many places been rebuilt in the fourteenth century, and Caen and Rouen were particularly strong. Yet various accounts of the conquest – including Monstrelet's and Hall's – stress how easy it was for the Lancastrians. Many towns surrendered without a fight.

Sir Charles Oman was convinced that Henry V's aim in 1417 was to conquer Normandy – he even wrote of the king 'specializing' in it. However, we do not really know what the King's ambitions were. Basset's Chronicle tells us, no fewer than three times, that he arrived in Normandy 'with the intention to conquer' ('en entencion de faire conquest'); and the Duchy certainly came to occupy a special place in his heart. It is certainly unlikely that he aimed to conquer the whole of the French kingdom, which was far too large. Yet he may have aimed wider than Normandy. Under the entry for that year, Basset sets out a list of over 160 French captains, and the geographical spread of the names is intriguing. About 100 were indeed in Normandy, but four were on the Somme, some in Maine and several in the Vexin (the area between Rouen and Paris). The reason for including the list is not stated, but these captains controlled the fortresses of a large part of northern France. These were the men who had the power not only to resist an invader but to negotiate a surrender of their fortresses. The list makes it difficult to say categorically that Henry V aimed only at the Duchy of Normandy in 1417. He may have set his sights higher, even before landing.[13]

Henry was very particular about the quality of the men he took with him, and excluded those whom he considered unfit on social grounds. On 2 June 1417 he commanded the sheriffs of the English counties on the south coast to be vigilant:

> In recent expeditions abroad many persons have taken to themselves arms and tunics of arms called 'cotearmures' when neither they nor their ancestors have used such in time past, you shall make proclamations that no man of whatsoever status, rank or condition he may be, shall take to himself arms or a tunic of arms unless he possess or ought to possess the same by ancestral right or by grant of some person having authority sufficient thereunto.

At around the same time, the Duke of Clarence – now Constable of the king's host for France – issued an ordinance regulating the duties of heralds. These were charged with ensuring that anyone claiming to 'bear arms' was entitled to do so. However, the new knight, Sir John Fastolf, had no difficulty with this requirement. Unlike Shakespeare 170 years later, his right to 'coat-armour' was never challenged. His arms were 'Quarterly or and Azure on a bend Gules three cross crosslets or'.[14] At some point he also acquired a motto: *me faut faire* ('I must be doing').

Henry V's new expedition set off in 1417 and landed at Touques, opposite Harfleur, on 1 August. Clarence took a leading role in the enterprise, along with the Earl of Dorset, now created Duke of Exeter. We do not know for a fact that Fastolf sailed with it: he may have joined it direct from Harfleur. However, given the relatively short duration of military contracts, he is unlikely to have remained in garrison there throughout the second half of 1416 and first half of 1417.

What was the strategy, once the army disembarked? The American historian Newhall, who conducted his research during the First World War, wrote, 'by rapid movements and vigorous attacks, [Henry] established himself on a line from Caen to Alençon, threw out a strong frontier towards Paris, and then proceeded to subdue the Cotentin at his leisure'. Curiously, if that was the royal plan, it broadly coincided with the one adopted by the Allies after D-Day in June 1944.

The two most difficult sieges were those of Caen and Rouen (the largest town ever taken by the English). We cannot be certain that Fastolf was present at either of these, but it is at least likely that he was at Caen. All the great lords – the King himself, Clarence, Gloucester, Salisbury, Warwick, Willoughby and others – were there and every available man seems to have been mustered. The English occupied the two great abbeys founded by William the Conqueror, outside the walls of the Old Town, but the citadel had to be taken by storm, to the cry of 'A Clarence, a Clarence, a Saint George!' The English marched south and Fastolf was certainly present at the taking of the castle of Courcy, in the canton of Morteaux-Couliboeuf, on 1 October, and of the cathedral city of Sées (of which we will hear more). Argentan, Verneuil and Alençon also fell at this time. They soon reached the borders of Normandy, though some places to the rear of the line of advance were temporarily left in enemy hands, one of these being Falaise (as it was again in 1944). It was around this time that Fastolf's name is first associated with Alençon and Fresnay-le-Vicomte, in the Sarthe valley, where he was issued with a consignment of bows and arrows, in lieu of wages.[15]

Despite (or because of?) the speed of the conquest, Fastolf sometimes experienced difficulties in ensuring that his men were adequately supplied. In the autumn of 1417 Henry V issued a typically forthright order:

> The King, to the Lieutenant of our town of Harfleur, the Treasurer of the town and any other relevant officials there, greetings. Because we have been given to understand that you have caused various supplies of victuals intended for our dear and faithful John Fastolf to be arrested in the said town; having ourselves heard the arguments about the matter presented before us, we now command you to cause the said victuals to be released forthwith, of whatever kind they may be, and to be delivered to the said John or to his agent. Given at our royal castle of Caen in the royal Duchy of Normandy, 2nd October [1417], by the king in person.[16]

It took three months to 'mop up' and capture Falaise, while the siege of Rouen lasted six. Yet, on the whole, as Monstrelet wrote:

[Henry V] conquered towns and castles at his pleasure, for scarcely any resistance was made against him, owing to the intestinal divisions of France. He thus easily gained possession of the towns of Évreux, Falaise, Bayeux, Lisieux, Coutances, Avranches, Saint-Lô and many more.

Fresnay-sur-Sarthe and Saint-Céneri-le-Gérei

The English first invaded the Sarthe valley in northern Maine in 1417. In 1420 the Earl of Salisbury led a second invasion, laying siege to Fresnay-le-Vicomte (now known as Fresnay-sur-Sarthe), defeating a Franco-Scottish force and capturing the Scottish paychest. Fastolf was probably too busy in Paris and Meulan to have been present, but he was appointed Captain of Fresnay, either in 1420 or in 1425, when the English invaded for a third time. He also became Governor of Maine and Anjou as a whole.

The conquests made by English armies produced fierce, if sporadic, resistance, but this in turn provoked determined repression, noted – if only in passing – by both Peter Basset and William Worcester. The woods and deep valleys of northern Maine made it a centre of operations for resistance fighters, in particular for local hero Ambroise de Loré. He was a thorn in the side of the English, but the fate of his base at Saint-Céneri-le-Gérei, high above the Sarthe valley, shows that the resistance was not everywhere and immediately successful.

Ambroise de Loré fought the English from the earliest days of the invasion – Basset names him as Captain of Sainte-Suzanne in 1417, when he was only twenty-one – and he kept up the resistance all through the 1420s, in various theatres of war, sometimes in collaboration with the Scots but sometimes alone. He survived the battles of Verneuil in 1424 and Rouvray in 1429. At the same time, the English were very persistent. They attacked Saint-Céneri on three occasions, in 1429, 1431 and 1434, and on the third occasion, the assault was successful and the castle was completely destroyed. Ambroise had fought with Joan of Arc at Orléans, but he could not save Saint-Céneri. Today there is nothing left of the medieval fortifications, though the old church, with its medieval wall paintings, continues to dominate the Sarthe valley.

In 1437 Ambroise de Loré became Provost of newly-liberated Paris, and he died there in 1446. The Canon of Notre-Dame recorded that by this time the old resistance-fighter had become deeply unpopular, because he maintained three or four mistresses and ran several brothels, though he also had a beautiful wife who came from a good family. As far as the Canon was concerned, the Provost's lax ways had resulted in an increase in prostitution. In some ways, he almost seems to regret the passing of English rule.

The capture of Rouen, early in 1419, opened the way to the conquest of Upper Normandy. The Duke of Exeter advanced along the north bank of the Seine, while despatching a minor expedition eastwards to Gisors. He accepted the surrender of Lillebonne and Tancarville and on 3 February Fastolf took control of the port of Fécamp, with its ancient and well-endowed abbey. The Abbot of Fécamp had fled rather than swear allegiance to the English king and a monk was appointed to act as receiver of the abbey's income. Fastolf was put in charge of a garrison there and ordered to draw his wages from the monastery. The burden this placed on Fécamp was recorded in the abbey's records for August 1421. The monks declared that they had been unable to enjoy their income that year 'because Sir John Fastolf, knight, Captain of the said place of Fécamp holds it and gathers everything into his own hands, without giving anything back'.

Henry V consolidated his hold on the Duchy. He promoted regional loyalty by assembling the Norman Estates (which had not met since the 1390s) and revived the office of Seneschal (which effectively meant the same thing as Steward), but he also appointed English office-holders, encouraged English settlers to come over and granted large numbers of fiefs to his followers. At some point Fastolf was made Captain of Condé-sur-Noireau in southern Normandy (though Basset names Sir John Popham as the town's first English captain). This was a dangerous border area, but Fastolf was also granted fiefs in Upper Normandy, close to Harfleur. His estate at Frileuse had been given to him for his lifetime only, but he was given an entailed estate in four lordships in the *pays de Caux* (so that the estate would descend from eldest son to eldest son after he died). However, in his case there was a disadvantage to this form of tenure: by 1419, he must have known that in the ordinary course of events he would have no legitimate children, since his wife was already past fifty. On the other hand, the feudal dues demanded of him in relation to his Norman fiefs – a fleur-de-lys for Graville, a chaplet of violets for Aurichier – were purely nominal. Indeed, a French historian has described this kind of arrangement as 'ridiculous and derisory', taking the view that it contributed to the resentment felt by French landlords of the English newcomers.[17]

The English had now conquered almost the whole of the historic Duchy of Normandy, including Richard the Lionheart's Château Gaillard at Les Andelys – though they never captured Mont-Saint-Michel. They did not stop at the uncertain borders. Jean Juvénal des Ursins, a French ecclesiastic and chronicler (1388–1473) records that they pushed into northern Maine as early as 1417, but they also conquered parts of the Vexin, while Henry also campaigned as far south as Orléans on the Loire, and as far east as Meaux on the Marne. The English evidently found it easy to penetrate the great river valleys of northern France. The area where they established control, outside Normandy, was known as 'the conquered country' – the *pays de conquête*.

Henry V was a very able general but he was also an opportunist. It was not so much his conquests as the murder of Duke John of Burgundy, at Montereau in

September 1419, which enabled him to bring about a diplomatic revolution, and it was this which truly transformed English prospects. The Dauphin Charles, heir to the French throne, was widely thought to be complicit in the murder, and the new Duke of Burgundy, Philip 'the Good', promptly allied with the English, while King Charles VI of France was persuaded to disinherit his own son. By the Treaty of Troyes in 1420, the English, the Burgundians and the French monarch all agreed that Henry V should become Regent for Charles VI and that, on the latter's death, the French Crown should devolve on Henry. To seal the bargain Henry married the French king's daughter, Princess Catherine. The allies agreed to make war on the Dauphin and his supporters until the rest of France was brought to heel. From now on, the English would be fighting to subdue rebels who had refused to recognize the new 'dual monarchy'. In the accounts of the fighting which follow, the term 'English' usually refers to mixed armies of Englishmen and of Frenchmen (mostly Normans or Burgundians) who supported the settlement at Troyes, while the term 'French' refers only to those who refused to accept the Treaty.

Shakespeare portrayed the Dauphin Charles as feeble and inadequate – a kind of Merovingian *roi fainéant*, but this is a caricature, as is the depiction in George Bernard Shaw's *Saint Joan*. Charles may have had an unfortunate character, but his position in Bourges, which was his capital between 1418 and 1436, was always stronger than we have been led to believe. Shaw described him as a 'rat in a corner' and even the meticulous McFarlane commented that he had almost 'given up' in 1422; but the reality was that he still controlled the largest part of the French kingdom and had many powerful friends and allies, even before Joan of Arc came to his rescue in 1429.

Charles chose, perhaps unwittingly, the stronger military position. In his classic account of the Franco-Prussian War, Michael Howard described the Loire as an immensely strong natural line of defence, and France to the south of it as an 'inner citadel', while Édouard Perroy (who fought with the Resistance during the Second World War) wrote that the so-called 'kingdom of Bourges' was 'superior to the Lancastrian government by virtue of the area under its control, its support by the appanaged princes and the ability of its civil service'. In addition, the Dauphin negotiated a renewal of the 'Auld Alliance' with Scotland. Though the Scots were always a small nation numerically, this brought him substantial assistance in the form of Scottish troops, who landed at La Rochelle in 1419 and 1424. Individual Scotsmen had joined the ranks of French armies before, but the arrival of two fresh armies, each of which may have numbered around 6,000 men, was something quite new. It was the Scots who enabled the Dauphin to win his first victory in the field, against Clarence at Baugé in 1421, and, because they spoke English, they also proved useful as spies.[18]

Nevertheless, as long as Henry V lived – and for some years thereafter – the English retained the initiative. In the absence of written documentation, it is difficult to be sure about strategy, but Henry seems to have aimed at 'rounding off' his conquests, pending some further diplomatic success. He, and his Burgundian allies, advanced up the valleys of the Yonne and the Seine. Sens surrendered to them on 10 June and Montereau (scene of Duke John's murder) was stormed on the 24th. Fastolf was certainly present at the siege of Melun, which surrendered, after a siege lasting six months, in November 1420. Jean Juvénal des Ursins and the Canon of Notre-Dame (once known as the Bourgeois de Paris) both tell us that some of the prisoners taken there were incarcerated in the Bastille in Paris, where Sir John was shortly to be appointed captain.[19]

Paris and Meulan

Though it was still ringed with walls and gates, Paris was the largest city in Western Europe. Despite the devastating effects of the Black Death in 1348, it may have been home to as many as 200,000 people, perhaps double that of London. It would have been beyond the capacity of an English army to capture it unaided, whether by storm or by siege, but the Burgundians had taken control of the capital in 1418. In 1420, Paris fell into Henry V's lap by courtesy of his ally the Duke of Burgundy (whose interests were increasingly focused on Brussels). This is the only time that an English army has ever occupied Paris.

On 1 December 1420, Henry, his brothers Clarence and Bedford, his new wife Catherine and her father Charles VI entered Paris in triumph. The Duke of Clarence took possession of the fortresses of the Louvre, Vincennes, Charenton, Saint-Germain-en-Laye and, last but not least, the Bastille, which guarded the Porte Saint-Antoine on the eastern side of the city wall. We learn from an entry in the Norman Rolls for 7 September 1420 that men from the retinues of Sir Walter Hungerford, Sir John Robessart and Richard Woodville were the first to garrison this place, though Thomas de Elmham tells the story that a party of twenty Englishmen took control by means of a trick. The Bastille was quite new: it had been constructed in the 1390s and it set a new standard for strength. In court proceedings in 1433, Sir John Talbot was to boast that the fortress of La Ferté-Bernard in Maine was 'as strong as the Bastille'.[20]

Fastolf was appointed Keeper of the Bastille for a year, under the terms of a contract dated 24 January 1421, his lieutenant being Morelet de Bethencourt. His time there was proudly recorded by William Worcester in a long list of his master's offices which he prepared many years later, but Fastolf's accounts, as well as the indenture relating to his captaincy, have also survived. The latter was signed in Rouen by, or on behalf of, Henry V, who was at that time leaving for England with his new Queen. Under the Treaty of Troyes, Henry was merely Regent of France, since Charles VI was still living, and he specified that 'for the retainer and attendance of the said John [Fastolf] towards the very excellent prince the King of France ... the said John [Fastolf] shall [also] have letters patent of the said King of

France sealed under his Great Seal'. Nevertheless, Fastolf agreed with Henry to keep the Bastille safe, and not deliver it up to anyone other than the King of England and his heirs. The garrison must at all times keep itself 'well mounted, armed and arrayed to ride and do service' to both monarchs. Fastolf was to have twenty men-at-arms and sixty archers under his command. These numbers seem very small, given the size of Paris and the much larger numbers maintained by the Duke of Burgundy at the Hôtel d'Artois (400 men in 1410), but the eighty men whom Fastolf contracted for were his own retainers, and possibly only the core of a larger force under his command.[21]

Fastolf's contract contained many standard clauses: for example, those relating to the division of booty, prisoners and other profits of war. Likewise the rates of pay were those which usually applied: 2s a day for the Keeper, 12d for the men-at-arms (plus the 'usual' *regard*, or bonus) and 6d for the archers. What seems to us extraordinary (but perhaps was not so unusual in its day) is the detailed provision as to the currency to be used. Fastolf and his men were to receive a quarter of their wages immediately, and they must 'take the gold noble of England' for four francs of the 'white money now in France'. As to the remainder, 'if the said money [the French currency] was changed and be put at a better alloy and value', the instalments would be paid monthly, but then the garrison would have to 'take the franc for three shillings sterling'. The explanation for these puzzling clauses is that the French monarchy had frequently tried to manipulate the coinage, but in 1421 Henry V was trying to improve the currency. He was in the process of issuing a new silver currency known as 'white money', and exchange rates needed to be specified. Sad to say, it is very doubtful if these efforts met with much success.

Fastolf's account-roll in relation to the Bastille is an even more surprising document. The date on it is Hilary Term (Spring) 1441, and yet it relates to service performed in Paris twenty years before. It appears to claim £34 4s 4d, part of a larger sum of £114 10s 8d due in relation to the service of eight men-at-arms and seventeen archers for the month of November 1421. It would appear that Sir John must have contracted to provide additional troops for guard duty, over and above the retinue referred to in the surviving indenture, but that he was not paid for them at the time. The fact that he claimed what was due after such a long delay, and was apparently paid, would seem to be a tribute to his own persistence, and to the efficiency of the English bureaucracy – though it seems to have worked in this case with the speed of the mills of God.

In March 1421, devastating news reached Paris. While the King was away in England for the Queen's coronation, Clarence had gone campaigning in Anjou with a force of only 1,500 men. He raided Angers and besieged the castle at Baugé, when a much larger Scottish force caught up with him. The English field army was heavily defeated and Clarence was killed. In the aftermath the Dauphin was able to campaign north of the Loire and recapture much of the territory previously overrun by the English. The Scots presented Clarence's banner to the Dauphin and the Earl of Buchan was made Constable of France. Clarence was only thirty-three and, at the time, he was heir to the throne. Fastolf had lost a master whom he had served for almost twenty years and in several theatres of war. Baugé was a serious setback for everyone, both in terms of strategy and morale.

Clarence's death had an immediate impact in Paris. Exeter took over but, almost immediately, rioting broke out in the capital. This may have been a response to the news of the English defeat at Baugé, or a reaction to Exeter's decision to arrest the Burgundian captain, John de Villiers, Lord of L'Isle Adam, on suspicion of treason. Either way, the rioting proved difficult to put down. In Fauquembergue's view, it was largely the Parisian bourgeoisie which restored law and order, but Monstrelet gave credit to the English:

> The Duke of Exeter, governor of Paris, for certain reasons best known to himself ordered the lord of de L'Isle-Adam to be arrested by some of his English, which caused a thousand or more of the commonalty of Paris to rise in order to rescue him from those who were carrying him to the Bastille. But the Duke sent six-score combatants, the greater part of whom were archers, to support them; and they by their arrows, and by proclaiming that what they were about was by the king's order, created so great an alarm that the people retired to their houses.[22]

Years later, drawing (as he tells us) on Fastolf's memories, William Worcester praised his master for his part in quelling the disturbances:

> And it fell in the 8th year of Harry the Vth, named king, when he was Captain of the Bastille of Saint Anthony of Paris, and Thomas Beaufort, Duke of Exeter, being then Captain of the city, it fortuned that for the arresting of the Lord L'Isle-Adam, who was in so great favour of the city that all the commons of the city stood suddenly to arms and rebelled against the Duke of Exeter and against his army and fellowship; so the Duke for more surety with his fellowship was coerced to take the Bastille for her defence. And at his coming the chief question he demanded of the said Fastolf [was] how well he was stored of grains, of wheat, of beans, pease [*pesyn*] and oats [*aveyn*] for horse-feed, and of other victuals; [Fastolf] replied for half a year and more sufficient. And it comforted greatly the prince.[23]

Worcester placed this story in a marginal note to his *Boke of Noblesse*, next to a passage extolling the military virtue of the ancient Romans. The message was that the English garrison in the Bastille had been able to hold out, when faced with a Parisian mob, because they had enough food, and that Fastolf was responsible for this.

There may be more to Worcester's story about the Bastille than an old man's faulty memory and a secretary's devotion to his master. We know that, shortly after he was put in charge of the fortress in February 1421, Fastolf was given permission 'to bring grain from Rouen for use of the fort of St. Anthony, Paris'. Another source suggests that grain was sometimes brought to the English garrisons on the Seine from as far away as Caen, and even from the Cotentin peninsula. Newhall thought that it was relatively rare for English captains to act as 'private commissaries' – most orders for supplies being placed by the royal household; but, as we shall see, Fastolf was always keen to turn a profit when he could. It is quite possible that he was already combining private and public enterprise when he was minding the store at the Bastille. One of the orders he gave there provoked litigation between his factor Guillaume Larbonde and another man who claimed the same boat. He even had the boat arrested while it was moored at the Port de l'École-Saint-Germain in Paris. This is typical of the style Fastolf adopted when litigating on his own account in England in the 1440s and 1450s.[24]

Paris was a great port, though she is 100 miles from the sea and the river is not tidal. She imported huge quantities of goods, especially corn and wine, which arrived by boat along the Seine, the Oise and the Marne, while cattle were driven live into the city, along the roads. The city's coat of arms displays a ship afloat on a rough sea and her motto was *fluctuat nec mergitur* ('she is tossed by the waves but does not sink'). Fastolf's experience of ships and the sea, gained in youth, may have stood him in good stead as Grand Master of Bedford's household from 1422 (as it did later in life, when he commuted between Southwark and Caister). The Canon of Notre-Dame, who was obsessed with both the weather and the price of food, tells us how, on one occasion in 1430, twenty-three barges (*fonces*) laden with provisions were making their way along the Seine, when the Armagnacs attacked them. (They captured thirteen of these vessels, killing some of those on board and taking 120 prisoners.) Four months later, he tells how the Regent arrived safely in Paris at the head of fifty-six boats (*bateaux*) and twelve lighters. The Parisians thought this was the most impressive convoy they had ever seen. It would be surprising if the exercise had been completed without Fastolf's assistance.[25]

Relations between Englishmen and Frenchmen, and between Englishmen and French women, had to be handled carefully. One night in October 1424, between midnight and one o'clock, two Englishmen arrived outside a house near the Pont Neuf which belonged to a woman called Jeanette Bardin. She was described in the official record as a *femme amoureuse* – literally 'a woman in love' but, in this context, a prostitute. The two men knocked loudly on her door. She asked what they wanted at that time of night: later she said that she was afraid that they intended to rob her or do something else that was very unpleasant. She told them that she would not let them in, but they replied that they were coming in anyway. Jeanette tried to make the Englishmen go away by promising to send down some supplies (*biens*), but they took no notice and tried to force an entrance. She started throwing pebbles down on their heads but in so doing injured one of them and he died a week later. As a result, Jeanette was locked up in the Châtelet. She claimed that she had genuinely been afraid, but had not meant to kill anyone; that she had always run an orderly house and had never caused any trouble for her neighbours, nor been the cause of any argument before. This is a story worthy of the pen of Guy de Maupassant and it is pleasing to report that, in this case, Jeanette was given a pardon, despite the fact that she was French and the dead man was English.[26]

Fastolf's responsibilities in Paris were not exclusive, for he was Captain of Meulan (30 miles away but still on the Seine), as early as 1417, in succession to Sir Thomas Rempston, and he was there again in October 1420, when he was paid for a total force of forty men (five mounted men-at-arms and five infantrymen, fifteen mounted archers and fifteen foot archers). When Henry V returned to France in June 1421, he marched south to the Loire and camped before Orléans, where Fastolf was present, along with his nephew Robert Harling. Sir John was also at Henry V's last siege of Meaux, where the king contracted the illness from which he died. Yet Fastolf was still Captain of Meulan on 19 January 1422, when this was one of the towns ordered to file a return of men prepared to keep watch and ward, and he was again Captain on 5 May 1422, this time with ten men-at-arms and thirty archers.[27]

Henry V's death in August 1422 changed everything and in particular it brought Fastolf's responsibility for Meulan to an end for the moment. Doubtless this was why he also ceased to be Captain of the Bastille around this time, since Sir Roger Fiennes seems to have taken over from him there, either in July or September 1422. However, around New Year 1423, news arrived that Meulan had been recaptured by the French. The Regent immediately assembled a siege army, including the Earls of Salisbury and Suffolk, Lord Scales, Fastolf himself, and Robert Harling his nephew. Monstrelet wrote:

> The fortress on the bridge of Meulan was surprised by the French under the command of Sir Jean de Graville. He had with him some able Captains and a body of five thousand men who slew all the English they found there, and used great diligence to put the place in better repair, and revictual it.[28]

To fully understand what happened, we need to understand that in the fifteenth century, the bridge at Meulan was of great importance. The town was even known as 'Bridge of Meulan' (Pont de Meulan) – but the eponymous bridge was in fact in two parts, which spanned the Seine on either side of a central island, the Île du Fort. What is now known as the Pont des Perches linked the town, on the north bank of the river, with the fortress on the island, while the Grand Pont linked the island with the south bank.[29] When Bedford and Fastolf arrived, they laid siege to the bridge 'on each side of the river', but the island fortress was the strongest part of Meulan's defences and the French would still have been able to bring in supplies by river (unless chains were stretched across the Seine to the east and the west).

The consequence was that the siege lasted several weeks. Monstrelet continues by telling us that Bedford 'had bombards and other warlike engines erected against the gates and walls to destroy them, and continued this siege with great perseverance from the beginning of January until the following March, when the besieged offered to capitulate'.

The crisis came at the end of February 1423, when a large force of French and Scots were summoned by Charles VI to relieve the English siege, but marched away again when there was a quarrel between the French leaders. The inhabitants of Meulan were so incensed by this that they opened negotiations with the English, tearing down the Dauphin's banner displayed over the gate, as well as their badges of allegiance.

Fastolf was now appointed as one of nine commissioners charged with negotiating with the Meulanais, and an agreement to surrender the town was signed on 1 March 1423. The Treaty of Meulan displays an attention to detail, and a legalism, characteristic of Sir John when he had more time to attend to his own affairs, though they may well have been drafted in committee. There is provision for the surrender of the bridge and the fortress on the Île du Fort within three days, together with all 'warlike stores' (cannon, gunpowder and crossbows). Next comes the enemy garrison, which had held the island fortress. Their lives are to be spared, regardless of rank, with the exception of (1) those who have previously been English subjects; (2) those who have previously sworn allegiance under the Treaty of Troyes; (3) those who were in any way accomplices to the murder of Duke John of Burgundy; (4) all Welsh, Irish or Scots soldiers; and (5) John Dourdas, Savary (a Bernardine monk), Olivier de Launoy, all those in charge of the enemy cannons, and 'those who formed the ambuscade by which the bridge was surprised'. All these are to remain 'at the disposal of the Lord Regent'. Any member of the garrison who holds any towns or castles elsewhere must surrender them, and release the prisoners they hold, without demanding a ransom. All valuables, whether silver plate, money, jewels or otherwise, must be handed over, without concealing or destroying any part of them. All horses, with their armour, must likewise be given up undamaged. Pending final implementation of the Treaty, the besieged must not allow anyone to enter or leave Meulan without permission, and must 'denounce and deliver up' the cannoneers, and any others who were not lucky enough to be amnestied.[30]

It is clear that, above all, the English hated and feared the skilled artillerymen to be found in enemy ranks. The way in which they were treated at Meulan in 1423 contrasts sharply with the way in which Ambroise de Loré was dealt with in September 1425, when he surrendered Sainte-Suzanne in Maine. Ambroise merely had to take an oath that he would refrain from making war on the English for twelve months, and he was released; but even on that occasion the Earl of Salisbury had the enemy cannoneers hanged, with cannons suspended from their feet.[31]

Chapter 4

From Triumph to Disaster, 1422–9

Grand Master of the Household

Henry V's death must have been a shattering blow for the English. What were they to do now? With hindsight, it is easy to conclude that the late King had left them with the impossible duty of making a reality of his Treaty of Troyes. Even at the time, the task must have seemed daunting. Charles VI of France followed Henry to his grave within a few months, causing even some loyal French to reassess their loyalty to the infant Henry VI. Fortunately, that child had a number of very able uncles. The most able was John, Duke of Bedford, who quickly (though not without argument) became Regent of France.

In *Henry IV* Shakespeare's Falstaff meets Bedford before the Battle of Shrewsbury and later in Yorkshire, and these are not happy encounters: Bedford clearly distrusts the fat knight, suspects him at least of incompetence and sees right through him. In reality Fastolf was closer to Bedford than ever he had been to Henry V. He became the Regent's right-hand man, entrusted with heavy responsibilities in France, and the Duke rewarded him handsomely by giving him no fewer than four houses in Paris. Waurin, who knew Sir John well, called him Bedford's 'first chamberlain', as well as 'Grand Master' of the ducal household, an office he held from the earliest days of the Regency; 'Grand Master' was the title Fastolf himself used in his most famous memorandum, written in the last year of Bedford's life. A list of Bedford's retinue prepared in the same year of 1435 refers to Fastolf as 'knight banneret, baron of Sillé-le-Guillaume, high seneschal, otherwise called master of the household to the Regent, governor of Anjou and of Maine for many years'.[1]

Fastolf held relatively few positions of authority in England, but the list of his offices in France is a long one. Bedford was the first Regent in English history, with vice-regal powers in France, and Fastolf was one of the most powerful men at his court. William Worcester wrote that he occupied a whole range of offices, at one time or another:

Lieutenant of Normandy beyond the River Seine
King's Counsellor
Grand Master of the Household

Governor of Anjou and Maine
Captain of Le Mans
Captain of Mantes
Captain of Alençon
Captain of Fresnay-le-Vicomte
Captain of the Bastille of Paris
Captain of Honfleur
Captain of Harfleur
Captain of Pont Meulan[2]
Captain of the Palace of Rouen
Captain of Fécamp
Lieutenant Captain of the castle of Calais
Sieur [of] Bec-Crespin [*Bekecrespyn*]
Sieur [of] Aurichier [*Dourechyr*]
Captain of Caen
Captain and Baron of Sillé[-le-Guillaume]
Marshal of Normandy
Grand Butler of Normandy
Constable of Bordeaux
Captain of Soubise [*Sulyse*] by [*Larroque-Engalin?*]

There is documentary confirmation of all these posts except for Mantes and Calais, but we know that, in at least two respects, Worcester's list is not wholly correct or complete. One charter preserved in the British Library shows that Fastolf was also appointed captain of the town and castle of Verneuil in August 1427 (for a year and in return for 1,500 *livres tournois*). Another charter shows that in 1431, he was lieutenant, rather than captain, of the town, castle and keep of Caen.[3]

Why did Bedford appoint Fastolf as his Grand Master? We know that Sir John had already been noticed at court: appointed Captain of the Bastille in Henry V's reign, he had justified that appointment by his careful management of supplies. In addition, he had shown that he had diplomatic skills at Meulan, but the fact that he was a Norfolk man may also have helped. There were several men from the County of Norfolk in Bedford's entourage, and Fastolf in particular had a useful knowledge of ships and barges. His wealth may also have assisted his cause, for he was in a position to supply his own retinue (and more) with tunics made in his Wiltshire manor of Castle Combe. William Worcester wrote that, throughout the whole period between 1415 and 1440, his master 'bought every year to the value of more than £100 of red and white cloth of his tenants'; and it has been estimated that this quantity alone was enough to clothe 200 men. The clothing consisted in large part of 'hubes' or 'houppelands' – a type of jacket which could serve as a uniform, when finished with an individual captain's coat of arms, or the cross of St George.[4]

Grand Master of the Household was a French office, and the French version of the title – Grand Maître d'Hôtel – tells us more about what it involved. In French *hôtel* meant 'household' but it also referred to the 'town house' of a great lord, of which there were about twenty in Paris, including the *hôtel* of the Abbot of Cluny (which still stands) and the Duke of Burgundy's Hôtel d'Artois (of which one tower remains). Bedford acquired several of these palaces, the main one being the Hôtel des Tournelles near the Bastille, though he was also given the twin Hôtels de la Petite Rivière and de la Grande Rivière in 1422 and the Hôtel de Clisson in 1424. After he married the Duke of Burgundy's sister in 1423, his Duchess had her own establishment and her coachmen lodged at the Hôtel de la Rivière. Bedford spent much time in refurbishing his *hôtels*, and the Burgundian court set the trend in terms of culture and fashion – in the 1420s there were some 600 persons attached to it. It would have been natural for Fastolf to copy Burgundian protocol in the way that he ran the Regent's household.[5]

Fastolf had at least one house of his own in Paris, close to Bedford's and near to the Port de l'École-Saint-Germain, but he must have spent most of his time on the Duke's business. In one sense he was a steward, busy with domestic concerns, but he could call on many hands to help him. He was *Grand* Master, and there were doubtless others who were merely 'masters': the Duke of Burgundy had no less than four *maîtres d'hôtel*, as did the Dauphin in Bourges. In Bedford's household John Barton was *maître* by 1429 and there were other Englishmen who acted as *serviteurs*, treasurers, chamberlains and *valets de chambre*. At the same time, the office of Grand Master placed Fastolf at the centre of power in Lancastrian France, because the Regent was king in all but name, his household troops formed the backbone of the army of occupation, and all important decisions were taken in his various Councils.

The ducal household was expensive to run and it existed on revenues drawn from all parts of English France. As the person in charge, Fastolf must have become familiar with the way in which a large organization was run, including the methods of accountancy. The objective was to provide the Duke with all that he needed – goods, services, men, horses, transport by land and by water, but Fastolf's job also involved him in legislation. Bedford issued Ordinances (*ordonnances*), just as the Duke of Burgundy did; and Sir John was involved in promulgating those made in 1423, when Bedford attempted to regulate various abuses and grievances. Article 6 was a response to the complaint that various members of the ducal household, when staying in the towns of Normandy, had found themselves lodgings in adjoining villages, rather than in the towns, as they were meant to do; but they still charged the cost to the Duke. This must stop. In future, everyone – regardless of rank or degree – must obtain permission before they went 'out of bounds', and expenses must be limited to a proper amount.[6]

The Regent moved between Paris, Rouen and Westminster, and Fastolf must often have travelled with him. William Zeman, an Englishman who became a butcher in Paris and worked for Bedford's household there, was sued for arrears of a rentcharge in relation to property which had been confiscated from an Armagnac and given to him. He pleaded that he was unable to appear before the Paris Parlement because 'the servants of the Regent often had to change their lodgings'. On at least one occasion, Fastolf gave a similar reason for being unable to attend court.[7]

That Bedford and Fastolf were mobile is also shown by the record of their attendance (and non-attendance) at the annual meetings of the Order of the Garter, normally held on St George's Day, 23 April. The minutes show that neither man attended in 1427, because they were 'carrying on the war in France'. In fact we know from Gruel's *Chronicle of Arthur of Richemont* that Fastolf was at the siege of Pont d'Orson – modern Pontorson, in the bay of Mont-Saint-Michel – on 11 March. However, both men did attend in 1428 and 1429. Between 1430 and 1432, the ritual was disrupted by the King's journey to France for his coronation, but then the situation appears to have returned to normal for a time, until Bedford died in 1435. In 1433–4, Fastolf was in England on no fewer than four occasions – in November, February, April and June – despite his heavy responsibilities in France.[8]

When he appointed Fastolf as Captain of Verneuil in 1427, Bedford referred to him as Counsellor (or Councillor), and McFarlane wrote that Sir John was paid an annual fee of £110 sterling as a member of the 'Great Council' (Grand Conseil) throughout the years 1422 to 1440 – and therefore under both the Regent and his successors. His name appears (though only once) in the lists of this Great Council printed by Benedicta Rowe for September 1425 and 1427–8, and he was certainly a member at the time of the Norman revolt of 1435.[9] There was also a Norman Council – in principle an entirely separate body – which retained responsibility for the Duchy and the *pays de conquête*; but whether Fastolf sat on this is unclear. It is quite possible that he was also a member of a third body, the 'privy council' which advised the Duke of Bedford personally.

The system of government in northern France was not static: it changed in several ways, and several times, during the thirteen years of Bedford's Regency. In 1428 the Regent devolved the task of preparing garrison accounts to civilians, which must have had a considerable impact on the activities of his household. More disturbing were the military successes of Joan of Arc and the Dauphin's generals in 1429–30, which caused Bedford to transfer the headquarters of his Grand Conseil from Paris to Rouen, leaving the former to his Burgundian allies for a time. The Grand Conseil and the Norman Council were also merged at this time. During the period April 1430 to January 1432, when Henry VI came to France for his coronation, the powers of the Regent were in theory suspended and Henry governed (again, in theory) through a unified Council, though he was still a mere boy. We know that a Grand Master of the Household was a member of this council, but we cannot be sure that this was Fastolf, since it was during these years that Cardinal Beaufort removed him from his positions as Captain of Honfleur and

Verneuil. He may have stood down as Grand Master but been reappointed when Bedford resumed office.[10]

We should not allow Fastolf's high office to exaggerate his importance in Bedford's life. He was the Regent's counsellor, not his friend. It may be significant that the list of the guests at Bedford's wedding in 1423 – which appears in Basset's Chronicle – originally contained Fastolf's name, but that it was subsequently

---

St George's Chapel, Windsor

Windsor, and Windsor Park, are the setting for Shakespeare's *Merry Wives of Windsor*, where Falstaff is lampooned, but Windsor Castle – the birthplace of Henry VI – was where Fastolf was elected a Knight of the Garter in 1426, and where the Order of the Garter had its home. This was the most exclusive club in England. It had been established by Edward III with a very select membership, and elections were held only when there was a vacancy. The Order is still in existence, as is the College of St George which supports it. Nowadays the Knights have their annual meeting in June, but in Fastolf's day this was held on the Feast of St George in April, which had been made into a full 'holiday' after the Battle of Agincourt in 1415.

Yet, if one goes to St George's Chapel in search of visible remains of Fastolf, one will be disappointed. His election as the 143rd KG is recorded, but there is nothing to commemorate him. The reason is not that he was suspended after Patay, but that the present Chapel was entirely rebuilt by Edward IV from 1475. Magnificent as the architecture is, it is not what Fastolf would have seen, and not where he would have attended divine service. The stalls, garter plates and heraldic achievements are those of later Knights. He would have sat in what is now the Albert Memorial Chapel, but that too was rebuilt in 1494–8. Predictably, this is now given over to Victorian memorials and murals.

Nevertheless, St George's Chapel has much to tell us about Fastolf's posthumous reputation, for there are no fewer than three Talbots with garter plates there, the earliest of which belongs to the 2nd Earl of Shrewsbury (*c*.1413–60), son of that Talbot who was Fastolf's greatest rival. We can see for ourselves that much of the damage to Fastolf's name must already have been done when Shakespeare came to write his history plays. While Fastolf had no issue, Sir John Talbot founded a great aristocratic dynasty, which wielded enormous power in Elizabethan England. It was Talbot's descendants who occupied the place of honour in Edward IV's new chapel at Windsor, and his family which enjoyed his reflected glory. Above all, it was his version of history which was accepted by Hall and Holinshed, some decades before Shakespeare picked up a pen.

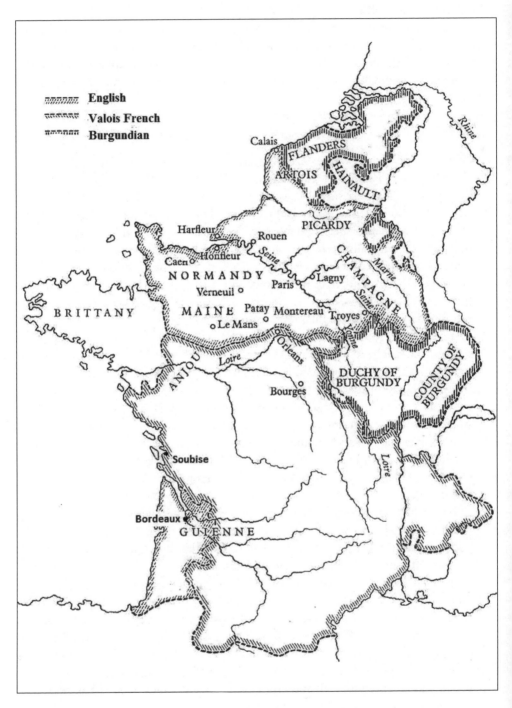

Map of the French kingdom in 1429

crossed out. The Regent was, after all, a royal Duke and his peers in France were the great Dukes of Burgundy, Berry and Brittany. He was also closely related to the English Dukes of Clarence, Gloucester and Exeter, while his most trusted English lieutenants were Salisbury and Warwick, Suffolk, Scales, Willoughby and Talbot – all members of the nobility.[11] Fastolf was simply not in the same league as these men socially, despite his election to the Order of the Garter and his membership of Bedford's own order of chivalry, the Order of the Root. Nor does he appear in the Beauchamp Pageant, which contains pictures of the French coronation of Henry VI, the appointment of the Earl of Warwick as King's Lieutenant in 1437, and of the Earl's death in Rouen in 1439. It was a very hierarchical society, men knew their place, and there was very little importance attached to notions of equality.

The Battle of Verneuil

In 1424 the Duke of Bedford assumed the titles of Duke of Anjou and Count of Maine and it was decided to expand the area subject to Anglo-Burgundian control by launching an invasion of these provinces. English strategy had changed a good deal since the fourteenth century: at that time, Edward III and his son the Black Prince had launched a series of long-distance raids known as *chevauchées*, with a view to inflicting maximum damage on the French countryside and population, and possibly – as Clifford Rogers argues – to provoke a decisive battle, in which they could defeat the enemy's main field army; but after Agincourt, the French were unwilling to risk a pitched battle and Henry V's war for Normandy was one of sieges. Bedford and Fastolf were to spend the rest of their military careers in the attempt to expand and then defend his achievements in northern France. Neither of them ever fought again in Aquitaine.

Unlike his elder brother, Bedford did not usually lead his troops in person, but he did take part in one great pitched battle, which was fought at Verneuil in mid-August 1424, where Fastolf was also present. Indeed, this was probably the first time that Sir John had ever been involved in a major battle. Though he had taken part in many sieges and skirmishes, he had missed Agincourt in 1415, and he does not appear to have been present at either Baugé in 1421 or at Cravant the following year. Verneuil made up for his absence: it was generally regarded as 'a second Agincourt' and it was at Verneuil that Fastolf was made a banneret, with the right to carry his own banner and lead his own contingent of men. Moreover, this honour was conferred on him before the battle, not afterwards as a reward, so that his participation counted that much more in terms of reputation. As a banneret he was also entitled to a higher rate of pay and enjoyed a higher status, both at the muster in France and back home in English society.[12]

There are several accounts of the fighting at Verneuil: English, Norman, Burgundian, French and Scottish. All agree on the importance of the encounter – and that it was a 'pitched' battle, where the two sides met quite deliberately. Hall says that Bedford had made up his made up his mind 'to search the Dauphin in every part to the intent to give him battle in a pitched field, and so to make a final end of his intended conquest', while the French wanted an opportunity to make use of their new mercenaries, Scottish and Italian.[13] All agree, too, that the English and their allies were heavily outnumbered. Bedford's army was Anglo–Norman, there being no Burgundians present on this occasion, and his forces probably numbered no more than 8,000 men, including household troops, men summoned from the Norman garrisons, and the Norman feudal levy. On the other side, the French were able to put anything between 14,000 and 18,000 men in the field, but no one disputes that it was the numerically inferior English who prevailed.

There the agreement as to what happened seems to end. Historians have taken very different views as to the principal cause of the English success. Sir Charles Oman (in his *Art of War in the Middle Ages* in 1924), Colonel Burne (in his *Agincourt War* of 1956), Ethel Carleton Williams (in her biography of Bedford in 1963) and more recently Peter Reid, in his *Medieval Warfare* of 2007, were all of the opinion that the battle was won in the usual English way. They relied on the account given by the Burgundian chroniclers Waurin and Monstrelet, who tell us that

> The archers were posted in front, each having a sharp-pointed stake in the ground before him; and the stoutest of these men were placed at the two ends of the battalion, by way of wings. Behind the men-at-arms were the pages, the horses, and such as were unfit for combat. The archers tied the horses together by their collar pieces and tails, [so] that the enemy might not surprise and carry them off. The Duke of Bedford [also] ordered 2,000 archers to guard them and the baggage.

Here we see the English winning the day by virtue of a classic combination of archers and men-at-arms. These were the tactics which had won the day at Agincourt, but also at Crécy (1346) and Poitiers (1356); but Michael K Jones, in a very influential reappraisal written in 2002, disagrees. He re-emphasizes the importance of morale – so central to Fortescue's *History of the British Army*, written in 1899. He argues that the archers were ineffective against the armoured cavalry sent against them, and it was the men-at-arms who really won the day. He explodes Colonel Burne's theory of inherent military probability (IMP), at least as applied to this case.

In the conventional narrative, the French deploy 'Lombard' (meaning Italian) heavy cavalrymen against the English lines, but their charge is rebuffed by the archers. The Italians then attack the English baggage-guard at the rear, but are thrown back once more. The English right, under Bedford, overcomes the French left, sweeps around to the rear of their Scottish allies, attacks them from behind and virtually annihilates them. In Jones's account, the battle should be divided into two halves. In the first half, the Italian cavalry – benefiting from its state-of-the-art horse-armour – not only breaks right through the English line, but metes out much the same treatment to the baggage-guard, causing large numbers of English to flee and report that the day is lost. In the second half of the fight, the Italians (like Prince Rupert's Cavaliers) are unable to pull up. This allows the experienced and well-trained English men-at-arms to re-form the line and fight their way to victory in a bloody mêlée. Tactics are secondary. What matters is discipline and courage.

It is likely that Fastolf was in Bedford's division (the other being led by the Earl of Salisbury), and indeed that he fought at the Duke's side, since as Grand Master he would have been in charge of the household troops. Fastolf may even have been the source of William Worcester's story that the Duke roused his followers with a speech, when it looked as if all might be lost. Hall has the Duke harangue the men even before the fighting begins, but Worcester has him shouting at them at a later stage:

> And when his chariots of treasure and vessels at the battle of Verneuil in Perche was bereaved from him by Lombards and other soldiers holding your adverse party, he commanded the host embattled not to break nor remove their array for winning, or keeping worldly goods, but only to win worship in the right of England that day, which he had the victory to his greatest renown.[14]

If English tactics at Verneuil are a matter for debate, there is no doubt that the battle was of the greatest importance strategically. It was at Verneuil that the Scottish army, which had been so useful to the Dauphin at Baugé, came to grief. Casualties among the Scots were very heavy and their leading commander, the Douglas and his son, were among the dead. The Scots continued to provide contingents for French armies for the rest of the decade – they were present in some numbers at the siege of Orléans (1428–9), but an entire Scottish army did not reappear in the field. More immediately, Verneuil opened the way to the south, so far as the English were concerned – and incidentally pointed in a direction the Burgundians were not much interested in. In this way, Bedford's victory was even more significant than Henry V's at Agincourt, since the latter had not brought any immediate territorial advantage in 1415. In 1424, the English high command was able to promise land in territories yet to be conquered, to those who had fought at Verneuil.[15]

Despite Bedford's supposed order, given in the heat of battle, to refrain from thinking about 'worldly goods', Fastolf won substantial gains as a result of the victory at Verneuil. In the course of the fighting, he and Lord Willoughby had captured the Duke of Alençon, the enemy commander, though it was Bedford who claimed the prisoner's Duchy, and the ransom due was never paid in full. In addition there was the opportunity to acquire estates in Maine and Anjou.

The Conquest of Maine

Colonel Burne suggested that, if the Regent had ordered an advance on Bourges after his victory at Verneuil, the war might have been brought to an end, but this theory was more appropriate to the conditions of 1944 than those of 1424. It also ignored the fact that Fastolf and others did try to advance rapidly after Verneuil, but ran into difficulties. The Regent in fact organized several expeditions into Maine and Anjou, and against Mont-Saint-Michel. His lieutenants included the Earl of Warwick (responsible for the east and south-east of Normandy); the Earl of Salisbury (in the south); and the Earl of Suffolk (who was ordered down to the border with Brittany). Hall's account of the southern thrust is confused, but he seems to be telling us that it took place in two waves, the first consisting of 2,000 men and led by Lord Scales, Sir John Montgomery and Fastolf, the second consisting of 10,000 and led by the Earl of Salisbury, Lord Scales and 'other approved captains'.

According to Basset's Chronicle, Fastolf, Scales and Montgomery were ordered to advance into Maine as early as 25 August 1424, only a few days after Verneuil had been won. They made rapid progress down the Sarthe, penetrating as far as Le Mans (and capturing Sillé-le-Guillaume); but they seem to have become over-extended. Some of the strongholds which surrendered to them reverted to Dauphinist allegiance very quickly, and they had to withdraw from some areas, only to return the following year.[16]

In a proclamation issued in Rouen on 20 October 1424, it was announced that Fastolf had set out from an area near Le Mans 'of which he had the government', with the intention of joining up with the Regent, but that the enemy had besieged Montfort (probably Montfort-le-Gesnois, 12 miles east of Le Mans). This resistance forced the English to take extraordinary measures, and the passage of almost six centuries does not disguise the note of panic in the repeated calls for assistance issued by the authorities in Rouen. The *baillis* of Rouen, the *pays de Caux*, Alençon and Évreux, were ordered to see that 'all men accustomed to arm themselves and to follow the wars, directly and without delay ... proceed, sufficiently mounted and armed' to Alençon, where they should present themselves to Fastolf and others 'commissioned for the expulsion of our said enemies who hold the siege before that our fortress [Montfort]'. It was emphasized that every available man should turn out. No excuses should be accepted, 'provided that the towns, castles and fortresses from which they shall set out, shall remain sufficiently garrisoned'. A further letter, issued eight days later by the *bailli* of the *pays de Caux*, confirms that all *Englishmen* in his bailiwick 'accustomed to take wages and pay from the king' should go as soon as possible to Sir John's aid.[17]

On 27 November 1424, Fastolf entered into an indenture of war with Bedford, recorded in Paris, whereby he agreed to provide and lead eighty mounted men-at-arms and 240 archers, for a year, beginning and ending at Michaelmas, for the invasion of Maine. This was a much larger command than he had enjoyed as a knight, but it was appropriate for his new status as banneret. Wages were to be paid at the usual rates (4s a day now for Fastolf), plus the normal bonuses (*regards*). The exchange rate was again specified, since the Regent was just as conscious of the need for sound money as Henry V had been. If booty was taken, one third of its value would be allocated to Bedford, but Fastolf was to have the right to the ransoms of any prisoners taken, except those of very high rank. The English had evidently not forgotten that the Black Prince had once captured the King of France, since the contract specifically provided that if any kings, princes or king's sons were captured, *and especially Charles who calls himself Dauphin*, these must be handed over to the Regent. The same rule would apply if Fastolf were to capture 'chiefs and Lieutenants having power from the said kings and princes, and also those who killed and murdered, or were accomplices to the murder of, the late Duke of Burgundy'. Finally, Sir John must protect 'the people and subjects obedient to [Henry VI] from all force, violence, pillage, robberies, seizure of provisions, horses, cattle, and all other exactions whatever'.[18]

Bedford seems to have anticipated that there would be bureaucratic difficulties in ensuring that Fastolf was paid, down in Maine. This was probably because the County was not part of the Duchy of Normandy, where the Regent's Treasurers were accustomed to operate. Repeated orders were therefore issued, late in 1424 and early in 1425, to members of the royal council and to various officials in Normandy, requiring them to pay Sir John what was owed to him. Large sums changed hands: on one occasion £973 3s 8d *livres tournois* (including £228 10s 10d for seven lances and twenty-five archers); on another, £1,489 11s 8d *livres tournois* for fifty lances and 150 mounted archers. We should remember, however, that these sums were not all Fastolf's to keep: he was paid gross sums for himself and his men. Furthermore, the term 'lance' was flexible. Sometimes it seems to refer to one man – 'a lancer'; at others to a military formation of varying size, consisting of a horseman and several attendants.[19]

There was a fresh invasion of Maine in 1425 and, according to Basset again, the English laid siege to Le Mans in June that year. The Earl of Salisbury bombarded the walls and towers with cannonfire and the city fell in August, when the citizens agreed to pay 1,000 *livres*, while the inhabitants had to choose between staying (and keeping their property) or leaving in safety (without it). Suffolk was made captain, with Fastolf as lieutenant, though Basset tells us that he was made captain and, shortly afterwards, Governor of the whole province of Anjou and Maine. He also tells us that Suffolk became Captain of La Suze.[20]

The capture of Le Mans and the conquest of Maine were feats of arms which Fastolf later claimed credit for, as one of the 'lords and helpers' of the Regent. Maine was one of the territories which formed part of the 'ancient inheritance' of English kings: it had been part of the Angevin empire created by Henry II, King of England between 1154 and 1189, and the English habitually referred to 'Maine and Anjou' as if they were one and the same, but this greatly exaggerated the extent of their conquest. They never did overrun Anjou, though they raided it (and Matthew Gough had adventures as far south as Courcillon, now Dissay-sous-Courcillon, between Le Mans and Tours). Neither Clarence nor Bedford nor Fastolf ever entered the capital city of Angers, while the indigenous House of Anjou, led by René, titular King of Naples and Jerusalem, remained at large and were extremely powerful allies of the Dauphin. René has become famous for his pursuit of lost causes in faraway places, but his hope of recovering his homeland of Maine did not prove to be in vain.[21]

On 22 April 1426 Fastolf was elected a Knight of the Garter. The election, which took place in Windsor, was a competitive process – the criteria being martial renown, gentility of birth and unblemished reputation. His rival that year was John Radcliffe, also cited for loyal service in Ireland, Normandy and France, and the two men received an equal number of votes; but Bedford (presiding over the election as the King's deputy) seems to have intervened in his servant's favour and Fastolf was duly elected as 'the more deserving'. Letters containing the good news were sent to him in France and Sir Henry Inglose duly acted as his proxy at the ceremony of installation.[22] Fastolf was also a prominent member of the Guild of St George in Norwich, but the pride he felt in becoming a Knight of the Garter must have been quite unique.

The Order of the Garter had been founded by Edward III in 1348, after his victory at Crécy and his successful siege of Calais. It was the oldest order of chivalry in England, indeed in the whole of Europe, and it was an elite brotherhood, consisting of the King, the Prince of Wales and twenty-four other knights; but, if membership was a great honour, it also brought obligations. The Garter had a strict code, and perhaps the most important part of it was summarized by William Worcester years later, when he wrote that Edward III had worn the Garter 'as a token of respect, to show that, when he was engaged in battle, he would not leave the field, but would stay, to await whatever fortune it might please God to send'. This unwritten rule was to assume great significance in Fastolf's life three years later.

Fastolf was made Governor of Le Mans and indeed of the whole province of Anjou and Maine. He was also awarded the barony of Sillé-le-Guillaume, which must also have had some lost feudal association with La Suze, since he is sometimes referred to as the baron of both places.[23] As a baron, he assumed a new position in French society, and we know that by 1431 he was using a new seal. In that year the Regent referred to Fastolf's use of a great seal 'with double tail' (*en double queue*). At Fresnay in 1432 we find him using a seal bearing his full coat of arms. This shows 'a helmet in profile, with a crest on top, flanked by palms, leaning on a collar of an order of chivalry, the shield carried, by its points, by two angels with wings outspread'. These are the 'achievements' he later displayed at his castle in Norfolk, including (surely) his Garter arms.[24]

The award of the barony of Sillé-le-Guillaume, with or without the enclave of

La Suze, was a sign of the depth of the Regent's appreciation of Fastolf, and the latter's commitment to the Lancastrian cause. He has often seemed to posterity like a man on the make – an 'old vulture' as one historian put it – but one of Bedford's problems was that there were not enough men like Sir John, who were prepared to accept the responsibility of becoming a member of the ruling class in the new dual monarchy. In November 1433, an address in Parliament recalled the victory at Verneuil as 'the greatest deed done by Englishmen in our days, save the Battle of Agincourt', but it also warned that 'few Englishmen abide or would abide [in France] for the great peril that they see there'. There is good evidence too that the interests of men like Fastolf came to differ markedly from those of the men who simply stayed at home. The latter ceased to have much interest in the pursuit of the profits of war, and therefore – eventually – in the war itself. Where they sat as Members of Parliament, they became increasingly unwilling to vote the taxes which were so vitally necessary to sustain the war effort.[25]

Maine and Anjou did not exhaust all Fastolf's time and energy: there was still work to be done elsewhere. Bedford was away in England between January 1426 and March 1427, trying to smooth over the differences between his brother Gloucester and his uncle Cardinal Beaufort. The fact that Fastolf was not present when he was elected to the Garter in April 1426 may suggest that Bedford did not take his Grand Master to England on this occasion. In the Regent's absence from Rouen and Paris, strategy was decided by the Grand Conseil, including the Earls of Warwick and Salisbury, and they authorized various minor operations. To the west, Sir Thomas Rempston was sent to invade Brittany and took possession of the small town of Saint-James-de-Beuvron, between Avranches and Fougères, where he fought off a far greater French and Breton force. (Burne wrote that this action had escaped the notice of English historians, but in fact it had been noted at the time by Basset and again in the sixteenth century by Hall.[26]) In the east, the Council gave orders for the relief of an English force, holding out in two of the town gates of Vertus, between Reims and Troyes. Warwick was to march from Paris with twenty-five lances and seventy-five archers, Fastolf with two lances and nine archers. They were ordered to proceed 'in all haste' – *en hastivement*. It was specifically provided that Pierre Surreau, Receiver-General of Normandy, should pay them for fifteen days' service and not insist on any muster or review of the troops as a precondition of payment, because this was simply not practical in an emergency – 'ce que faire ne les pouvaient pour la hastivité que le cas requérait'. Meanwhile, on 11 March 1427, Fastolf was ordered to muster at the siege of Pont d'Orson, on the border of Normandy and Brittany, with a retinue of fifty men-at-arms and archers. The records would seem to show that the English were hard-pressed and that Sir John – like many others – was being asked to fight on at least two fronts at more or less the same time.[27]

Soon after his return to France, Bedford replaced Fastolf as Governor of Anjou and Maine, and this may well have been caused by his disappointment with his Grand Master's performance in the field. Basset and Hall tell us that Sir John had recently assembled a large force, laid siege to the town of 'St Owen Destays' (Saint-Ouën-des-Toits), to the west of Laval, and had obtained its surrender.[28] The lives of the inhabitants were spared and they were allowed to keep their arms, but there was one exception: a 'railing and slanderous person' who was 'put to terrible execution'. Fastolf had then besieged La Gravelle (also near Laval), and this place had agreed to surrender if no relief came within twelve days. Hostages were delivered to the English, and Fastolf returned to Bedford's camp to inform him of the situation. However, La Gravelle refused to abide by its agreement, when Fastolf rode back there to take the surrender. The hostages paid the price for this treachery: the English paraded them under the walls of the town and executed them in full view of the garrison, but the hard fact of the matter was that La Gravelle remained in French hands, and Bedford may have held Fastolf responsible.

The Regent had brought a new man from England, and this was Sir John Talbot, Lord Furnival. Talbot had wider military experience than Fastolf, both on the Welsh borders with Prince Henry and as lieutenant in Ireland, and it has to be said that he was probably the better field-commander. He proved an instant success on the battlefield. In May 1428 the French took Le Mans again, but the English took it again within a few days, thanks to a daring attack which Talbot led personally. The recapture of Le Mans was the kind of dashing assault which led Edward Hall to describe Talbot in extravagant terms. He wrote that 'This holy Captain and son of the valiant Mars entered into Maine and slew men, destroyed castles, and burned towns.'[29]

The Siege of Orléans and the Battle of the Herrings

Historians have long discussed when the turning point came in the struggle between the Lancastrians and the Valois, but there is no doubt that the unsuccessful siege of Orléans, between September 1428 and May 1429, was the high water mark of the Anglo-Burgundian tide of conquest. Before that siege, the English were within striking distance of the Dauphin's capital of Bourges. After it, they were always on the defensive and they never again reached the Loire. J F C Fuller considered the raising of the siege of Orléans one of his 'decisive battles of the Western World'.

There were serious discussions in the Regency Council in 1428, as to what the English should do next. Bedford was in favour of completing the conquest of Maine and Anjou, and it is likely that Fastolf agreed with him. He now had estates in Normandy and in Maine, which would remain vulnerable to attack so long as the enemy controlled Anjou. The Earl of Salisbury disagreed. He had recently brought an army of fresh and reliable troops from England and he had ambitions to conquer territories further south. His plan was to take Orléans, before advancing south of the Loire, where no English army had penetrated since Fastolf had marched down to Bordeaux with Clarence in 1412. The details of the debate are lost, but it was Salisbury's plan which was adopted. Perhaps it was important that Henry V had, on one of his most audacious expeditions, attacked Orléans himself.[30]

To approach Orléans, the English would have to cross the Beauce – which was very different country from the valley of the Sarthe. In the flat and featureless plain, it was both more difficult for the enemy to lay an ambush, and more difficult for the English to find cover, if they were attacked – but at first all went well. The English marched south across the plain and stormed the town of Janville, after a siege lasting two weeks. The defenders retreated into the castle, where they held out for a further two weeks, before surrendering the place to Salisbury. In typically ruthless fashion, the Earl had some members of the garrison put to death and took the rest prisoner. According to one French account, he left his cannon, munitions and equipment in Janville before advancing further south. Thereafter, the English used Janville as a base: when the French recaptured it the following year, they found large quantities of guns and ammunition, together with stores of food and other merchandise.[31]

Orléans still lay over 20 miles away by road, a good day's march for an army. It was a large city, and the English must have known from their experiences at Harfleur and Rouen that long sieges could be costly and difficult. They did not expect, and did not receive, a great deal of help from their Burgundian allies. They prepared for the siege of Orléans by capturing Meung-sur-Loire, then Beaugency (which lay downstream from Orléans) and then Jargeau (which was upstream). These were all places where the river could be crossed easily, while at Meung and Beaugency there were forts on the bridges, as well as in the towns. Possession of these strongholds meant that a French army approaching Orléans from the south would have to go as far as Blois to cross the Loire safely. According to Basset's Chronicle, each of the three towns fell after a siege lasting two weeks, and the inhabitants surrendered on the basis that they were allowed to keep their lives, goods and inheritances. The English were evidently prepared to grant favourable terms to secure the bridgeheads on the Loire. Possession of them enabled the Earl of Salisbury to march along the south bank of the river – the *côté devers la Sologne* – as well as the *côté du Beauce*. On the former he sacked the rich basilica at Cléry-Saint-André and established a garrison in the Tourelles, a strong fort directly opposite Orléans itself. The English captains of war now controlled the area: they held several conferences in Meung, Beaugency and Jargeau, where they were out of the firing line of French guns.[32]

It has been suggested that the siege of Orléans was doomed from the start, because the English did not succeed in cutting the city off. Instead of building forts and digging trenches all around the city, they spread themselves too thinly in forts that were out of supporting distance of each other. However, this view seriously underestimates the efforts the English did make to surround the town, and it ignores the fact that the siege was almost successful.

Orléans was certainly a tough nut to crack: the city had thirty-four towers, with a company of militia in each one, together with capable leaders, cannoneers and handgunners, and it lay between the Forest of Orléans to the north and the Loire to the south – natural defences which made siege operations very difficult. Nevertheless, the English almost completed the encirclement of the city with forts, building at least nine themselves. They captured the Tourelles on the south bank of the river and built new towers to the north-west, which they called 'London', 'Rouen' and 'Paris', as well as holding other strong points to the east, west and south. They suffered a significant stroke of bad luck when their commander-in-chief, the Earl of Salisbury, was shot in the head by a stone cannonball, fired from a *veuglaire*. The Armagnacs portrayed this as divine retribution – for Salisbury's lack of chivalry in attacking the patrimony of Charles, Duke of Orléans when he was still a prisoner in England, and for pillaging the basilica at Cléry. However, although the Earl died at Meung eight days later, the English still had many good captains.[33]

Bedford threw himself behind the siege. Suffolk was put in charge in place of Salisbury, and Talbot, Scales, Rempston and Fastolf were all ordered down to Orléans. According to Basset, this was with a view to encouraging, as well as reinforcing, the siege army. Fastolf's special interest in matters of supply, as Grand Master of the Household, should not lead us to think that he was a mere quartermaster: he was one of the leading English generals, recognized as such by contemporary French chroniclers and historians. According to Peter Basset's Chronicle, he helped to construct some of the forts around the beleaguered city, and the documentary record shows that he contracted to serve on the Loire for successive periods of four, and then two, months as early as July 1428 (though he initially discharged these duties through a deputy).

The *Journal du siège d'Orléans* relates that, when Fastolf arrived first in the English camp, he came with 1,200 men as well as 'victuals, bombards, cannons, powder, missiles (*traits*) and other war materials', while the accounts of Pierre Surreau show that on 3 December 1428 Sir John mustered with twenty men-at-arms and sixty mounted archers at Meung, which had become the English headquarters (*quartier-général*), and where he was obliged to muster thereafter, on a monthly basis. Eighty men was the same number as he had commanded at the Bastille seven years before, indicating once again that it was his own retinue that was being referred to here, but Surreau's accounts show that he was also paid for the service of another forty-four men-at-arms, 'in taking the field and in bringing supplies to the siege' ('pour leur service à tenir les champs et conduire les vivres de ce siège'). This was a role Fastolf was to perform again quite soon.[34]

The siege of Orléans turned into a titanic struggle, which lasted all through the winter of 1428–9 – Régine Pernoud describes it as an early example of total war. The fighting involved the civilian population of Orléans, and both sides had allies.

The English had considerable numbers of troops with them who had been recruited in Normandy but were not native-born Englishmen – men whom the Valois would later brand as *faux-français* ('false French'). One French historian calls the attacking force 'the Anglo-Norman army'. However, they did not have the assistance of the Burgundians, who withdrew their forces part-way through the siege. On the other hand, the French inside the beleaguered city still had some Scots in their ranks: Jean-Pierre Bernard has shown that when a distribution of food was made to the troops on 25 March 1429, these included 560 Scotsmen, who received 3^1/2 tonnes of wine and 3^1/2 *muids* of wheat (about 2.7 litres of wine for each man, and about 1.7 kilos of wheat).

The English siege did begin to bite, and both armies needed to find fresh supplies if they could. On the French side, control of the Loire was the key to survival. So far as the English were concerned, their possession of Paris, and of bases such as Janville and Meung, was critical, but they also increased the wages paid to at least some of the troops. In particular, in February 1429 Bedford and his Council ordered that the monthly rate paid to archers be increased from 100 *tournois* shillings a month to 120, 'to help them to afford the cost of food, which is high at the said siege … since they were not able to live on their ordinary wages'. The measure displays humanity, but a modern economist might question whether it would really reduce price inflation to pump more money into the local economy.[35]

Fastolf was sent to Paris in search of food and other items. A convoy was assembled there which, according to Waurin, consisted of 400–500 wagons stocked with victuals, artillery and other supplies. There were crossbow-shafts, cannons and cannonballs, but also barrels of herring which were needed as Lent was approaching, when meat was forbidden on religious grounds. Command of this convoy was entrusted to Fastolf, both because he was still Grand Master, but also because he was known for being 'a wise and prudent soldier' ('moult sage et prudent suz armes'). Frenchmen from Paris, including the heavy-crossbowmen known as 'The Fifty' (la Cinquantaine) joined the expedition, commanded by Simon Morhier, master of the Queen Mother's household at the Hôtel Saint Pol and Provost-Marshal of Paris.[36] As for the English, official documents show that they mustered at Corbeil, south-east of Paris on 7, 8, 9 and 11 February 1429, to form part of the escort, including forty-nine men-at-arms and 123 archers mustered by Fastolf personally. Some troops came from as far away as Alençon and Honfleur. Sir John was later paid a total of £1,349 15s 10d *livres tournois* for the men under his direct command.

Fastolf set off on the return journey from Paris on 10 or 11 February 1429. While crossing the Beauce, the convoy approached a place called Rouvray and it was here that it was attacked by the French and that Fastolf won the greatest victory of his career. The conventional wisdom is that this 'Battle of the Herrings' took place at the village of Rouvray-Saint-Denis (which indeed lays claim to it), but it is much more likely that it was in fact fought near the hamlet of Rouvray-

Sainte-Croix (which does not).

The texts of the various French chronicles are thoroughly confusing. Michaud and Poujoulat's 1837 edition of the *Journal d'un bourgeois de Paris* has 'Tonmray St Denis', while their edition of the *Mémoires concernant la Pucelle* simply says 'Rouvray'. On the other hand, Alexandre Tuetey's critical edition of 1881 has Rouvray-Saint-Denis, as does the modern version published as a Libre de Poche. However, when we consult Tuetey's footnotes, we find that two of the three manuscripts he relied on in fact referred to 'Toumray' or to 'Tommiray'. It was Tuetey who identified this name with Rouvray-Saint-Denis, citing evidence that the latter had a fortified church and had fallen to the Earl of Salisbury in September 1428, but neither of these facts supports his conclusion. Likewise, Colonel Alfred Burne visited Rouvray-Saint-Denis when writing his *Agincourt War* of 1956, but his conclusion that this must be the site of the battle was based on little more than village gossip and his own so-called 'theory' of inherent military probability (IMP). Neither he nor Tuetey seems to have been aware of the existence of a second place called Rouvray, and Burne was certainly unaware of the existence of Basset's Chronicle, for he consistently deplored the general absence of English chroniclers for the period.[37]

The *Journal d'un bourgeois de Paris* is not the only French chronicle which refers to the Battle of Rouvray. Perceval de Cagny states that Fastolf's convoy was attacked between Janville and a place called Saint-Pierre-Avy. In 1902 Cagny's editor identified this as Saint-Péravy-Epreux, which is near Rouvray-Saint-Denis; but there are two Saint-Péravys in the Beauce, as well as two Rouvrays, and the second (Saint-Péravy-la-Colombe) is less than 5 miles from Rouvray-Sainte-Croix. The answer cannot lie in the study of the place-names alone.[38]

Even if the texts were unanimous, the contemporary French writers could well have been wrong about the geography. They were not in the field, with Fastolf and his wagon-train. They were probably sitting in Paris, or Orléans, or Bourges when they heard reports of events. It is the English and Burgundian writers – Basset, Waurin and Monstrelet – who are more likely to have been accurate when it comes to the detail. Peter Basset or his co-author Christopher Hanson could actually have been with Fastolf, and, even if they were not, they asked him for advice when they wrote. As for Jean de Waurin, he was a Burgundian who marched with Fastolf that year and wrote his chronicle in the late 1450s, while Fastolf was still alive.[39]

Peter Basset tells us that the battle took place 'near a village called Rouvray'. Waurin and Monstrelet each refer to 'Rouvray-en-Beauce'. This does not, of itself, rule out Rouvray-Saint-Denis, but the critical point is that all three say clearly that the battle was fought between Janville (which was an English base) and Orléans, and that Fastolf was heading for Orléans when the French attacked him. Basset adds that Fastolf had spent the night at Janville, and he includes a detail, which has the ring of truth, that it had been very cold that night and that there was a heavy frost when the English left Janville in the morning ('il avait effort gélé et faisoit grant froit'). If these accounts are accepted, the battle must have been fought near Rouvray-Sainte-Croix, which lies well to the south of Janville. It cannot have been fought near Rouvray-Saint-Denis, which is north of it. It would not have made sense, from the English point of view, to retreat to Rouvray-Saint-Denis having passed through Janville and, likewise, it is unlikely that the French would have advanced north of the English base there when they decided to attack Fastolf's relief column.[40]

It may well be thought that Rouvray-Sainte-Croix is simply too small to have attracted anyone's attention. It might also be said that the more southerly of the two Rouvrays cannot have been the site of the battle because it lies too far to the west, and is not on the main road from Paris to Orléans. However, it is not the size of Rouvray-Sainte-Croix which mattered, but the fact that it was (and is) a distinct settlement, in the middle of a large plain, and that although it does not lie on any of the modern routes between the capital and Orléans, it does lie on the old road from Janville (where there was an English base) to Meung (where the English had their HQ and where Fastolf was contractually obliged to muster). He had no reason to head for the centre of Orléans, which was still held for Charles VII, and he had no reason to go to the east of the city, where there was a large forest. The English siege army lay in garrisons all around the beleaguered city, but mainly to the north-west, and the distribution point for supplies was Meung.[41]

The attack on Fastolf's relief column, wherever it was made, came during the afternoon of 12 February 1429. The 'English' were greatly outnumbered, and there were only some 500–600 who came from England itself (being 'Anglais natifs du pays d'Angleterre'). The Dauphinists were led by Charles of Bourbon, Count of Clermont. Waurin says at one point that they were 3,000 or 4,000 strong; at another, he tells us that they numbered 6,000. Either way, these were largely fresh troops who had not been engaged in defending Orléans, although Dunois (the illegitimate half-brother of Charles, Duke of Orléans) did contrive to lead a contingent from inside the beleaguered city, including some Scots. The encounter became known as the 'Battle of the Herrings', because the English deployed their wagons as a stockade and some of these were loaded with barrels of fish.

One account of the battle tells how the English were warned of the enemy's approach by their scouts, who were standing guard in nearby garrisons, but Basset's account seems more reliable. He tells how Fastolf's men were on the march when they saw the enemy from afar, approaching across a vast heath ('en unes grans lands'). Fastolf ordered that a wagon-park be formed with only two points of exit or entry, guarded by the archers, while the men-at-arms took up positions nearby. The civilians, boys and horses were placed in the middle of the park, and Fastolf gave orders that each archer drive a sharp stake into the earth in front of him, to break the force of any cavalry charge.[42] Then they waited. There was a delay of some two hours, during which the French prepared themselves for battle and kept out of range of the English longbows, but their preparations were hindered by a disagreement as to tactics. Some wanted to dismount in order to fight, while others were in favour of a cavalry charge.

Eventually, the Scots led a charge against the wagons but it was badly executed and the English archers inflicted heavy casualties. Bowmen were most effective when they shot from fixed positions, and on this occasion they had wagons as well as stakes to protect them. Waurin explains that they were 'well shielded by their carts, so that they could fire most effectively' ('moult bien targies de leur charroy à tyrer très raidement'). The remaining, mostly French, contingents were slow to join the Scots in the bloodbath. The Valois historian Thomas Basin was in no doubt that the 'rain of arrows' ('pluie de flèches') unleashed by the English archers was decisive in breaking up the French cavalry charge. Scottish casualties were particularly heavy, because the Scots had borne the brunt of the fighting. The accounts of the battle given by the contemporary author of the French *Mémoires*, and by the modern writer Régine Pernoud, leave the impression that the French would have won the battle, if it had not been for the stupidity of the Scots.

Like Basset, Waurin considered that Fastolf had won a great victory. He stressed that both sides had troops of excellent quality, but that the French had expected an easy victory. Yet not only did the English prevail, they suffered very few casualties (perhaps only one man 'of note', who was nephew to the Provost of Paris). Afterwards, they were filled with joy and gave thanks to their Creator. Then, having stripped the corpses which lay on the battlefield, they took their rest at Rouvray. More importantly, they were able to proceed on their way next day, bringing vital supplies to the siege army at Orléans. Sir John's arrival was greeted with 'great joy and honour' and the English celebrated their deliverance by dubbing new knights.[43]

In William Worcester's account of the battle, it is portrayed – along with Verneuil – as Bedford's revenge on the Scots for the defeat and death of his brother Clarence at Baugé. Naturally, it was God who had caused their downfall. It is difficult for us to sympathize with these attitudes, but there is a case for saying that the Battle of the Herrings did see the 'final break-up of the Army of Scotland',[44] while the English siege-army before Orléans was resupplied and French morale briefly dented. Waurin tells us that the Dauphin heard the news of the setback with great sadness, while the author of the *Journal du siège d'Orléans* felt that his own side had behaved in a cowardly fashion, by failing to support their Scottish allies. The Count of Clermont was blamed for the failure and he left the beleaguered city soon afterwards, with 200 men. The battle did not secure any significant strategic advantage for the English, but it did have a temporary effect on morale. Perceval de Cagny wrote that 'after the Battle of the Herrings, the English in the forts around Orléans made sure that no foodstuffs reached the inhabitants'. Had it not been for the arrival of Joan of Arc at the end of April, Fastolf's victory might have proved critical.

Fastolf's victory at Rouvray has been much discussed by English historians. It earned him his sole mention in Sir Winston Churchill's *History of the English-Speaking Peoples*. Some fifty years before that, in 1899, J W Fortescue, who wrote a jingoistic history of the British Army, praised Fastolf's generalship, but suggested that his tactics derived from Bohemia (which is now the Czech Republic). The use of wagons as barricades supposedly provided 'the first glimpse of a lesson learnt by England from the military genius of a foreign power. For the tactics of the wagon were those of John Zizka, the greatest soldier of Europe in the fifteenth century.' John Zizka was a Czech general who fought in the 1420s for the Hussites (the local equivalent of the Lollards) and did indeed use a tactic called the *Wagenburg*, which involved the use of farm wagons as a stockade; but Fortescue was stretching a parallel too far here. There is no reason to think that Fastolf had ever heard of Zizka, and he did not need a foreign general to teach him how to use carts and wagons. They were an essential part of the Regent's commissariat, and he would have been well used to organizing convoys of them each time the Duke moved from one of his *hôtels* to another. For that matter, the Ancient Britons had used wagons to defend themselves against the attacks of Julius Caesar.[45]

Despite Fastolf's achievement in mid-February 1429, the English lifted the siege of Orléans at the beginning of May. They retreated quite suddenly, abandoning a great quantity of stores and equipment in the process, without attempting an assault on the city, without fighting the French in a pitched battle and, as it turned out, without keeping even a foothold on the Loire. Why did they decide to withdraw? The short answer might be that they were simply amazed by the phenomenon of Joan of Arc, who arrived in Orléans at the end of April, and did not know how to cope with her. Words certainly failed them. There is a story that Joan addressed one of her famous 'summonses' to Fastolf, demanding that the English army leave France, and that he answered it with insults. The Maid sent several such messages to the English captains outside Orléans and there are other stories linking her name with other English commanders – Sir William Glasdale for one, but all sources are agreed that all she received in reply was abuse. The English called her camp-follower, whore, witch and cowherd (*vachère*). A young girl who disapproved of bad language, Joan's strongest riposte seems to have been 'miscreant mackerels'.[46]

If Peter Basset is right, the fighting around Orléans continued to go well for the English until Easter 1429, with 'marvellous skirmishing and other deeds of arms on both sides', but it would be nearer the truth to say that the French assaults on English positions were becoming more effective even before Joan of Arc arrived on the scene. Within days, she herself recaptured the Bastille Saint-Loup (or Saint-Lô) which lay to the east of the city, where several hundred English soldiers were killed or taken prisoner. On 7 May, she took the Bastille des Augustins on the south bank of the Loire, before leading a successful attack on the Tourelles, at the far end of the bridge. Several hundred more English were killed, while some of them –

including Glasdale – were drowned when the bridge collapsed, presumably dragged down by their armour. What happened next day is best told by the French chronicler Perceval de Cagny:

> On Sunday 8 May, the lords of Fastaff [sic], Willoughby, Scales and other Captains who were in the forts on the French [north] side, had seen the attack from a distance, which the Maid had launched on the Wednesday against the *bastille Saint-Lô*, and that she had taken it and killed those inside; and they had seen the attacks she had made on the Saturday against the Tourelles and on the *bastille* on the bridge … On this Sunday then, in the morning, they set fire to their lodgings and made off, most of them on foot, towards Meung and Beaugency. And it was in this way that the noble city of Orléans was freed by the Maid, the messenger of God …

Jean Chartier, Charles VII's official historian, adds the detail that Fastolf was in the tower known as 'London' when the decision was taken to lift the siege, and relates that when the English marched away to their headquarters at Meung, they left behind large quantities of wagons, foodstuffs and above all artillery. The French walked into the forts which the English had built at such cost, and either burned or demolished them. Fastolf must have been utterly dismayed: he had watched while Joan of Arc ran riot, and had seen several of his colleagues killed. Now the entire field army was in full flight, for the first time in living memory. Even the loyal Burgundian Jean de Waurin thought that the lifting of the siege of Orléans was 'shameful', while the Italian Morosini wrote that 8 May 1429 was the worst day of the war so far, for the English.[47]

The English high command must have decided in conference that it was hopeless to prolong the siege, if the French would not agree to a pitched battle outside the walls – which Joan counselled against, at least on that Sunday. The siege had lasted all winter, but no end was in sight. The Parisian, Norman and English troops were all far from home and had taken a battering from the French guns, and the Burgundian contingent had withdrawn. Despite Fastolf's success on the 'Day of the Herrings', the English had difficulty in keeping their siege army supplied and land convoys were liable to be attacked.[48] The French, on the other hand, had been able to use the Loire as a lifeline: Joan of Arc had arrived by boat, via the Porte de Bourgogne. Her charisma made all the difference to morale, but she also brought supplies, demonstrating that the French had won the war of logistics. The loss of the Tourelles must have been the last straw. The English could no longer prevent the French from resupplying Orléans from the south.

We cannot leave the siege of Orléans without including a French view of Fastolf at this time. As early as 1439 a play was performed in Orléans entitled *Le Mistère du siège*. Contrary to what Colonel Burne thought, the title did not mean that the French thought that there was anything mysterious about what had happened –

mistère was simply a word for 'play', but the Orléanais certainly thought that the relief of their town was miraculous. The anonymous author was a patriotic supporter of Charles VII and probably a citizen of the heroic city, and Fastolf has an important part to play, in the guise of Messire Jehan Facetot (though he is sometimes called Facestot and Fastot). In this account of the conflict, he is a formidable English general, and one who has the ear of the Regent. Talbot sends him to Paris, along with the *bailli* of Évreux, with a view to bringing fresh supplies, especially of artillery, and he goes to see Simon Morhier, the Provost of Paris. When he first makes an appearance, he tells the audience that he is setting off to bring help to his comrades:

> I must go, without further delay
> To help the English host …
> Load up the artillery
> Gunpowder and all the equipment.

> *Aller me faut sans plus attendre*
> *Aider à l'oust des Anglais …*
> *Faites charges artillerie,*
> *Poudres et tout abilement.*[49]

Do we detect an echo of Fastolf's motto, *Me faut faire* ('I must be doing'), in the first line of this stanza?

Chapter 5

Soldiering On, 1429–39

Joan of Arc

It is very noticeable that Basset's Chronicle, which was written at Fastolf's request, finishes at the very moment when Joan of Arc arrives on the scene in April 1429. Basset has just told us about Sir John's 'noble and glorious victory' at the Battle of the Herrings, and has begun to relate other 'marvellous skirmishes' and feats of arms at Orléans, when he feels obliged to list the names of some of the men on the other side: the Duke of Alençon, Dunois, La Hire, Gilles de Rais (later convicted of mass murder). Almost as an aside he mentions Joan, referring to her simply as La Pucelle – 'the Maid'. Then the narrative breaks off. It is almost as if she has personally closed a chapter in English chivalry.

The French sources are abundantly more copious. If we have to excavate a thick layer of Shakespearean interpretation before we arrive at the historical Fastolf, there are many levels of ideology and iconography between us and Joan of Arc. Successive generations of French kings, ecclesiastics and playwrights have buried her with paper, and in Perroy's view even the records of her retrial in the 1450s are suspect. The beautiful stained glass windows in the cathedral at Orléans portray her as a combination of the Virgin Mary and Christ – a figure who receives an annunciation but also undergoes a kind of crucifixion – and she was made a Saint of the Catholic Church in 1920. Orléans has five statues of her, and in the house where she is remembered as the heroine who liberated the city in eight days, the implication is that she did it single-handed.

The essential facts are clear enough. Though she may have dressed as a man, Joan was a peasant girl with no previous military experience, who succeeded in galvanizing the Valois army. Her companion in arms, Dunois, had no doubt about the startling effect she had on the men who saw her. He testified that

> Two hundred Englishmen had been able to put 800 or 1,000 of the French royal army to flight before, but now 400 or 500 hundred French were able to combat almost the entire English army, pressing the besiegers so hard that they had to take cover in their shelters and forts.[1]

The doubt as to whether Joan's arrival at Orléans was the turning-point in the

Hundred Years' War relates to those who never saw her – not to those who did.

Did Fastolf see her? Shortly after her arrival at Orléans, she was informed that he had resupplied the whole English camp – and might attempt to do so again. This must be the explanation for the rather strange evidence, given by Joan's squire Jean d'Aulon at her retrial in 1456:

> After dinner, my lord Dunois came to the Maid's lodging, where she and I had dined together. While he was talking with her, my lord told her that he had heard for certain on good authority that one Ffastolf, who was one of the enemy's captains, was soon to arrive in the enemy's camp, both to bring them succour and to reinforce their host, as well as to revictual them, and that he was even now at Janville. The Maid was highly delighted with this news – or so it seemed to me – and spoke the following words to my lord Dunois, or something similar: 'Bastard, Bastard, in the name of God, I command you to let me know as soon as you hear of Fastolf's coming. For if he gets through without my knowing it, I swear to you that I will have your head cut off.' To which my lord Dunois answered that he did not doubt it, and that he would certainly keep her informed.

We do not know whether Fastolf was in fact at Janville at the end of April 1429. What is important is that Dunois and Joan thought that he was, but this was not the end of the story. D'Aulon told how he and Joan had retired for the night:

> But when I was beginning to doze, the Maid suddenly jumped out of bed and woke me with the great noise she made. And when I asked her what the matter was, she replied, 'In God's name, my mission is to march against the English [mon conseil m'a dit que je voise contre les Anglais]; but I do not know if I must go against their forts or against Ffastolf, who is to resupply them.' Thereupon I got up and armed the Maid as quickly as I could.[2]

Joan's indecision was brought to an end by the fact that, when she left her lodgings, she immediately heard a commotion. Fighting had broken out around the city and, characteristically, she threw herself into it. She went on to lead the assaults against the forts we have heard about – the Bastille Saint-Loup, the Bastille des Augustins and eventually the Tourelles – but her dilemma with regard to Fastolf demonstrates that he was feared by the French, as a key commander at the siege of Orléans, with special responsibility for supply. The essential facts of d'Aulon's evidence are confirmed by the author of the *Mémoires concernant la Pucelle*, who relates that, at a critical juncture, Fastolf was on his way from Paris with a large number of men, foodstuffs and artillery, but he left his supplies at Étampes and moved on to Janville without them, when he heard that the French had retaken Jargeau.[3]

Following the liberation of Orléans, Joan went on to free the neighbouring towns, before leading the French army across Burgundian-controlled territory, capturing Troyes and enabling the Dauphin to be crowned as Charles VII in Reims, in July 1429. Strategically, her brief career meant not only that the English were driven back from the Loire, but that they lost key positions in Champagne, the Île de France and even Normandy. Pierre Cochon, who was an ecclesiastical notary in Rouen, recorded the fall of Richard the Lionheart's great Château Gaillard, noting that the English had considered it 'one of the strongest places in Normandy'. The English counter-attacked where they could – and even managed to recapture Château Gaillard and Louviers – but the momentum of their conquest was lost. Moreover, though they organized a major expedition to bring Henry VI to France, they only managed to crown him in Saint-Denis, near Paris. A coronation in Saint-Denis was in no sense equal to one in Reims, where French monarchs had been crowned since the days of Clovis, King of the Franks in the fifth century.[4]

In the late Middle Ages, belief in God and the Devil was universal, and the 1420s were a time of religious excitement. Just as some of the Valois commanders (and chroniclers) thought that Joan was a messenger from God, the English thought she was an agent of the Devil. Fastolf, as a man of conventional beliefs, would like as not have shared Bedford's opinion that she was a witch. There were many French, particularly in the University of Paris, who thought the same. The Canon of Notre-Dame deeply disapproved of her as a superstitious hypocrite, a false prophet who claimed to have a direct line to God, a 'creature in the form of a woman' who attacked Paris on a Saint's Day and a heretic who put on men's clothing (a sure sign of heresy).[5] So far as the English were concerned, what else but sorcery could account for the girl's astonishing success, when English arms had previously enjoyed almost complete military superiority? Bedford wrote to the Council in England that, when the Maid first appeared at the head of a French army, this was 'a great stroke upon your people that was assembled there in great number, caused in great part, as I trow, of lack of sad belief and unfaithful doubt that they had of a disciple and limb of the fiend, called the Pucelle (Maid) that used false enchantments and sorcery'. The Duke had no doubt about the effect of this on English morale: 'The which stroke and discomfiture not only diminished in great part the number of your people there, but as well reduced the courage of the remnant in marvellous wise, and encouraged your adverse party and enemies to assemble then forthwith in great number.' In 1430 an order was issued to the authorities in Kent, telling them to apprehend deserters from the army, said to be returning home because of the widespread fear of 'the Girl', Joan of Arc ('terriculamenta Puellae'). For Fastolf, however, the worst was yet to come.[6]

The Battle of Patay

Word spread of the English withdrawal from Orléans. Within a few days, the

English were in retreat all along the Loire. Jargeau was retaken on 12 June 1429, Meung on the 15th, Beaugency on the 17th. At Jargeau, the Earl of Suffolk surrendered, with one of his brothers, while another was killed, along with a total of some 300 other English. Pierre Cochon reported that the French had captured many prisoners, along with cash, artillery, ammunition and other *matériel*. The *Mémoires* record that Fastolf, Scales and Talbot attacked the bridge at Meung in an attempt to retake the town, but had to break off their attack when Beaugency fell to the French. By 18 June they were in full flight. The French, in hot pursuit, caught up with the English at Patay, only a mile or two from Rouvray-Sainte-Croix, and this may have been more than coincidence. The French may have known that they could find their enemies somewhere on the road between Meung and Janville, just as they had done four months before. Unfortunately for Fastolf, the result of the encounter was very different. The Battle of the Herrings was his greatest success. The Battle of Patay was a debacle.[7]

According to Monstrelet, Joan of Arc had given characteristically bold advice. When asked if she had any orders for the French army, she said 'That she knew full well their ancient enemies the English were on their march to fight with them, – but in God's name advance boldly against them, and assuredly they shall be conquered!'

The English at Patay were outnumbered, but the main problem was that they were operating, once again, in the open plains of the Beauce and were vulnerable to attack from the resurgent French army. They had won their most famous victories in France when they had been able to choose the battleground and deploy their infantry in an orderly way, in combination with archers who had the time to construct some kind of defences. Henry V had famously required that his archers fight behind a stockade of stakes ('pauchons estoquiés devant eux'). At Rouvray, Fastolf had provided them with a laager of wagons. What if there was no time or opportunity to cut stakes, or form the wagons into a circle, or for that matter find the cover of woods or hedges?

Waurin was an eyewitness at Patay. According to him, Fastolf must have gone back to Paris after the English withdrew from Orléans, with orders to bring relief once more, this time to those besieged in Beaugency. Accompanied by Sir Thomas Rempston and 5,000 men, he made for Étampes and then Janville, where there was a heated debate among the English commanders about strategy. The French were known to be mopping up the English garrisons around Orléans, if they had not already taken them, and the question was whether to withdraw further, or attempt to re-establish a line on the Loire. Fastolf urged caution: he argued that the English had suffered many casualties during the long siege, that the troops were demoralized ('effraez') and that the enemy now had the upper hand. An attempt should be made to negotiate a truce, so that they could regroup. His advice could almost have been drawn from the pages of Vegetius. The late Roman author had repeatedly urged that battle should be avoided unless the time was right.

Talbot's advice was in favour of an immediate counter-attack. Famous for his lightning raids, he did not believe in retreat in any circumstances. He even declared that, if he was left alone with his own retinue and a few volunteers, he would still 'go and fight in the cause of God and St George', and it was this emotional appeal which seems to have won the day. When Fastolf saw that he was overruled, he left the council table and went off to his lodgings, but he accepted the will of the majority. Next day, the army rode into open country with banners and pennons flying – a demonstration that the English were ready to fight – but even now Sir John had not given up hope that there might be a change of mind. He attempted to speak to his colleagues on the march, explaining the risks as he saw them. He pointed out that they were heavily outnumbered and warned that they were jeopardizing all their previous achievements, but Talbot was deaf to his pleas.

There was marching and counter-marching out on the Beauce, the details of which are now unclear. It is said that at one point the English proposed that the issue be decided by a match between picked champions – three knights on either side – but that Joan of Arc declined the challenge. (Such a story would seem improbable, but this was the Late Middle Ages, when chivalry could still overrule realpolitik.) At another point, a party of English managed to recapture Meung, where they spent the night, but, in the meantime and unbeknown to Talbot and Fastolf, the English garrison in Beaugency surrendered and marched off in the direction of Paris, as required by the terms of their parole. On 18 June, the French regrouped and set off once more in search of the English.

Fastolf's worst fears now came true. The English had formed up in conventional fashion, with vanguard, mainguard and rearguard, and set off into the plain, and we are not told that they deployed scouts. The vanguard consisted of artillery, supply trains and merchants. Fastolf, Talbot and Rempston were with the mainguard, but the French came up behind the English rearguard. When it was realized that they were there in great numbers, Talbot had very little time to make his dispositions: he gave orders that the vanguard should take cover behind a line of hedges and that a group of 500 of his best archers should defend the hedgerow and prevent the French from breaking through the gaps in it, but these hasty preparations were inadequate. The French cavalry swept down on the vanguard, overwhelming the archers and taking Talbot prisoner. By the time Fastolf caught up with what was happening, it seemed to him that the battle was effectively over. Waurin wrote that 200 Englishmen were killed and 2,000 captured. Berry Herald put the numbers at 300 and 2,200 respectively. In any event, it was a crushing defeat.

Waurin assures us that Fastolf still wanted to fight:

Then, Sir John Fastolf, seeing the danger in flight itself, but knowing that everything was going very badly, said to me directly, that I should take care of myself, because the battle was lost; but that in any case he wanted to return to the fray and await its outcome there, according to whatever God might ordain for him, and said that he would rather die or be captured than flee dishonourably, and abandon his countrymen.

But it would have been suicide to join the mêlée at this juncture. In Waurin's view, there was no choice but to retreat, and Fastolf now did so. The French *Mémoires* record that Fastolf (whom the author calls 'Fastot') fell back on Meung once more, which he 'pillaged', before making his way north to Corbeil.[8] Waurin simply says that he fell back on Étampes, marching next day to Corbeil and from there to Paris:

> John Fastolf left with his small company, feeling full of regret and in the greatest turmoil a man can experience, and the truth is that he would indeed have returned and thrown himself into the battle again, if it had not been for those who were with him, especially Sir John (the Bastard of Thian) and others who dissuaded him.

Waurin's account is so favourable to Fastolf that one cannot help wondering whether the latter had a hand in its composition. Nevertheless, Waurin does not forget to tell us of the recriminations which followed when Fastolf's sorry party reached Paris:

> He was the subject of bitter reproaches and it was for this that the Order of the Garter was taken away; but afterwards, when various accounts were given of the way in which he had argued with his companions, and when many other reasonable arguments for his conduct, for which there was good evidence, were deployed, the Garter was given back to him [though] I know that there was a great dispute between him and the Lord Talbot when the latter returned from the imprisonment he had been subjected to since the day of the aforesaid battle.

As we shall see, this is a series of understatements. It was to be many years before Fastolf was able to clear his name.

There have been many accounts of the Battle of Patay written since 1429, many of them highly unfavourable to Fastolf, but it is interesting that Colonel Burne, who was a fellow soldier, was not critical of Sir John's conduct, nor were the main French accounts of the day. Thomas Basin (1412–91) mentions only that 'Fastolf, who was in command of part of the army, succeeded in escaping and that this was thought by the English to be very dishonourable and shameful.' The implication is that the French would not have considered it shameful, if one of their commanders had escaped inevitable defeat, and chosen to fight another day.

Likewise, Jean de Bueil's *Le Jouvencel* positively commends Fastolf for his 'good conduct' at Patay, and, later on, he gives an unverifiable account of meeting Fastolf, whom he describes as 'Msr Jehan Helphy ... a noble knight, wise and wealthy'. Berry Herald mentions that Fastolf fled the field of battle, but does not criticize him for it. Pierre Cochon points out that Fastolf escaped lightly because his men were mounted and were able to make their escape more easily. Lastly, in *Le Mistère du siège d'Orléans*, Fastolf's reputation as the victor of Rouvray remains intact. He is not made into a scapegoat for what occurred at Patay. There is no accusation, or dramatic representation, of cowardice or dereliction of duty. With some irony – since the speech begins once again with a play on Fastolf's motto – the playwright has him order the retreat as if there is no alternative:

> We must do this, or we shall die
> Within forty-eight hours.
> Let us save ourselves, if we may,
> Rather than give our lives away.
>
> *Faire le fault, ou nous mourons*
> *Avant qu'il soit deux jours entiers.*
> *Et nous sauvons, si nous voulons,*
> *Ou vouloir mourir volontiers.*[9]

Fastolf was treated much more fairly by the French playwright than ever he was by Shakespeare.

The debacle at Patay produced a crisis in Lancastrian France. The French swept the English away from the Loire altogether, out of the Beauce, and back to Paris. The French *Mémoires* related how the small English garrison at Montpipeau near Meung simply gave up and marched away when they heard the news of the defeat. Talbot's capture, in particular, was very demoralizing. Back in Rouen, Pierre Cochon wrote that the English were now very downcast and that many simply wanted to go home. It was widely said that one Frenchman was now worth three Englishmen – not a statistic that anyone would have thought credible before.

As the newly-emboldened French armies pressed forward, the English had to abandon some of the orderly practices they had developed in Normandy. The normal procedure with regard to pay was that the Regent entered into contracts (indentures) with the captains, and issued warrants to his ducal Treasury authorizing payment of wages, which were not actually handed over until the captain presented his men for inspection, but after Patay it was necessary to cut the red tape. On 25 August 1429 Fastolf was specifically authorized to pay an emergency levy of men sent to Saint-Germain without a formal muster ('sans monstres'). On 29 August he entered into a contract in relation to a levy raised at Verneuil which specified that payment be made 'from the finances and revenues of the taxes, aides and *appâtis* coming from the said place' – not from a central treasury. His first month's pay was to be in the form of payments in kind.[10]

Fastolf continued to be very active during the emergency created by the English defeat at Patay, but Bedford probably felt that he needed to do something in response to complaints which were evidently being made about his Grand Master. Monstrelet even tells us that Fastolf was deprived of his status as a Garter Knight, but this is not accurate. What the Duke did was to suspend Sir John from the Order. This puzzled Anstis, the Garter's eighteenth-century historian, because there was no recognized procedure for suspension, but the answer to the problem is that Bedford did not have time for legal niceties. Acting in the wake of a crushing defeat, he imposed a temporary suspension, pending further investigation, whether or not he had formal power to do so.[11]

There was clearly an argument that what Fastolf had done in 'flying the field' at Patay was militarily justified, but Fastolf, Talbot and Bedford were all Garter Knights and these men lived by a strict code of honour. The Garter statutes may not have contained any clause which specifically provided for what had happened, but 'flying the field' had been prohibited by the statutes of the French Order of the Star (founded in 1351), and there was a strong presumption that Garter Knights did not abandon a comrade under any circumstances. Only a year after Patay, Sir Lewis Robessart, who was elected in 1421, showed what was expected of the brotherhood: when heavily outnumbered at Conty near Amiens, he stood his ground and fought to the death. Even William Worcester recognized that 'No such [Garter knight] was ever seen to withdraw or flee from a battle or a feat of arms.'[12]

Though he was suspended from the Garter, Fastolf suffered no further penalty for his alleged pusillanimity at Patay. He continued to hold high office under Bedford. He helped to defend Paris when it was attacked by Joan of Arc in late summer 1429. He was sent to the English siege of Louviers in 1430. He commanded a field army in 1431, and was at the siege of Pouancé in 1432, alongside Willoughby and Scales. He remained an important landowner in both Normandy and Maine and continued to employ an attorney in the Paris Parlement. However, Talbot continued to blame him for what had happened, and was determined that the matter should not be forgotten. He pressed his complaint after he was released from captivity in 1433 and it took Fastolf thirteen years to clear his name.[13]

An informal tribunal of Garter Knights eventually accepted Fastolf's defence, but the English have never truly forgiven him, because it was Talbot who became famous. He became known in England as 'the English Achilles', was celebrated in Burgundian folk-tales and was even called *le roi Talbot* in France. Fastolf retired from active service in 1439 but Talbot continued to put his armour on, and in 1453 died a hero's death at Castillon, where he is honoured with a monument. More importantly, it was Talbot's version of what had happened at Patay that influenced the majority of Tudor chroniclers and, through them, William Shakespeare.

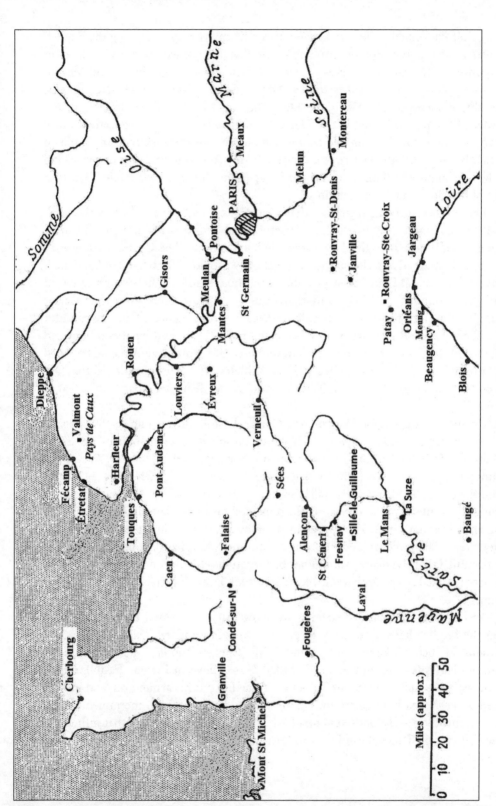

Map of northern France to illustrate Sir John Fastolf's military career, 1415–39

Fastolf at Auxerre

Fastolf is allowed to speak for himself only once in Shakespeare's history plays, and, when he does, it is as a mere messenger, bringing news from the Duke of Burgundy to his ally the King of England. There is a kernel of truth here, in that Sir John did play a part in the diplomatic process, and the one conference he is known to have attended did involve English, French and Burgundians.

In November 1432 the Italian Cardinal Albergati convened a peace conference at Auxerre, in territory belonging to the Duke of Burgundy, and the English sent an embassy consisting of Bishop John Langdon of Rochester, Thomas Bekyngton (the Duke of Gloucester's nominee) and Fastolf (who was Bedford's). These three were empowered 'to treat for peace with Charles of Valois', and on this basis the Victorian writers Dawson Turner and the Reverend Duthie portrayed Fastolf as both a diplomat and a soldier. For them, Sir John was 'ambassador to the Council of Basle' and hence 'famous at home and abroad'. Yet the episode is not even mentioned by Gerald Harriss in the *Oxford Dictionary of National Biography*, and it does not fit with the rest of what we know about Fastolf.[14]

There is no evidence that Sir John ever went to Basle (where the Council of that name was first convened in 1431). The Council was a body composed of churchmen and academics and its primary objective was to promote Christian unity, suppress heresy and reform the Church. Peace was naturally on the agenda, but when Fastolf was sent to Auxerre, he was not going to meet a representative of the Council of Basle (though Albergati also participated in that Council). He was going to meet the Papal Legate. Albergati had been appointed to work for peace by Pope Martin V, and reappointed for that purpose by Eugenius IV in 1431.

The Duke of Bedford has sometimes been portrayed as a warmonger, along with his brother Gloucester, while Cardinal Beaufort has been regarded as the leader of a 'peace party', but both royal Dukes were prepared to at least talk about peace in 1432. The situation was much more fluid than hindsight would suggest. Everyone had to face facts, and, as we have seen, the English position in France had become very difficult. In particular, the Regent had recently failed to retake Lagny, only 20 miles east of Paris. Fastolf had personal experience of the seriousness of this setback, since the revenues of Normandy had been temporarily diverted to pay for the siege of Lagny, and payment of his own men at Caen and Fresnay-le-Vicomte had been delayed.[15]

Despite Henry VI's youth, which made it difficult to think of compromising his rights, Parliament had voted to 'ordain and advise' Bedford and Gloucester to treat for peace:

> As every man with understanding may well consider, it is not suitable or fitting, nor in accordance with God's will nor that of the world, for a Christian prince to refuse peace offered with reasonable conditions, nor the

resulting treaty … and also considering the burden of the war, and how grievous and heavy it is to this land; and therefore how beneficial peace would be for it.[16]

Why was Fastolf chosen as an ambassador? He was a member of Bedford's Grand Conseil and he did have some experience of negotiations but, on the face of it, he lacked the qualifications of his fellow envoys. Bishop Langdon had been educated at Oxford, was a member of the Regency Council in England, and had been at the Council of Pavia; Bekyngton was Gloucester's chancellor (and later became secretary to the King and Bishop of Bath and Wells). In fifteenth-century terms, these men were professional diplomats. Accordingly, it is tempting to think that Sir John was sent to Auxerre for another purpose: for example, to provide an armed guard. Guards were certainly needed, but there is no support for the idea of a limited role in the document which contains the terms of Fastolf's appointment. All three envoys were given full diplomatic powers. That being so, it seems reasonable to suppose that Sir John was chosen because he knew Bedford's mind as well as the situation on the ground in both Normandy and the pays de conquête, in a way that Langdon and Bekyngton could not. This kind of knowledge could have been particularly valuable in the context of discussions about truces, which normally preceded any peace treaty.[17]

In the event, nothing went right at Auxerre. It had even been difficult to agree the venue. Nevers and Auxerre had each been proposed, but Bedford had objected, on the grounds that 'each of the said places were difficult and dangerous as regards the roads for the king's men who were appointed to meet there'. (He had good reason to be concerned, since someone had tried to murder him on the road from Paris to Calais in December 1425.)[18] Albergati had insisted on Auxerre, and the English and Burgundian delegations had made their way there, but the French were late and the conference did not start until November 1432. When the three sides did meet, the talks broke down almost immediately. The English delegates were not prepared to agree that Charles, Duke of Orléans, and other prisoners taken at Agincourt, should be released so as to take part in further negotiations. For their part, the French were unwilling to consider any territorial concessions and refused to recognize the Duke of Burgundy's title to the province of Champagne. Exasperated at the lack of progress, Albergati prorogued the conference, and it was to be three years before there was any further meaningful discussion between the three sides.

The Congress of Arras and the Fastolf Memorandum

One of the myths about Fastolf is that he was an ambassador at the Congress of Arras in 1435, but a Roll of Arms prepared for the Congress has survived, and his coat of arms is not listed. Indeed, it would be surprising to find it there, since the

English ambassadors were the greatest dignitaries in England and English Normandy. Fastolf was not in this league, despite his baronial status in France.

The background to the Congress was that Cardinal Albergati had convened another peace conference, this time in the Duke of Burgundy's city of Arras, capital of Artois. Bedford's views might have been of great significance there, but by the time the delegates assembled in August 1435, he was too sick to attend. One of his last acts was to authorize Fastolf to submit a memorandum 'upon the management of the war in France, upon the conclusion of the Treaty of Arras'. The document which has survived in fact deals with two separate issues: the attitude which the English ambassadors should take towards certain peace proposals, and how the war should be conducted, if the negotiations broke down.

It was well known that the first item on the French agenda would be to insist that Henry VI renounce his claim to the French throne – something that was totally unacceptable to Bedford. Nor would the idea have appealed to the Duke of Gloucester, nor to many other soldiers. Accordingly, Fastolf's Memorandum began by denouncing the whole idea of giving up the claim to the French Crown, and even suggested that it was beyond the competence of mere ambassadors to discuss the royal title: 'It seemeth that it [neither] [be]longeth nor sitteth to the said persons to touch nor speak of so high and great matters, saving only by the commandment of my lords of the king's council ...'. Jocelyne Dickinson thought that, when he referred to 'the said persons' Fastolf meant the enemy, but, while this is a possible reading, it seems more likely that it was the English ambassadors who were being referred to. It was, after, all, for them that Fastolf was writing.[19]

If the English did compromise the king's claim to be King of France, they would be admitting that all previous wars they had waged were 'usurpation and tyranny'. To concede that the king should pay homage to Charles VII for any part of the French kingdom would be to give up the most important prize won by Edward III at Brétigny in 1360. Moreover, the French would only take advantage of any sign of weakness, and the English would 'stand in adventure daily to lose [what they retained] by subtle means of your enemies'. It was axiomatic for Fastolf that the French could not be trusted: they had broken every treaty they had ever entered into, from the time of Richard the Lionheart in the twelfth century. The English should not be afraid. Fortune might have ceased to smile on their war effort for now, but one heaven-sent victory could change all that. The conclusion was obvious:

> The king should pursue the rights he is possessed of in France with all his power, regardless of any outcry and of the devastation of the country which result, for it is better to lay waste to a country temporarily than lose it altogether.

In some respects, Fastolf sounds like a mouthpiece for Bedford, but in others his advice represented a profound change from the Regent's policies. For example, he advises that the most important military matters should in future be decided by English councillors, not by Frenchmen. He has evidently had enough of them:

> Item, that the king ordain in this land [France] sufficient councils of Englishmen, expert and knowing in the war, and that the war may be counselled and governed by [them] in particular [*bi speciallie*], and not be managed [*demened*] so much by the French Council as it has hitherto been the case.[20]

This advice would not have been acceptable to Bedford: it was a criticism of his way of governing, and it was also somewhat impracticable, politically. In the Regent's mind, the English ruled northern France by virtue of Henry VI's title as King of France, not by virtue of armed might alone. If that was so, Henry could hardly disregard the views of his loyal Norman subjects, as expressed in his Council. However, Fastolf was not a politician or a lawyer: he was a practical man, who thought that military decisions should be taken by Englishmen, especially in a time of crisis.

Sir John packed a wealth of other advice into his Memorandum of 1435. The garrisons in Normandy should be 'well stuffed and purveyed of payment', because a well-supplied garrison was of great 'comfort' to local people. A field army of 500 men should be placed on the borders of Normandy, to make war in Anjou, Maine and the Chartraine, while holding off the threat of invasion from the Duke of Brittany. Two more armies, each of 7,000 men, to be led by two competent 'chieftains', should be sent out from England via Calais or Le Crotoy, the first to make 'sharp and cruel war' in Picardy and Artois, Champagne and Burgundy, the second to do the same in the region of Chartres and Anjou. These forces should 'hold the field continually and *oostay*' (Fastolf's word for the *chevauchée*). They should fan out, riding 6, 8 or 10 leagues apart, and lay waste to the countryside, between 1 June and 1 November. The English should come as avenging angels,

> burning and destroying all the land as they pass, both houses, corn, vines, and all trees that bear fruit for man's sustenance, and all beasts that may not be driven should be destroyed, and those that can be spared, over and above the needs of the host, should be driven to Normandy, to Paris and to other regions in the king's obedience.

The raiders should show no mercy, and they should refrain from ransoming the territories they passed through, because that would weaken the effect. Three years of this sort of treatment would bring the Valois kingdom to its knees. The cost to the English Exchequer would be minimal, since troops sent out from England would only be paid five months' wages each year. For the rest, they could live off the French countryside. At the same time Fastolf urged that the English should take 'all manner of ordnance for the field, as *ribauquins*, culverins, artillery, wood-axes, hatchets and bills, to cut vines and trees with, gunners, carpenters and other means necessary for the conduct of the said ordnance ...'.

All this represents a complete reversal of the strategy pursued by Henry V and Bedford since 1417. The siege warfare employed during the conquest of Normandy and the largely static defence forced on the English by the reverses of 1429 were to be abandoned. Fastolf was advocating a return to the strategy pursued by Edward III, when the emphasis had been on the sending of expeditions, not on occupation of territory. The new strategy would have meant rejecting the idea that French non-combatants should be treated as if they were English subjects, who were entitled to protection from Crown forces.

The Fastolf Memorandum of 1435 is a very unusual document. We have recently been told that 'there was no native English tradition of manuals and treatises on warfare and chivalry written during the course of the Hundred Years War'.[21] Hitherto, advice about military strategy had been confined to the council chamber, or the pages of Roman and French authors (such as Vegetius and Christine de Pisan). Accordingly, we are not really sure why Henry V chose to land at Harfleur in 1415 or why he landed at Touques in 1417. Royal strategy was decided by the king and did not need to be put into writing. In 1428, the Earl of Salisbury had largely dictated the decision to attack Orléans because he had brought an army of 7,000 men with him from England. The matter was discussed in council, but the minutes (if any were taken) have not survived. The Fastolf Memorandum is based on rational argument rather than self-interest. Fastolf works out, on paper, what the objective is and the means required to achieve it.

Where did Fastolf get his ideas from? He probably had access to literature on the subject of strategy. We know that, at least in later life, he owned a copy of Vegetius's treatise and some of the works of Christine de Pisan, which circulated widely among the English military class, and it is conceivable that he may have been aware of a 'General Rule' which Vegetius at any rate had proposed: 'It is preferable to subdue an enemy by famine, raids and terror, than in battle, where fortune tends to have more influence than bravery.'[22]

However, Vegetius had written 1,000 years before and was an imprecise guide to what needed to be done in the fifteenth century. More useful, perhaps, were contemporary chronicles which related the history of the Hundred Years' War in the fourteenth century, when Edward III, the Black Prince and Henry of Grosmont, 1st Duke of Lancaster had developed the practice of riding in force across the length and breadth of France, burning and destroying wide swathes of territory. In particular, the Prince's two *chevauchées* of 1355 and 1356 had been spectacularly successful. Later *chevauchées* – those led by Sir Robert Knowles in 1370, John of Gaunt in 1373 and Gloucester in 1380 – are generally thought to have been failures, but this may not have been the version of events relayed to men like

Fastolf. According to Froissart, Gloucester had looked back on his *chevauchée* with fond memories:

> I have not forgotten my last expedition through France. I might have had with me about two thousand lances and eight thousand archers. When we crossed the sea, we entered France by way of Calais, and continued our march through the country, without meeting any one to oppose us or offer us battle. Such formerly was the success of Sir Robert Knowles, Sir Hugh Calveley, Sir Thomas Grandson [and] Sir Philip Gifford.[23]

Experience is the best teacher; and when Fastolf proposed a resumption of the *chevauchée* in 1435, he was probably drawing on his own knowledge of France more than on books and chronicles. After all, he had taken part in campaigns which were *chevauchées* in all but name – in the Cotentin in 1412, in the Angoumois and Saintonge in 1413, and in Normandy in 1415–16. He was also in a position to contrast one kind of warfare with another, since he had experienced the sieges of Harfleur and Rouen, as well as pitched battles at Verneuil, Rouvray and Patay. In addition, he moved in the company of other soldiers, not least when he attended the feasts held in honour of St George at Windsor and Norwich. Moreover, his proposals made a lot of sense in 1435: the war of conquest had ground to a halt; to renew it would have been unacceptably slow and ruinously expensive, if applied to Dauphinist France as a whole. The conquest of Normandy by this method had taken two years, while Maine and Anjou had only been partly subdued.

Fastolf's new remedy might well have worked – but what of morality and the law? Those on the receiving end would be innocent civilians and – under the Treaty of Troyes – subjects of the same king. Sir John knew very well that the reign of terror which he urged would involve breaking both the letter and the spirit of the Ordinances issued by Henry V and Bedford, which he had helped to implement and perhaps even draft. He therefore tried to justify what he proposed by suggesting that the areas affected by his multiple *chevauchées* had deserved their fate, because the inhabitants had either rejected the allegiance they owed to Henry VI, or were about to do so: 'For it is thought that the traitors and rebels must needs have another manner of war, and more sharp and more cruel war, than a natural and ancient enemy.' At the same time, Fastolf seems to have been concerned about the adequacy of this reasoning, and added a second argument:

> It is thought ... that the king may, and ought reasonably, make all this cruel war without any note of tyranny, seeing that he has offered unto his adversaries, as a Good Christian prince, that all men of Holy Church, and also of the commons and labourers of the realm of France, dwelling or being out of fortress, should dwell in peaceful security ... but that the war in either party should be and rest only between men of war and men of war,

the which offer the said adversary has utterly refused.[24]

It is not clear what this 'offer' was, or when it was made, but the broad thrust of the argument is clear enough. Following St Thomas Aquinas, Fastolf drew a distinction between the just and the unjust war, between the acts of a lawful sovereign and those of a tyrant. For him, tyranny meant the absence of legitimate power, and a king like Henry V was not acting tyrannically when he made war, even on fellow-Christians, because he was merely pursuing what was rightfully his. He was not merely engaging in a private feud, as the Burgundians and Armagnacs had been in France, after 1407. Further, the English would have been quite content to pursue the war with conventional forces, but the French had resorted to guerrilla warfare and had used highly unconventional means of resisting English rule, including the use of peasant armies and women fighters. (Fastolf did not refer to her, but Joan of Arc was the most unconventional war-leader one could imagine.) By implication, the conclusion was that the English would be justified in waging unrestricted warfare themselves. Fastolf was not alone in thinking this way. In the 1440s, the English Council solemnly decided that it was necessary to launch a further expedition across the Loire, and 'there use the most cruel and mortal war'.[25]

Fastolf's primary objective in writing the Memorandum of 1435 was to persuade the English delegation at Arras to reject French demands, but it is possible that there was also a hidden agenda, which was to make the case that the Duke of Bedford was right and the Duke of Gloucester was wrong, when it came to strategy. The two brothers had clashed when they met in Calais in the spring of 1433: Gloucester had wanted Calais to be at the heart of English strategy, while Bedford's mind remained fixed on Normandy. In this debate Fastolf was bound to be on Bedford's side, as a matter of personal loyalty and also because of his experience in Normandy. He seems to have had no comparable experience of Calais.[26] The Memorandum of 1435 advocates the *chevauchée* as a means of defending Normandy and Maine, rather than Aquitaine or Calais, and it is the Dauphin whom the author still regards as the main danger, not the Duke of Burgundy. In this respect, Fastolf was in danger of becoming out of date, because by 1435 Duke Philip – never a reliable ally – posed a very real threat to Calais. Gloucester was more aware of this danger than Bedford: he had pursued his own agenda in Hainault in the 1420s and he still harboured ambitions in Flanders.

In any event, Fastolf's advice was ignored, both at Arras and afterwards. The Congress had a dramatic outcome, but not because it involved any peace treaty between the English and the French. What happened instead was that the English walked out, but the French and the Burgundians stayed on. Charles VII agreed to apologize for the murder of Duke John in 1419 and also mortgaged the province of Picardy, and several important towns on the Somme, to Duke Philip. Philip took legal advice and, having satisfied himself that the Treaty of Troyes had always been unlawful, he renounced it – and the English alliance along with it. A separate peace was concluded between France and Burgundy, leaving England diplomatically isolated. Yet no English minister could seriously contemplate the resumption of the *chevauchée*. It was so far removed from practical politics or strategy as to sound like a counsel of despair.[27]

The Changing of the Guard, 1435–9

Despite their reconciliation with Charles VII, the Burgundians had hoped to stay neutral after the Treaty of Arras, but this proved to be impossible. Their volte-face was regarded as rank treachery in England, and Philip the Good became an object of hatred at court, in Parliament and in London, where the mob sacked the houses of Flemish merchants and murdered their inhabitants. English sailors intercepted Burgundian vessels in the Channel, while the Calais garrison staged raids into the hinterland, which was now almost entirely under Burgundian control. Since neutrality was not an option, Philip decided to strike back.[28]

Fastolf's centre of activity in the late 1430s was in Normandy. He must have passed through Calais on many occasions (and Worcester's list of offices names him as lieutenant captain of the castle there), but his knowledge of it must have been limited and he had many responsibilities which kept him in the Duchy, not least his position as one of Bedford's executors. Bedford had died in September 1435 and the natural leader of the operation to defend Calais was therefore Gloucester, who was now appointed Captain of Calais. Duke Philip planned no fewer than three attacks. He laid siege to Calais in 1436 and to Le Crotoy at the mouth of the Somme in 1437, while in the following year he aimed to break the dykes and take Calais by a process of inundation. None of these projects came to anything, but nearly all the towns in the Calais March fell to him in 1436. His repeated attacks kept Gloucester's mind focused on Flanders.

Yet Normandy still had to be defended, for while the Burgundians attacked Calais, the Valois French were not idle. The French counter-attacks came in several different areas and nowhere in Lancastrian Normandy was safe. Soon after 1435 the town of Verneuil, where Fastolf had been captain and where Bedford had won his greatest victory, was recaptured by the Count of Dunois, who was now in a position to threaten the entire Duchy from the south. There were rumours of invasion from Brittany in the west. The castle of Rouen had to be reinforced because of rumours of a plot. Two French captains managed to seize Dieppe, on the Channel coast.

From Fastolf's point of view, the worst disasters involved Caen and the *pays de Caux*. Monstrelet tells us that in 1434 large numbers of 'common people' arrived from the direction of Bayeux and surrounded the walls of Caen. William Worcester refers to the incident in his *Boke of Noblesse* and again in his *Itineraries*. In the first of these Fastolf's 'rescue' of Caen is used to illustrate the principle that a small group of disciplined men can prevail over a large ill-disciplined mob. In the second,

The Castle of Caen

Caen was the capital of Lower Normandy. It had been an important centre in the time of William the Conqueror, before he became King of England. Edward III had captured it during the first phase of the Hundred Years' War, but he did not stay to rule. The difference when Henry V took it in September 1417 was that Caen became a seat of English government. Bedford convened the Norman estates there, and he and Fastolf founded a new university in Caen in 1431.

Caen was above all a stronghold: a document of December 1431 refers to Fastolf as the Captain of 'the town, castle and keep' ('ville, chastel et danjon'). Yet it was never entirely secure, though it remained in English hands for thirty-three years. Ambroise de Loré led his partisans against the town in 1431 and a Valois army besieged it in 1435. Fastolf was proud of the fact that he helped to rescue the town on that occasion, but the English needed to repair the castle and town walls in the aftermath of the siege. William Worcester tells us that Fastolf 'made the counterwall on the south-east side of the castle towards the gate'. Though it is impossible to verify this by reference to French documents, the Museum of Caen considers it likely that Sir John superintended the repair of a section of wall between the Tour Mathilde and the Porte du Vaugueux, but Sir John did not stay long enough to see how his handiwork stood up to bombardment. He retired to England in 1439.

Ten years later, Charles VII deployed overwhelming force against Lancastrian Normandy, and his forces enjoyed complete supremacy in terms of equipment and morale. His Breton allies took the rock of Tombelaine, near Mont-Saint-Michel, which had been thought to be impregnable, while Saint-Sauveur-le-Vicomte in the Cotentin (a thorn in the French side in the fourteenth century) was taken without bombardment. In June 1450 Charles joined the siege of Caen in person. In Monstrelet's account, the French dug trenches, captured an outlying fort, undermined sections of the town walls and breached the walls of the castle in several places. Notwithstanding all this, the chronicler considered that the castle had been tenable:

I must say that it is the strongest in all Normandy, fortified with high bulwarks of a very hard stone, situated on a rock … It has a very strong keep, consisting of a large and high square tower, surrounded by four massy ones from the foot of the ditch to the level of the ground, the whole strengthened by a high wall all round, with towers at proper distances, and a very deep ditch cut out of the solid rock.

Yet Somerset surrendered Caen to the Count of Dunois after a siege which lasted only seventeen days. Charles VII made his triumphal entry into the city on 6 July 1450.

we learn that Sir Richard Harrington was the *bailli* of Caen and that Fastolf brought help from outside.[29] One of the *pièces justicatives* attached to the *Chronique du Mont-Saint-Michel*, edited by Siméon Luce in 1879, adds that Caen was attacked by members of the French nobility as well as by Monstrelet's 'common people', and that Fastolf was compelled to send for help to Domfront, where Lord Scales was in charge. Sir John's letter pleaded for help: as many men-at-arms and archers as could be spared must be sent to Caen as soon as possible. However, the messenger who took the letter went on foot and had difficulty finding Scales. He spent four days on the journey, running up bills at Harrington's expense, and to no great effect. Fastolf had to fend for himself at Caen. Nevertheless, his 'rescue' of it was a feat of arms to be proud of, and he continued to play a part in the aftermath. In March 1436 he corresponded again with Lord Scales (who was now at Vire), about the fate of a rebel called Borchier, said to have been captain of the commoners who had marched against the town. This time the messenger went on horseback.

In 1435 there was a serious rebellion in the *pays de Caux*, where Fastolf owned extensive estates. English and French accounts both give the impression that this was a kind of nationalistic peasants' revolt, and the 'peasants' certainly managed to take Fécamp, Valmont, Tancarville, Lillebonne, Montvilliers, and even Harfleur, while the French commander Richemont sent in regular forces. By the beginning of 1436 there were between 2,000 and 3,000 French troops in the *pays de Caux* and only Caudebec remained in English hands. The English commanders in Rouen were reduced to a state of panic. By the beginning of 1437, it was felt necessary to appoint four English scouts to keep watch outside the gates of Rouen by night, though this was the capital of the whole Duchy of Normandy.

Sir John may have rescued Caen but this did not turn back the tide of invasion, which even reached Granville, in the south-west corner of the Cotentin peninsula. The *bailli* of Valogne and Cotentin, Hugh Spencer, wrote to his fellow English commanders in Coutances, Saint-Lô, Caen and Rouen, to tell them of the gravity of the situation and make suggestions as to mutual defence and support. In Caen, the messenger Martin Doublet delivered letters to Harrington and Fastolf, informing them that

> The so-called Duke of Alençon, Charles of Anjou and the Count of Padirac, enemies of our lord the King, were due to join the lords of Loheac, la Roche, de Bueil and other adversaries who had advanced on Granville … where they are building fortifications.

Fastolf and Scales wrote to England, describing the Valois attack on Granville, and appealing for help.[30]

The insecurity felt by the English at this time is manifest in a letter written to Fastolf by John Appleton ('Appulton'), the English captain of Pontdonné and La Haye-du-Puis, around 1435. Appleton wants a favour. He recommends his daughter, who is a young widow, and asks Fastolf to look after her. He requests the grant of an estate at Piron (recorded later as one of Sir John's properties in Normandy). The grounds for this are that the previous tenant, Degory Gamel, proved unable to pay the rent, but Appleton promises to pay without fail. His letter explains that the English have their backs to the wall: the *pays de Caux* has been destroyed and the Cotentin is in danger of meeting the same fate. If Fastolf is not disposed to grant him Piron, perhaps he can have the estate of Beaumont instead? In any event, Appleton is unwilling to do business in Rouen, because the roads are not safe, and he will not go near the place, not even for 200 francs.[31]

The situation in English France was now extremely difficult, if not desperate, but it increasingly fell to others to lead the counter-attack: to men like Scales, Talbot, Willoughby and Sir Thomas Kyriell. These men were generally younger than Fastolf (with the possible exception of Willoughby, whose age is unknown). Talbot was born around 1387, Scales around 1399, Kyriell in 1406. Fastolf may have started to feel his age, and to give priority to other responsibilities than the military. In September 1435 the English recaptured the town of Saint-Denis, just north of Paris, but the French had inflicted numerous casualties with their culverins and they remained in good spirits when they surrendered. They told the English to say hello for them to the French kings buried in the Abbey of Saint-Denis, implying that they would be back. Among the English dead was Sir Robert Harling, and his bones were taken back to England for burial. He was commemorated in the church at East Harling in Norfolk. Fastolf was his uncle and his executor.[32]

Valois forces recaptured the bridges on the Seine, including those at Meulan, and they stopped the traffic on the river between Rouen and Paris, so that the latter was cut off. The Provost Simon Morhier attempted to remind Parisians of Charles VII's participation in the murder of the Duke of Burgundy in 1419, but it seems that many of them decided that, if the son was prepared to forgive his father's murder, so could they. Some of the most important Burgundian commanders in Paris defected to Charles almost immediately, including L'Isle Adam, who joined Dunois and Richemont as they closed in for the kill. There was no 'Battle of Paris' but the city did fall to Charles VII's forces in April 1436, despite efforts by Talbot, Scales and Willoughby to save it. The English garrisons took refuge in the Bastille but were greatly outnumbered and surrendered without making a last stand, though the fortress was well provided with stores and ammunition, as Fastolf had recommended.[33]

Englishmen with properties in Paris were forced to abandon them. The Regent lost the Hôtel des Tournelles and other palaces he had once occupied in splendour. As for those French who had 'collaborated' with the English, Charles VII was lenient because most of them were very useful to him, but it was impossible for those at the very top to stay in power. The Chancellor, Louis of Luxembourg, was expelled and took up a post in English Normandy. Likewise, the Provost Simon Morhier escaped and was rewarded with a place on the Council in Normandy and the office of Treasurer of the Duchy. Louis Galet, one of four officers (*échevins*) who had frequently dealt with Fastolf, was also transferred to Normandy. Charles VII lost no time in transferring the principal French institutions, including the Parlement and the Chambres des Comptes, back to Paris. At the same time, he did not move back there himself. The royal palace was abandoned, and the royal dukes, great aristocrats and churchmen followed suit. The French capital was a shadow of its former self in the late fifteenth century, not as a result of the Anglo-Burgundian occupation, but because the richest men in the land moved elsewhere.[34]

Bedford's death in September 1435 brought about a change of government in Normandy. Richard Plantagenet, Duke of York, was appointed Lieutenant (rather than Regent) the following May. Despite his high birth and his great wealth, York was only twenty-five and he lacked experience. This may have added to Fastolf's authority in the Duchy, rather than diminished it: he became one of York's advisers and continued to sit on the Grand Conseil, but he was also heavily involved with the administration of Bedford's estate. On 20 May, he was one of six councillors authorized to treat for peace – the others being York, Louis of Luxembourg, Salisbury, Suffolk and Raoul le Sage. At first sight this seems a little odd, since there was no realistic prospect of peace – or even a truce – at the time, but the appointment was a sign of Henry VI's personal preference for a peaceful settlement of his dispute with the Valois, which was to have an increasingly baleful effect on Fastolf's fortunes. It was also important as an expression of confidence in York and in prominent members of the Council he had inherited from Bedford. The King was making it clear that these men did have full powers to engage in diplomacy, however important the subject matter of the negotiations, and Fastolf remained, for the time being, one of the most experienced and trusted men in Normandy.[35]

But things could not stay the same without Bedford. Fastolf enjoyed a good relationship with York, but he was not as close to him as he had been to his old master. The new lieutenant had his own household and retainers of his own generation. Fastolf ceased to be Grand Master, and York even took over the captaincy of Caen, relieving Fastolf of this office at the end of November 1436.[36] It was around this time, too, that Sir William Oldhall became a member of the Council in Normandy. Unlike Fastolf, he went on to hold high office in France under York's successor Warwick and during York's second lieutenancy between 1441 and 1446. Most importantly, York continued to favour Talbot, who had been one of his annuitants since 1425, and Talbot, appointed 'marshal of France' on 8 May 1436, still harboured a grudge against Fastolf, as well as eclipsing him militarily. His recapture of Pontoise in February 1437 was particularly impressive.[37]

York's first lieutenancy was only ever intended as a stop-gap. He stepped down after a year and was replaced by Warwick in June 1437. Richard Beauchamp, 13th Earl of Warwick (1382–1439) had fought at the Battle of Shrewsbury in 1403. He was a Knight of the Garter and a jouster with an international reputation, as the finely illustrated Beauchamp Pageant makes abundantly plain. In his youth he had visited the Holy Land as a pilgrim and, like Henry IV, he had been a crusader in Prussia. He had also been Captain of Calais and was at Henry V's bedside when he died, and he became the tutor of Henry VI. He was an extremely wealthy nobleman and he was entirely suitable to serve as lieutenant in France. However, like York but for different reasons, he was a poor substitute for Bedford so far as Fastolf was concerned. Whereas York was too young, Warwick was too old: in his own words, he was 'full farre from the ease of [his] years'. Perhaps the most important personal objection was that he was Talbot's father-in-law.

Warwick's lieutenancy did not last long – he died in Rouen in 1439 – but York, now appointed lieutenant a second time, with greater powers and for a period of five years, did not travel to Normandy until June 1441. By this date, and probably in the year of Warwick's death, Fastolf had returned to England, shipping all his possessions back home with him.[38]

Fastolf performed one last duty for the Crown before leaving France, and this was in the Channel Islands. The Islands, which had remained in English possession continuously since the twelfth century, were an intrinsic part of the defences of the Duchy of Normandy, and particularly of the Cotentin. In Bedford's time they had been a useful naval base, though they had also been a target for French raids. The Norman Rolls record a grant of the Islands to Humphrey, Duke of Gloucester on 9 April 1437, and the Fastolf Papers confirm that Fastolf was Gloucester's lieutenant-governor in Jersey, Guernsey, Alderney, Sark 'and all adjoining parts' in the sixteenth year of Henry VI's reign (1437–8), and, further, that he made a journey to Jersey and Guernsey in the eighteenth year of the reign, which necessitated repairs to his ship:

> Item, to various expenses and stock for two ships called ballingers, of which particulars appear in two schedules or scheduled indentures annexed, on a voyage to the islands of Jersey and Guernsey, according to the accounts of the ostler and filed in two books
>
> 73s 2d
>
> Item, to various repairs made on the ballinger called *The George*, at Yarmouth, after the voyage to Jersey and Guernsey
>
> £7 8s 5d[39]

The changing of the guard which took place in Normandy after 1435 had unforeseen consequences for Fastolf. While he was still Captain of Fresnay-sur-Sarthe and Alençon, he had been informed that some treasure (consisting of silver vessels and coin) had been discovered, buried in the earth at Sées. This was a cathedral city, with bishops who traced their origins back to the fifth century, and an imposing Romanesque cathedral. The treasure had been discovered in the grounds of the bishop's palace, but, in Sir John's view, since the bishop was loyal to Charles VII, he was entitled to seize the treasure for himself, as enemy property.

Instead, he elected to treat it as Crown property (as if it were treasure trove under English common law). He called in the bailiff of Alençon, the viscount of Falaise and 'other notable men' to act as witnesses, took possession of the treasure, and delivered it to Bedford, taking care to get a receipt.

If we can believe Fastolf's account, he had behaved entirely properly, but some years later the legality of his actions was called into question by a new bishop of Sées – the third since the events in question. This man had lived all his life in territory owing allegiance to the Valois, and had been appointed by the Pope at the suggestion of the English lieutenant who succeeded York in the late 1440s (Edmund Beaufort, 2nd Duke of Somerset). The new bishop, claiming that the treasure belonged to him and clearly regarding Fastolf as some kind of brigand, claimed 5,636 shillings *tournois* by way of damages. Perhaps his complaint should have been directed against the English authorities, but since Fastolf was one of Bedford's executors as well as a protagonist in his own right, he sued Sir John; and he was able to obtain interim relief when all Fastolf's property in Normandy was 'put in hand of justice'. This included his 'goods, heritages, rents and revenues'.[40]

One would not expect a man like Fastolf to take this lying down, and in April 1449 he petitioned the Crown for relief, but his efforts were in vain, since this was the very year in which Charles VII's 'recovery' of Normandy began, and all remaining possessions which the English had in France were overrun. Fastolf's lawsuit therefore became pointless. This is a vivid demonstration of the way in which he suffered at the hands of the King of England, as well as at the hands of the French. In their anxiety to please the French, Henry VI's ministers failed to support the very men who had won Lancastrian France in the first place, and done their best to defend it thereafter.[41]

Castle Combe: the so-called Weavers' Cottages

Fastolf's coat of arms

The beach at Étretat

The tower of the Dukes
of Burgundy in Paris

The Pont des Perches
at Meulan

The church at Saint-Céneri-le-Gérei

Windsor, the Albert Memorial Chapel, where the Knights of the Garter met

The Basilica at Cléry-Saint-André

Remains of the medieval bridge at Meung

The River Sarthe at Fresnay

The gatehouse at Fresnay-sur-Sarthe

A medieval watchtower
at Calais

The Hôtel Cluny, Paris

The castle at Meung-sur-Loire

The bridge at Beaugency

The keep at Beaugency

Joan of Arc's memorial
at Beaugency

The Castle of Caen

The castle at Sillé-le-Guillaume

The collegiate church
at Sillé-le-Guillaume

The Surienne Tower, Fougères

The Great Tower at Caister Castle

The outer and inner baileys at Caister Castle

Fastolf's coat of arms
at Blickling Hall

Sir John Talbot

Sir John Fastolf in
Southwark Cathedral

The Shakespeare memorial in
Southwark Cathedral

The barge-house at Caister Castle

The Great Tower
at Caister Castle

Feathered angel,
Norwich Cathedral

The site of the high altar,
abbey church, St Benet's

Magdalen College, where the
Fastolf Papers are kept

The tomb that Fastolf never had – Sir Ralph Fitzherbert and his wife at Norbury, Derbyshire

The gatehouse at St Benet's Abbey

Chapter 6

The Army of Occupation

The nature of the Hundred Years' War changed completely when Henry V conquered Normandy and his brother Bedford conquered Maine. In the fourteenth century, Edward III had sent innumerable expeditionary forces into the French kingdom, but his aim was not to conquer it. His forces sometimes occupied strategic castles and ports for long periods of time – for example, Saint-Sauveur-le-Vicomte and Cherbourg in Normandy, Brest in Brittany, and above all Calais; but the king's strategy was essentially to fight his way to the conference table, whether by way of *chevauchée* or battle. These required the men to ride, march and fight, but not to man garrisons far from home for long years at a time. Henry and Bedford required much more of their armies. They had to assist in the work of governing the conquered territories, for the English occupied Maine for twenty years and Normandy for thirty. Fastolf was there for almost the whole of that time.

Discipline and Justice

The Lancastrian administration in France gained a reputation for being fair but firm. Henry V was known as a strict disciplinarian, cold and severe, but he repeatedly ordered his troops to behave towards French civilians as if the latter were his own subjects. The scene in Shakespeare's *Henry V*, where the king orders that his old friend Bardolph be hanged for stealing a pyx, is based on a real incident which occurred in 1415. Four years later, with Normandy at his feet, the King ordered his captains 'to make proclamation that no Englishman do harm a Norman subject'.[1] He also issued Ordinances, running to dozens of articles, in an attempt to impose discipline on his army. The documentary evidence takes a good deal of unravelling, but it looks as if he did this in 1415, 1417 and 1421. It was not an original idea to issue a code like this – Richard II had done it before his Scottish expedition of 1385, but it was a sensible measure, because an English army was a motley collection of units, though it needed to operate as one. In the army of 1415 there were men from many parts of England in the host, as well as Welsh and Irishmen. The Ordinances of 1421 also referred to French troops who fought on Henry's side.

These Ordinances are draconian. There is no laxity, no second chance, no concern for modern notions of 'human rights'. Nor is there any sign of the eighteenth-century idea that all men are born equal. They discriminate between men according to 'degree' or, as we should say, class. No assault must be made on any castle or stronghold, by archers or 'any other of the commons', unless 'a man of estate' be present. On the other hand, 'everyone of our side, of whatever condition or nation, [must] bear the arms of St George on front and back.'

The maintenance of discipline is the key. The troops must respect churches and the sacrament of the Mass; they must not capture churchmen or women, nor utter the cry 'Havoc!' or 'To horse!' at the wrong moment. There are rules about the taking and assignment of lodgings, the fair division of booty and the issue of safe conducts. When Henry V issued new Ordinances at Mantes in July 1421, further clauses were added. These prohibited the capture of children under the age of fourteen (unless of gentle birth); ordered that soldiers should not enter the bedchamber of a woman in childbirth; and outlawed the taking of horses without compensation. All men were to obey the king's sergeants and gatekeepers. No one was to rob, pillage or invade the lodgings of other soldiers, and

> Prostitutes [must] not be allowed to stay with our host, especially at sieges of towns, castle, or fortresses, but ... be located at least one league removed from the army ... Such women are not to stay within towns, castles or fortresses or maintain any house, large or small, on penalty of breaking of their left arm if, after one warning, they are found at large or hidden in the prohibited place.

Henry disapproved strongly of prostitution, just as Joan of Arc did a few years later.

After the fall of Rouen in January 1419 the King required that the knights and squires of Normandy appear before him to hear his commands, while on another occasion when he wanted his Ordinances published (probably in 1421) he commanded 'that a copy be given to every lord and governor of men in the host so that they might have full knowledge and inform their men of the aforesaid articles'.

The penalties prescribed for contravening the Ordinances included death (by beheading or hanging), the loss of an ear, and various types of financial sanction (which could involve the loss of armour or the forfeiture of a prize). Further Ordinances were issued by the Earl of Salisbury before the invasion of Maine in 1425. These repeated much of what Henry had commanded, but some refinements are worth noting. The Earl sought to repress prostitution by punishing the customer as well as the provider of the service. No soldier should 'hold any common woman within his lodging upon pain of losing a month's wages', though the 'common woman' should still have her (left?) arm broken.[2]

Bedford convened the Norman Estates on more than twenty occasions. The main purpose was to vote taxes, but he was also prepared to listen and his Ordinances show this very clearly. They were issued at Caen in 1423 and again in

Rouen in 1428, and refer to the 'grievous complaints and piteous clamour' of the people of Normandy. Fastolf certainly had a hand in this legislation, which is mentioned over thirty years later by William Worcester and described as

> The statutes made by John, Regent of France, Duke of Bedford, by a Parlement at Caen, in the 2nd year of the blessed Henry VI, named king, upon the conduct of the war, that I delivered to your highness ensealed, the day before your departing out of London, that remained in the keeping of Sir John Fastolf for great authority, three years.

Bedford's Ordinances seek to regulate relations between English and French in Normandy and require, above all, that justice be done by the French. The military and civil authorities must work together to achieve that goal. Articles 1 and 2 provide that competent men be found to serve as *baillis* and *vicomtes*, as well as captains of the English garrisons. Too many English captains have been taking bribes and levying illegal tolls in the towns and fortresses, and along the rivers, of the Duchy. This must stop (Articles 7 and 8); but it is for the civil authorities, not English captains, to enforce the law (unless it be a purely military matter concerning the profits of war – Article 9). It has come to the Regent's notice that some captains, men-at-arms and archers ('gens de trait') have been acting as vigilantes, in some cases holding innocent men to ransom, on the pretext that they have arrested 'Armagnacs' or 'brigands'. This is causing honest men to desert the Duchy, which will eventually ruin it. All such behaviour must stop (Article 10). In Article 11, Bedford labours the central point: it is the *baillis*, under him, who are the principal officers of justice ('les baillifz son soubz nous les principaulx chiefs en Justice'), and it is to them that English captains, knights, squires and all other men must defer. Severe penalties are to be exacted for failure to comply. For a first offence a man will be fined 10 *livres tournois* if he is noble, and 100 sous if he is not. For a second offence, the fine will be 100 *livres tournois* for a nobleman and 50 for a commoner. For a third offence, noblemen and commoners alike will have their goods confiscated and their bodies will be punished 'criminellement' (Article 12). The new decrees are to be proclaimed in a loud voice and to the sound of the trumpet ('à haulte voix et à son de trompe'), before they are enforced (Articles 14 and 15).[3]

The central problem was one of allegiance, and it had come to the Regent's attention that too many people were calling the Dauphin 'King' and his followers 'the French', whereas the correct form of address for those who adhered to the Dauphin's cause was 'Armagnacs', since they were rebels and traitors. We know from his private correspondence that Fastolf was scrupulous in observing this requirement. Around 1430, Stephen Scrope used intemperate language in a letter he wrote to him when he was in Calais. Fastolf objected strongly to his stepson's tone, but note the terms of the reprimand:

> I marvel greatly of those words, for I cannot remember in any way that I
> ever said anything to you or anyone else which deserved this lack of
> respect. And though I pay attention to whatever you write to me, for I must
> treat you with respect, I would not have you write in this way to any other
> man, for the words you used are not appropriate, unless they be used
> between adversaries, as between an Englishman and an Armagnac
> (Arminake).[4]

The English were not alone in using 'Armagnac' as a term of opprobrium. The
Canon of Notre-Dame consistently did so. During the civil war which plagued his
country, he always took the side of Paris and the Parisians: he disliked anyone who
governed the city oppressively or failed to provide good government. He hated
those who pillaged and robbed, behaving in an un-Christian manner 'like
Saracens', but above all, he hated the Armagnacs, who raided right up to the gates
of the capital. When Joan of Arc attacked Paris, the Canon even called her 'the
Armagnac girl' – 'la Pucelle aux Armagnacs'.[5]

Bedford's Ordinances were issued for Normandy, but the English
administration faced the same problems in maintaining law and order in Paris.
There is a remarkable series of pardons, collected by Longnon in the late
nineteenth century, which show that justice was sometimes tempered with mercy,
though the impartiality of the justice that was done must sometimes have been
questionable. These pardons were issued in the name of Henry VI, but since he
was a child at the time, they must in reality have been granted by Bedford,
sometimes to members of his own household.

In September 1424 three English soldiers, Alexander Russell, Thomas
Tournoul (Turnhill?) and William Marshal escorted the Countess of Salisbury
when she travelled up to Paris, possibly from Melun, by river. Their job done, they
decided to have a drink at a tavern called The Arms of Brittany ('L'écu de
Bretagne'). They did not have the right change and, when it came to pay for the
drink, the landlady attempted to cheat them. (At least this was what Alexander
Russell thought.) There was a row and words were exchanged. Eventually Russell
got up to leave, shouting: 'By the Devil, how are we ever going to get out of this
place, if you are not willing to let us pay!' Robin Morhillon, who was some kind of
French policeman, intervened at this point, but this only made things worse.
Morhillon demanded to know: 'What do you think you are doing? Who are you?'
Russell replied in terms which were self-evidently true, but probably seemed
arrogant in the circumstances: 'You can see and hear for yourself, by the language
we speak, both who we are and what kind of men we are.' Morhillon was not put
off by the fact that these men were plainly English soldiers. He accused them of
robbery. Russell called him a liar. Morhillon told Russell to shut up and said he

would enforce the king's peace. Russell said that on the contrary, he would do that. Morhillon pulled out a dagger but Russell's friends broke up the fight. Yet, when the three Englishmen came to leave the pub later on, Morhillon had another go. He seized Russell by the shoulder, crying, 'Aha, traitor, villain, now you are going to prison!' Russell said, 'You lie, you know very well I am no traitor!' Grappling with his assailant, Russell spun Morhillon round and stabbed him three times in the stomach with the butt of his dagger ('dague d'estoc'). We do not know what became of Morhillon but, presumably, he survived. For his part, Russell was thrown into the Châtelet prison, where he stayed for three months in very miserable circumstances, before asking for mercy. The normal penalty for any kind of felony was death, but he was pardoned, on the grounds that 'he did not know the customs of our kingdom of France, and because Morhillon did not make it clear who he was, or what he was, and was not carrying his baton marked with the fleurs-de-lys, but only a simple sword'. The citizens of Paris may have wondered why ignorance of the law was an excuse in this case, though Russell remained in prison, at least for the time being, on bread and water.[6]

There was another brawl in Paris (not mentioned in Longnon's collection) in May 1432. A native of Calais, Jean Wistrelant, was given letters which he was supposed to deliver to Fastolf in Paris. He travelled up to the capital via Rouen, in the company of some merchants, and delivered the letters at the Regent's palace. He went down to the kitchens, where the travellers were given some cod to eat, and then on to a tavern nearby. It was when they left the tavern that the trouble began. As he made his way back to Bedford's palace by the Rue Saint-Antoine, Wistrelant was accosted by an Englishman named Thomas Massinger, whom he had met in the garrison at Pontoise three years earlier. Massinger demanded a sum of money, the two men quarrelled, and Massinger drew his sword, shouting, 'Bloody son of a whore, I'll flatten you!' Wistrelant was wounded, but he fought back and killed his assailant – or so he thought. In fact, the man he killed was an innocent third party, who had placed his body between them. Now Wistrelant too was locked up in the Châtelet. We are not told what became of him, but perhaps the significant thing is that he was not a member of Bedford's household or army and could not expect any special treatment. There is certainly no record of a pardon.[7]

Violence was to be expected when one had to deal with fit young men who were customarily armed and were trained to fight. In 1432 there was a quarrel in Alençon between William Bernard (whom Fastolf had appointed clerk of the Watch) and another Englishman called Sanson. The latter had failed to report for duty on several occasions and Bernard had tried to discipline him with fines, but Sanson refused to pay and now drew his dagger, even threatening to shoot his enemy with a longbow. In addition, he shouted that he would 'crown' him. The two men eventually came to blows, and Bernard killed the other man with a blow from his *guisearme*.[8]

Colonialism and Resistance

McFarlane described the conquest of Normandy between 1417 and 1419 as 'the English revenge for 1066'. What he meant was that Henry V redistributed the land he conquered from the French, and on a feudal or 'neo-feudal' basis, though the land settlement was not as comprehensive as that which William the Conqueror imposed on Anglo-Saxon England after the Battle of Hastings. 'The fiefs of [Normandy's] lords – most of whom had retreated before the English advance – were shared out amongst the English captains; between July 1418 and June 1419 six Norman counties were conferred upon their leaders.'[9] There is more controversy as to the extent to which the Lancastrian land settlement involved a transfer of population from England to France and whether Normandy became a colony, 200 years before the foundation of Virginia, but the Canon of Notre-Dame, who generally blamed the Armagnacs for the woes which afflicted France, had no doubt that the English ejected many people from their homes. He condemned their actions in a purple passage:

> Alas! First all Normandy was lost and the great majority of people who were accustomed to till the fields and mind their own business with their wives and families, and to live peaceably, the merchants, churchmen, monks, nuns, people of every condition, were thrown out of their homes and made to wander abroad as if they were brute animals.[10]

While Henry V and Bedford recognized the privileges and status of those Frenchmen who chose to stay, they also encouraged colonists to cross the Channel. By 1439 – the year of Fastolf's return to England – English settlement in Normandy and Maine was substantial enough to constitute an obstacle to the peace negotiations held that year: by this date there were settlers in every part of Normandy and the *pays de conquête*. There was a particularly large distribution of land after the victory at Verneuil in 1424. The method of granting estates was intended to preserve them in English hands, and under Henry V it was common to grant entails, although under Bedford a wider variety of tenure was common.

Fastolf was one of those rewarded with land and office, at first in Normandy and later in Maine, but it was always subject to strict military obligations. Those who were given houses in the towns were obliged to play a part in keeping watch (by way of the *guet et garde*), and in 1427–8 Sir John received 200 *livres tournois* for guarding the town of Alençon.[11] The obligation might vary from place to place, as the wife of the owner of the largest house in Calais explained: she related the facts to a Burgundian writer of short stories, as a prelude to a tale of intrigue and adultery:

> Once a week every householder must in person stand guard on the town walls for a whole night. Through his friends, the knights and gentlemen serving your overlord, his eminence the Cardinal [Beaufort], who are

staying in his house, my husband has contrived to stand only half a watch. His tour falls next Thursday, from curfew to midnight.[12]

If all had gone according to plan, there should have been several thousand English settlers in Normandy who, together with the loyal French, would have manned the walls of the towns and fortresses – but all did not go according to plan. It proved impossible to attract enough settlers. The system of *guet et garde* produced little more than a 'Home Guard', and it was starved of both men and resources. As time went by, security got worse, not better. The administration had to rely more and more on the purely English element in the garrisons, and the English Exchequer and Parliament had to be resorted to for subsidies more often, not less.

The re-capture of La Ferté-Bernard in Maine by the Dauphinists in February 1427 showed the dangers of relying on local French forces. Robert Stafford, the English captain, explained that he had been in Le Mans when a rumour reached him that La Ferté had been 'sold'. He rushed back to find that the plot had not yet succeeded. He manned the gates and other strong places with local men whom he thought he could trust, and some Englishmen. He deployed scouts outside the town 'by land and by water' ('par terre et par eau'), but in the event he simply did not have enough men – only twenty-four to guard both the castle and the town. The enemy were able to enter La Ferté at night because the townspeople were in league with them and knew the town better than the foreigners.[13]

There was a change of policy after 1429, and again after 1435. In short, the neo-feudal system was abandoned and there was an attempt to recruit a purely professional army. An Ordinance was issued which positively forbade the recruitment of anyone who held land in Normandy, and there is a document from the Fastolf Archive in Paris which suggests that this was enforced. In 1433, ninety-eight archers were prevented from drawing wages, on the grounds that they were householders and inhabitants of Alençon ('hosteliers et habitans du dit lieu d'Alençon'), and a certain Robin Daunoy was likewise disqualified, though he was among the more highly paid men-at-arms. At the same time, English captains of war were now rewarded with pensions rather than with land. In some cases, French landowners were allowed to take possession of their estates once more.[14]

In an attempt to encourage loyalty to his sovereign as Duke of Normandy as well as titular King of France, Bedford founded two schools of law, canon and civil, in Caen in 1431, and William Worcester records that Fastolf played an important part in this. He notes that, during the time his master was Captain of Caen,

a university for learned clerks ['clericorum studentium'] was established in the said town of Caen by statute ['privilegio']... by the Regent the Duke of Bedford and by Louis of Luxembourg, Archbishop of Rouen and Chancellor of France ... with his [Fastolf's] help and counsel ['suo auxilio et concilio'].[15]

While similar institutions were founded in different parts of France at this time, the new University of Caen has been seen as part of the attempt to foster Norman autonomy, along with Henry V's creation of a separate Grand Conseil and Chancery, and his revival of the office of Seneschal of Normandy. On the other hand, it would be wrong to think that Bedford (and therefore Fastolf) were opposed to the influence of Paris, simply because they fostered Caen. One of the few things we know about the workings of the Grand Conseil is that it confirmed the privileges of the University in Paris on 26 December 1431, and Bedford also conferred honours on leading members of the academic establishment there.[16]

Unfortunately, by the time these changes of policy were put into effect in Normandy, the damage had already been done: the Lancastrian land settlement had alienated too many French whose opinion counted. For those displaced from their land, it meant internal exile, and it was only natural that the exiles wanted to return to their homes. Charles VII's cause received a great boost when he issued the Edict of Compiègne in 1429, promising that those who had been ejected – or their heirs – would be restored to their lands when he came into his own again. Many French captains now had something concrete to fight for, in addition to Joan of Arc's idealism.

Despite the ease with which Henry V had conquered Normandy, there was active resistance to the English from the earliest days of their conquest. Jean Juvénal des Ursins conceded that the towns (apart from Cherbourg and Falaise) were captured after relatively short sieges, but he also wrote of patriots who took to the woods and started to fight back, led by a man called Mixtoudin, who led an attack on Pont de l'Arche near Rouen. Resistance in the countryside continued to pose a problem for the English throughout Bedford's Regency. In April 1424, the ducal Council decided that it was necessary 'to send prudent and powerful knights into certain *bailliages* of the realm, to ride in arms through those *bailliages* in order to expel and extirpate the enemies, brigands, and pillagers therein, and to maintain the king's subjects in peace and tranquillity'. In pursuance of this policy, Fastolf was appointed governor of a large part of Lower Normandy, from Pont de l'Arche in the east to Caen in the west, and from Caen down to Alençon, 'to receive all manner of complaints, punish crimes, execute royal orders, resist the enemy, and suppress brigandage'. Similar measures were taken in relation to other parts of Normandy and the Île de France.[17]

The resistance in Normandy was led by men like Phélippot le Cat in Cherbourg, Pierre de la Haye and Robert de Floque in Évreux and, more spectacularly, Ambroise de Loré, who operated around Fresnay in the Sarthe valley, where Fastolf was captain for many years. Ambroise was said to have been captain there himself between 1418 and 1420 (when it was retaken by the English) but he remained active for many years thereafter. Though taken prisoner, he was released (or escaped) and took command of operations in Maine in 1427. According to one French source, he assembled around 150 men and led them from Sablé to Sainte-

The Barony of Sillé-le-Guillaume

Sillé-le-Guillaume, to the north-west of Le Mans, was an ancient centre of lordship, with a fort on the lake which dated back to the time of Charlemagne. When the French king gave the Duchy of Normandy to the Viking Rollo in the tenth century, it became a frontier town, with the Dukes of Normandy and Brittany competing for power in the area. Basset's Chronicle mentions a French lord of Sillé in 1415 (he was killed that year at Agincourt) and again in 1417 and 1424, during the build-up to the Battle of Verneuil. The lordship is mentioned alongside Mont-Saint-Jean ('Montjehan'), which is close by and La Suze, which is 25 miles away. This may indicate a feudal connection between these places, now obscure but doubtless well known in its day: when William Worcester compiled a list of Fastolf's titles and properties in later years, he named him as the Baron of Sillé-le-Guillaume and La Suze. In the Late Middle Ages, Sillé was important as the site of a castle and a collegiate church with twelve canons, and as a place where pilgrims stopped on their way to Santiago de Compostella or Mont-Saint-Michel.

The history of Fastolf's relationship with the barony is complex. French records confirm that English troops entered the Sarthe valley as early as 1418, but Fastolf and Lord Scales only took possession of the town and fortress in 1424. Basset's Chronicle records that they took it from the brothers Pierre and Olivier le Forestier, who were Bretons and had been at the Battle of Verneuil. It also notes that the lives of the Breton captains were spared, but only on condition that they became hostages for the payment of a large ransom.

The English hold on Sillé was interrupted in the late 1420s, when Ambroise de Loré retook the town, but it was in Fastolf's hands once again between 1430 and the late 1440s. However, he did not enjoy his new status as *baron* for long, nor was Sillé hugely profitable. McFarlane's study of the Fastolf Papers led him to conclude that the income from it, worth 1,000 marks a year in time of peace, declined to an eighth of that sum in 1444–5, and Sir John lost everything – and received no compensation – when the province of Maine was surrendered in the late 1440s. Yet the place had been hard-won: small wonder that Fastolf was bitter about the policies pursued by Henry VI's ministers.

There is a fifteenth-century castle at Sillé today, but no evidence that Sir John built any part of it. It would have been surprising if he had, for it is doubtful if he ever had the time to reside there. The fighting in many parts of northern France continued to be fierce after his acquisition of the barony and his services were constantly required elsewhere, to meet Valois counter-attacks in Normandy and around Paris. Accordingly, there is no Château Fastolf, nor even a Tour Falstaff in Maine. What we see at Sillé today was built by French noblemen, who came into their own again after the English had vacated the area.

Suzanne to take on a force of 2,000 to 3,000 led by Fastolf himself. After fighting with Joan of Arc at Orléans and along the Loire in 1429, de Loré accompanied Joan and Charles VII on their *chevauchée* to Reims, returning afterwards to his home territory. His main theatre of operations was in the neighbourhood of Fresnay, Saint-Céneri and Sillé-le-Guillaume, where Fastolf had his barony, but after the French recaptured Paris he became Provost there.[18]

Ambroise de Loré did not act alone. Basset's Chronicle tells us that as early as 1421–2, a group of disaffected knights led by Sir Olivier de Mauny broke through into the Cotentin and did widespread damage in the peninsula. Stories like these show that French 'guerrillas' resisted the English from the earliest days of the occupation and kept up a stubborn resistance throughout. They also imply that there was support for the resistance among the indigenous population, so that English garrisons must have been constantly on guard, even when they were not formally on watch. The French resistance was quite capable of taking a walled town by *escalade* as well as by storm. Monstrelet tells us that they succeeded in scaling the walls of both Hamme-sur-Somme and Compiègne in the same year (1423) – and on both occasions 'through neglect of the watch'. They took Gerberoy in the same fashion in 1449. Even the Canon of Notre-Dame, who did not welcome Armagnac victories, wrote that in 1423, 'The English sometimes took a fortress from the Armagnacs in the morning but lost two to them in the afternoon; and so this accursed war went on and on.'[19]

In Maine the English met with stiff resistance, despite their victory over the Valois field army at Verneuil. In 1426 there was a conspiracy to betray Alençon, which was well to the rear of the line of advance. Basset and Hall each tell us that a Gascon captain in English service agreed to betray the town for 4,000 crowns, but changed his mind at the last minute and revealed the plot to Salisbury. The Earl ordered Fastolf and Willoughby, at the head of 2,000 men (which probably means no more than 'a large force') 'to encounter with the buyers of the king's town'. A French commander, unaware of the Gascon's double-dealing, came to the stated rendezvous with only 200 horsemen and 300 infantry. Hall relates the outcome:

> And, abiding for the Gascon, he there displayed his banner, thinking triumphantly to enter into the town; but it happened otherwise. For, before they were aware or suspected any rescue, they were environed with the English army, and slain and taken every creature, save Peter Danthenazy and twenty-five others, which by the swiftness of their horses saved themselves.[20]

There was always trouble from those whom the English called 'brigands'. Henry V had authorized bounty hunters to bring them in, dead or alive: he offered six *livres tournois* a head. Bedford used a combination of carrot and stick: he granted general amnesties in 1422, 1423 and 1431, as well as granting individual pardons to repentant criminals. However, there were many executions: 152 between June 1419 and April 1420. Were these men common criminals or patriots? The answer has been much debated by English and French historians alike, and opinion has not always divided on national lines. Even Jean Juvénal des Ursins, who supported the Dauphin, recognized that there were 'countless numbers' of brigands operating 'in the Île de France and in the forests of Hallate, Senlis and Montmorency' – men who killed anyone who fell into their hands, and by implication would have turned to a life of crime whatever the circumstances. Likewise, the Canon of Notre-Dame complained of unspeakable atrocities committed by Armagnacs and brigands. On the other hand, Benedicta Rowe has been accused of 'bad faith' in arguing that many of those condemned for brigandage in Normandy deserved their fate. In Fastolf's eyes, it cannot have made much difference which category a rebel fell into. He and his fellows were required to hunt down anyone who broke the law, whatever the motive.[21]

The English used the carrot and the stick: they laid on dinners, processions, plays (*mystères*), jousts and other forms of entertainment, especially in Paris. In August 1425 a kind of blindman's buff was staged in an *hôtel* there, where the blind were given large sticks and invited to hunt down a boar, but gave each other a good thrashing instead. A dinner for 8,000 people was thrown in June 1428, but in April 1431 they hanged a large number of 'robbers' and 'murderers' (after a period of lax Burgundian rule). The coronation of the boy-king Henry VI in December 1431 was supposed to be a time of great rejoicing and spectacle, but if the journal of the Canon of Notre-Dame is anything to go by, Paris was unimpressed. He sniffed at the fact that English cooks served meat on the Sunday night which had been pre-cooked the previous Thursday. Not even the sick in the public hospitals, who were used to eating leftovers, thought that this was acceptable (some evidence, perhaps, for the superiority of French cuisine, a hundred years before the Renaissance). At the same time, the English were niggardly when it came to the games and sports they organized on the day after the coronation, and the French were in any event unable to follow the proceedings, because the organizers insisted on speaking English. At this rate, it was going to take a long time to win the hearts and minds of the Parisians.[22]

The English also took harsh reprisals when there was open rebellion, but there were still numerous plots. John Strecche noted one in Rouen (to capture and kill Henry V), as early as 1419. Ten years later there was a somewhat incompetent conspiracy to release prisoners kept in the castle at Verneuil. One of the plotters did not know how to whistle, though this was the agreed method for giving the signal to attack. The man had to blow a trumpet instead, and one must assume that he at least knew how to do that, but the plot failed when it was betrayed to Fastolf, who was Captain of Verneuil at the time.

Other conspiracies had to be taken much more seriously. There were plots in Cherbourg and Louviers in 1429, Argentan and Chartres in 1432 and in the

Cotentin in 1440. There was a daring attack by partisans on Caen in 1431, and no fewer than four minor plots which came to light in Rouen between 1424 and 1429. The famous Ricarville plot in 1432 involved some very determined men, although the authorities regarded it as a 'mad enterprise'. The conspirators captured the Grosse Tour, in the centre of Rouen, and held out for twelve days. The garrison was compelled to summon reinforcements from other places held by the English – including Caen where Fastolf was captain. In September 1433 there was a plot to infiltrate 200 Scotsmen into Paris via the Porte Saint-Denis and Porte Saint-Antoine: they were to disguise themselves as English soldiers by wearing the cross of St George.[23]

The English Garrisons

It was the captain's responsibility to superintend building works, and although the English did not build new castles in occupied France, they were compelled to repair existing structures. The exception to this was the construction of a new palace for the Regent in Rouen between 1419 and 1439. William Worcester noted that Sir John was 'Captain of the palace of Rouen, where he made the very strong tower there above the River Seine on the east side'.[24]

As in feudal England, many soldiers in neo-feudal Normandy spent most of their time on 'castle-guard' (*guet et garde*), rather than in battle. The chroniclers tend not to deal with this aspect of army life, since it was too humdrum and there were not enough 'feats of arms' to satisfy their readers, but the archival sources are replete with references to it. In 1420 there were about 4,500 troops in the Duchy, distributed between some forty garrisons. After the victory at Verneuil, the numbers were reduced to around 3,000 but they were brought back up to around 6,000 after the setbacks of 1429 and 1435, only to be taken back down to some 2,500 at the time of the Truce of Tours in 1445. As Captain of Caen, Fastolf was paid for two mounted men-at-arms, fifteen foot-soldiers and fifty archers in 1432, while he had three cavalry lances, twenty-seven infantry lances and ninety archers there the following year. At Fresnay, the numbers were twenty-four mounted men-at-arms, fifteen foot-soldiers and 120 archers in 1432, and thirty-one horse lances, nine of foot and 140 archers in 1433–4. One is struck by how few reliable men there were to defend the places where he was captain. Numbers like these were to prove woefully inadequate when Charles VII launched a serious invasion to recover his patrimony. They were scarcely enough to maintain law and order.[25]

So long as the troops kept to the garrison towns, they were subject to military discipline, but one cause for complaint was that some English soldiers – men-at-arms and members of the rank and file – had started to reside in other towns and villages. Apart from anything else, this made it harder for the captain to find them if he needed to form a posse in pursuit of local 'brigands'. Bedford's Ordinances of 1423 provided that all soldiers must reside in the appointed places and that anyone who did not have a captain should find one within fifteen days (Articles 3 and 4). However, this did not entirely solve the problem. Even the captains were sometimes guilty of extortion and robbery. Such behaviour was prohibited, on pain of confiscation of goods and the death penalty ('la hart') (Article 5), but infringements still took place.

It is impossible to know the extent to which Bedford's Ordinances were observed. Benedicta Rowe concluded that 'on the whole the evidence of such certificates as have survived goes to show that the garrisons behaved themselves'. She was referring to certificates issued from time to time by the *vicomtes* (the local French magistrates), of which she cited those relating to Coutances (January 1429), Château Gaillard (March 1429) and Caen (July 1433). These three do paint a picture of contentment. In Coutances, the *vicomte* reports that he has asked if there are any complaints; the town crier has called for them to be made known on the last three market days, and no one has complained. To make sure that the people are not simply afraid to come forward, he has caused discreet enquiries to be made among the people of note, the butchers, bakers and inn-keepers of the town, but still no one wishes to complain. It therefore appears to him that the lieutenant's men have behaved themselves, and in particular paid their bills as they should have done. Much the same story is told in relation to Château Gaillard and Caen a few years later. It is only in Falaise, in 1435, that we find evidence of any wrongdoing, and this relates only to a missing 'pipe' of cider, taken by Denis Peinton [Paignton?] from Jean Foucault of the parish of Coutrailles. The claim has already been settled by a payment of 40 shillings *tournois*, made by the Receiver-General of Normandy. Can we really believe that this is all the French had to complain about?[26]

A much bleaker picture of the occupation emerges from some of the Valois sources. In the pages of Jean Juvénal des Ursins, we read how English troops, engaged on the Sarthe in 1417, put some of their prisoners in dungeons and drowned others in the river. Juvénal des Ursins also relates that some of those incarcerated in Paris after the capture of Melun in 1420 – admittedly those put in the Châtelet rather than in Fastolf's Bastille – were given hay to eat, called 'dogs' when they begged for food, and starved to death. He tells us that Henry V set a very bad example, despite his reputation for impartial justice. When complaints reached him about atrocities, he replied that he was only following normal procedures. If he marched against a town, he would lay siege to it and when marching through hostile countryside, he would burn it. 'War without fire', he said, 'was useless – like sausages without mustard' ('guerre sans feu ne valait rien, non plus que andouilles sans moustarde'). The royal example of ruthlessness was followed by Fastolf's colleague Richard Harrington, *bailli* of Caen in April 1435. Harrington's men apprehended a woman called Joan the Bold in Falaise. Joan was suspected of giving counsel and shelter to local 'brigands'. She was ordered to be buried alive ('enfouie toute vive').[27]

Some efforts were made to mitigate the excesses which some troops were undoubtedly guilty of. Guy du Melle, priest of Champhaut near Argentan, fell under suspicion of having dealings with the enemy and was harassed and robbed by English soldiers. They threatened to strangle or drown him and lay in wait for him several times. The priest fled to Fastolf (who was Governor of Alençon at the time) and Sir John issued him with a safe conduct. In December 1434, an assize was held in Falaise which heard evidence of other abuses, in particular:

> Horrible murder and slaughter done near Vicques on the nobles and common people of the region by several English, French and other men-at-arms, of whom it was said that Thomas Watrehoux (Waterhouse?) and Roger Yker (Hiker?) were the leaders, Captains and undertakers.

Orders were issued at Rouen for Fastolf and other officers to apprehend Watrehoux, Yker and their accomplices as soon as possible, and we learn that the culprits were duly arrested, imprisoned in Falaise – where they confessed their crimes – and executed.[28]

As a captain, Fastolf sometimes experienced difficulties with the officials responsible for paying the garrisons. One problem stemmed from the fact that he commonly held more than one captaincy – and it was sometimes necessary to appoint a 'lieutenant' – literally, a person to act in his place – while he in turn acted as lieutenant for others. However, while this was clearly convenient from the military point of view, the practice was not always acceptable to the civilian paymasters, who were cautious men, anxious to avoid paying twice for the same thing. When Fastolf was appointed Captain of Verneuil in 1427, Bedford directed the Treasurer and Governors-General 'of France and Normandy' to make sure that he was paid, through the Receiver-General's office, without contradiction or difficulty ('sainz aucun contradict ou difficulté'); but there was a considerable problem nonetheless, at the end of 1431. Fastolf was acting as Lieutenant of Caen, at a time when he was also Captain of Fresnay. Because of French attacks in the south, the Council in Rouen ordered twelve of the fifteen mounted lances at Caen to be sent down to Fresnay and Alençon, in exchange for an equal number of infantrymen, but this created a shortage of cavalrymen in Caen. Sir John responded to this by sending an extra cavalryman to Caen to serve in his place, but the Norman Treasury refused to pay for the additional man.

This mysterious episode, which was noted by the American historian Newhall almost a hundred years ago, may well be illuminated by British Library Additional Charter 47305, not cited by him. This contains a letter dated 27 September 1431, written by Fastolf when he was in Rouen, to the Vicomte of Caen, pointing out that he had entered into an indenture with a man called James Dryland, and had purported to appoint the latter as Lieutenant of Caen in his place. However, the expedient did not work. It is a fundamental principle of the law of agency that 'a delegate cannot delegate' (*delegatus non potest delegare*). Translated to fifteenth-century France, this meant that while a captain was entitled to appoint a lieutenant, a lieutenant could not lawfully appoint a lieutenant. In Fastolf's case, we know that the Treasury was willing to pay him as Captain of Fresnay (where rates of pay were normally higher), but was unwilling to pay for the self-styled 'Lieutenant of Caen'. Surreau's officials even withheld the pay of the entire Caen garrison while this dispute was resolved.[29]

There were other arguments about the rate of pay. On one occasion, the Duke of Bedford had to countermand his own staff, to ensure that his Grand Master was properly paid. It had evidently been normal practice to pay the financial controllers in the Norman garrisons at the same rate as the cavalrymen, but on 20 November 1431 the Duke gave orders that the controllers should in future be paid at the lower rate fixed for the infantry. The saving which would accrue would help to pay for a special levy or *creue* of men, who were required to reinforce the districts where Fastolf was in charge. (These were recognized as especially vulnerable because they were on the very edge of enemy territory – 'grandement en frontières des ennemis et adversaries'.) Bedford was perfectly well aware that he was taking extraordinary measures here and that his proposals would encounter resistance from the ducal Treasury, but he insisted that his orders be obeyed. The letter containing his commands confirms that Fastolf was a key figure in the government of Normandy: the Duke refers to him as 'our dear and loyal knight and Grand Master of our household Sir John Fastolf, Captain in charge of the said place of Fresnay and our Lieutenant in charge and Captain of the said place of Alençon'.[30]

Garrison duty could be hazardous. A document dated 16 January 1433 which, on the face of it, explains a minor breach of protocol, provides an insight into the dangers. Fastolf had submitted a *contrerolle* for his garrison at Alençon. This was a routine procedure, part of the system of financial control developed by the Regent's administration as a check on the reliability of musters, but in this case the document had been signed by a clerk, rather than by the controller in person. The writer felt obliged to explain why, and the explanation gives us some idea of the risks which Englishmen in France had to run:

> This was done under his sign manual by Thomas Hartley, the clerk of the late John Ferreld esquire, controller of the garrison of Alençon, who served for the quarter terminating on 29 September last, in the absence of the said Ferreld, who was recently killed, murdered and slaughtered ('qui naguère a été tué, muldry et ocis') by the enemies of our Lord the King, while on the road back from Paris.[31]

English captains could be held to account for their actions, at least at the suit of other Englishmen. Under the provisions of the Treaty of Troyes, they were obliged to use French courts, including the high court of justice in Paris known as the Parlement. The case of <u>Overton v Fastolf</u> concerned the accounts which Sir John said that Thomas Overton should have kept, when he acted as his receiver. As the name of the suit suggests, Fastolf was the plaintiff, and he claimed 20,000 francs from Overton. Overton filed a defence and counterclaimed, arguing that Fastolf had unjustly had him committed to prison – at first in Falaise and later in Paris. Fastolf replied that he had been fully entitled to imprison Overton, in view of the serious risk that he might abscond. At the heart of the case was the accusation that Overton had been guilty of unlawful exactions in Anjou and Maine, starting in 1428. He had allegedly cheated Fastolf by failing to render a proper account, but in bringing the suit, Sir John was also complaining indirectly about the exploitation of the king's French subjects.[32]

The arguments were not confined to mere accountancy. Each man put his character before the court. Overton referred to Fastolf as a fugitive knight ('chevalier fuitif'), because of his conduct at Patay. This must have hurt: in reply, Sir John said he was a knight, indeed a Garter Knight, an honourable man, and a trusted servant of the Regent of France. Further:

> He was of noble birth, of a noble line, and that from his youth he applied himself to the service of the King, in arms, in the countries of England and in Ireland, and on a journey to Jerusalem; and that it was, since that time, through his valour that the town of Soubise was taken, and its captain, the Sire de Heilly was captured; and that, when the late King first landed, he was the first to disembark and jump into the sea up to his sword-belt, and the King gave him the first house they saw in France, and he was Captain of Harfleur, according to the arrangements made by the Duke of Exeter; and that in the field he always vanquished anyone who offered him the pledge of battle [*gaige de bataille*] in the town of Calais; and that all along he had been esteemed as wise, courageous and valiant; and he recited several other acts of valour, and honourable exploits.[33]

Overton was a worthless impostor. He had claimed to be a clerk, educated at Winchester, but had been unsuccessful in claiming benefit of clergy. He had originally been nothing more than a common archer, along with thousands of others who had landed at Touques with Henry V. He owned 'not a furrow of land in France'. He had lived in sin with his French 'concubine' and had several bastards. He was totally untrustworthy and should under no circumstances be allowed to go free. He was passionately fond of dice and 'as likely to go and play in Bruges as in Ghent'.[34] Fastolf had rescued him from obscurity in Harfleur, where Overton had 'neither horse nor ass, neither proper clothing nor footwear' – and look how the man had repaid him!

Fastolf also gave further and better particulars of Overton's wrongdoing. He said that Overton had falsified returns when the troops had been mustered, that he had claimed for men whom he had never retained, that he had failed to pass on the rations he had indented for, and overcharged for safe conducts. His behaviour was oppressive, destructive of all discipline and morale, and had materially contributed to the English defeats at Orléans, Patay and elsewhere. These were very serious accusations. The English prided themselves on their fairness. Even Sir John Talbot, whose name was supposedly used to scare French children, was known for his impartial justice: there is a story in the *Hundred Tales* that (like Henry V) he once punished one of his own men for stealing a pyx from a church.[35]

Yet Overton admitted nothing. On the contrary, he counter-attacked by criticizing the Regent himself. He said that there was no hope of justice under Bedford, though the latter was supposed to be the guardian of the State. The Duke was surrounded by avaricious men who were only concerned to flatter him and, as a result, the whole realm was on the road to rack and ruin. Unwisely, Overton published his views by writing to various people in England about the case. He also insulted the judges of the Paris Parlement, calling them 'stuffed rosaries' ('chappeles fourrez'). This was the last straw as far as Bedford was concerned: he intervened in the case, throwing his weight behind his servant Fastolf. He demanded that Overton do penance, in his shirt-tails and without a hood, for the insults he had heaped on the English administration.

In later years, Fastolf had time to develop his thoughts on the importance of good government, and he conveyed them to posterity through the medium of his secretary. Certain sections in William Worcester's *Boke of Noblesse* might even suggest that the old knight became something of a critic of English rule. The *Boke* contains a sustained 'Exclamation' against the 'oppressions and tyrannies and cruelties' which some English officials had visited on the 'poor commons, labourers and peasants'. The inhabitants of Normandy – and the writer was referring to the French as well as to English settlers – had been 'surcharged grievously with the payment of taxes, *tailles*, subsidies and impositions beside their rents', so that their loyalty had been tested to destruction. The case of <u>Overton v Fastolf</u> springs to mind when we read how things are supposed to have deteriorated after Fastolf's departure: 'the officers then being needeth not to have so many lieutenants or under officers as they have had, which wasteth and destroyeth your said people by undue charges to enrich [themselves]'.[36]

Oppression had led to disloyalty and even treachery. Monstrelet and Waurin both tell us of a miller in the town of Verneuil who was supposed to keep watch but was beaten up by an English soldier for sleeping on the job. In the end, the man got his own back, because he betrayed the town to the Valois. One Sunday morning in July 1449, he sent the other watchmen home and allowed French troops to attach ladders to his watermill. They climbed in over the town walls, and when the garrison escaped into the castle, the miller completed his revenge by drawing off the water in the moat. Edward Hall has a similar story to tell about a raid on Laval in 1429.[37]

Masters of the Narrow Sea

Shakespeare's John of Gaunt spoke of England in unforgettably moving terms in *Richard II*:

> This happy breed of men, this little world,
> This precious stone set in the silver sea,
> Which serves it in the office of a wall,
> Or as a moat defensive to a house.

Once again, this is stirring stuff, but it is bad history. The English Channel was not a 'moat' in the Late Middle Ages, though it had become one by the late sixteenth century. No late medieval admiral could control the Channel in the same way as Elizabeth I's commanders did when the 'invincible' Armada arrived in 1588: it was beyond the capacity of their ships and sailors to do so. Moreover, there was no Royal Navy to speak of, except for a few brief years in Henry V's reign. Ships and shipping were organized for war on an ad hoc basis, and it was the soldiers rather than the sailors who did the fighting, even at sea.

When Fastolf was a young man, the coastline of England was very vulnerable to attack. The year 1405 was one of particular danger, since the French had entered into formal alliance with Owen Glendower in Wales and the Castilians in Spain. The Castilians used galleys, raiding and burning all the way from Cornwall to Southampton, before taking refuge in Harfleur for the winter. Don Pero Niño's standard-bearer tells us that Spanish galleys sailed into the North Sea in 1406, making an unsuccessful attempt to raid East Anglia, engaging in battle with an English fleet in the Channel and using a fire-ship to destroy English shipping. In February 1405 Prince Thomas was appointed admiral and orders were given that four ships be sent to him, with 255 mariners on board. Michael de la Pole, 2nd Earl of Suffolk, took part in naval operations in May, and Fastolf joined him. It seems more than likely that he first acquired experience of war at sea that year, in between tours of duty in Ireland. Accounts relating to the expenses of Suffolk's retinue show that 16d was paid for a horse of John Fastolf's at Sandwich and 5s 6d to buy him a warm doublet.[38]

It was Henry V who transformed the situation. The King built an impressive fleet, increasing the number of his ships from two in 1410, when he took control of the royal council, to six at his accession in 1413, and thirty-four by 1417. The fleet was based in Southampton, the point of embarkation for the expedition of 1415, and a base during the conquest of Normandy between 1417 and 1419. One by one, the ports of northern France fell into Henry's hands, and they remained under English control for a generation. The Dauphin was reduced to using La Rochelle on the Atlantic, and Fastolf and his fellow captains could travel back and forth from England without risk of molestation by enemy ships or pirates.

The situation began to deteriorate almost as soon as Henry V died. Many of the best master-mariners were laid off, and many of his best ships were sold. This did not lead to a sudden collapse, but it did weaken the English war effort. It meant that, when the French hired Castilian ships once more in 1424, they were able to bring an entire Scots army over to help them, and there was little the English could do.[39] The alliance with the Burgundians, who controlled the Low Countries, held until 1435, but when the Duke of Burgundy rejected it, the English were found sadly wanting at sea. The French recaptured both Dieppe and Harfleur (scene of their first triumph) and, although the English were able to retake it, this took five years, and they never recaptured Dieppe. Piracy revived and the pirates (who included Englishmen from the West Country) were able seamen. When the Lancastrian Empire fell apart in 1450–1, the French were able to blockade Brittany, La Rochelle and the Gironde estuary, and they were largely unopposed. Anglia no longer ruled the waves.

There were advocates of a naval strategy, both in Parliament and outside, and in the Fastolf Memorandum of 1435, Sir John urged that the wool trade with Flanders be protected:

> The sea [should be] kept mightily, as well for the king's worship and the realm's, as for the salvation of the merchandise and of the navy of England and of Normandy ... and the navy [should] make sharp war and keep the course of merchandise as much as they can or may from Sluys.

Fastolf was not alone in taking this line: it was becoming a persistent theme of English writers to stress the importance of the English Channel. The most urgent message was delivered by the author of the *Libelle of English Policy*:

> Cherish merchandise, keep the Admiralty,
> That we be masters of the Narrow Sea.

By and large, this was whistling in the dark. The advice was not heeded and English seapower simply withered away.

In the absence of a navy, the government of Henry VI found it necessary to commission privateers, and Fastolf invested in at least one such venture – an episode which undoubtedly demonstrates his patriotism, though it had unfortunate consequences. In 1447 he lent £100 to Thomas Daniel, a squire in the royal household who had eventually became a Justice of the Peace, sheriff, tax commissioner and 'guardian of the seas'. On this occasion Daniel was ordered 'to go with his posse on the sea for the safe keeping thereof, with full power to lead, rule and govern all masters and mariners and others of his company, and to punish the same, and to fight the king's enemies'. He enlisted the services of Robert Winnington of Dartmouth, recommended by the king as a useful man for 'cleansing' the seas and 'rebuking' robbers and pirates.

On 25 May 1449 Winnington reported back that he had seen action in the Channel. He had been told to make sure that all foreign ships there should 'strike' (lower) their colours in the presence of an English ship. So when he came across a Hanseatic salt-convoy he told them to strike, 'in the King's name of England'. They told him to take a shit ('go skyte'), in the King's name of England. The English were outnumbered but they were not deterred: perhaps they were used to receiving this kind of reply. They waited for the wind to change and they attacked. A ferocious sea-battle ensued, in which Winnington's crew suffered many casualties but seem to have overcome the Germans. Yet it is unlikely that Fastolf made much of a profit. Winnington's activities did severe damage to English diplomacy and, in retaliation for the attack on their fleet the merchants of the Hanse seized all English property within their jurisdiction and a general war broke out. When Fastolf prepared a claim against the Crown five years later, he included the sum of £100 lent to Thomas Daniel. Meanwhile, relations between the two men had deteriorated considerably. There is a record of proceedings between them in the Chancery court in 1452–4, when Fastolf accused his opponent of malicious falsehood: Daniel had allegedly had the audacity to say that he was Fastolf's heir![40]

The Patent Rolls record that in the early 1450s Fastolf spent the sum of £100 in 'victualling, repairing, maintaining and keeping' a ship which 'would otherwise have perished'. This vessel, originally named *Le George of Prussia*, but at some point renamed *Danyelleshulk* (Thomas Daniel's hulk?), had been captured 'contrary to the league between the king and them of Prussia'. On 10 January 1451 commissioners were appointed to sell the ship and repay Sir John the £100 he had invested, subject to the King's right to reclaim it from the buyer, if the vessel was required for military purposes within four months.[41]

Despite the mixed fortunes he enjoyed with his maritime investments, Fastolf knew what he was writing about when he advised Edmund Beaufort in 1448 to protect the coasts of Lancastrian France:

> Item, that of the ports of the sea there, as Harfleur, Honfleur, Le Crotoy, Cherbourg, and others, being in our obedience, be purveyed a navy of ships to help resist against your enemies when it shall need, forsean alway that by the admiral of England and Normandy the sea be well kept because of conveying of victuals, and for coming over the sea of soldiers when it shall be necessary.

As so often with Fastolf's memoranda, this was sensible advice. The problem with his naval strategy was not that it was wrong, but that the government ignored it.[42]

Chapter 7

The Fall of the Lancastrian Empire, 1439–53

The Falstaff Moment

> I know thee not, old man: fall to thy prayers;
> How ill white hairs become a fool and jester!

The moment when Henry V rejects Falstaff, his old friend, at the end of *Henry IV* is world-famous. Despite the promise made in the Epilogue, that the old knight will be brought back to entertain the audience, he dies before the action in *Henry V* begins, so crushed is he by the treatment he has received at the hands of the new king. There was no such dramatic moment in the career of the real Falstaff, but his military career did come to an end in 1439, when he sailed home from France, though he had another twenty years to live. Moreover, his retirement did owe much to the changing of the guard in English Normandy: after the death of the Regent, nothing was quite the same there.

The English position in France was not hopeless. Normandy had been gravely weakened by the events of 1429 and 1435, but much of the lost ground was made up by 1439, including in the *pays de Caux*, where Fastolf owned several properties, and many fortifications were rebuilt, including the castle of Rouen. On the French side, Joan of Arc's victories along the Loire and the coronation of Charles VII at Reims had increased the prestige of the Valois monarchy, but the court continued to be plagued by new factions, and there was even a series of noble revolts, starting in 1437, in which the new Dauphin (later Louis XI) played a part. Philip the Good of Burgundy may have ceased to be an active ally of England, but he was not a reliable ally to Charles VII either and by 1440 he was largely reconciled with the English, without becoming party to a new alliance. Meanwhile, many French and Burgundian soldiers, laid off after the Treaty of Arras, joined the notorious *écorcheurs* ('skinners'), creating widespread disorder in many provinces of Valois France.[1]

Yet in 1439 Fastolf came home from France and took up residence at Southwark. He did not withdraw from public life, but he took no further part in the fighting. In the dedication of his translation of the *Epistle of Othea*, addressed to Fastolf and written around 1440, Stephen Scrope mentioned that Sir John was feeling his age:

> And now, seeing that the natural course of events, through the turning and passing of 60 years upon you at this time of age and weakness, has started to reduce your physical labours, taking away your natural strength and power from all labours which involve the carrying out of chivalrous deeds
> …

Whereas Shakespeare recognized seven ages of man, Scrope referred to three 'areas' of human activity:

> And he exercised his knightly labours in three areas … in the first place, in victories, deeds of chivalry and arms, in defending the said Realm … from his enemies. The second was in helping to form policy, giving the benefit of his wisdom on high matters, giving counsel in order to promote justice and tranquillity, and in keeping the peace for the common welfare of that noble Kingdom. The third was in spiritual matters [spiritual and ghostly deeds], even for the health and welfare of his soul.[2]

Fastolf was now moving from the first into the second of these areas. He probably felt that, at the age of fifty-nine, he had done enough as a soldier, but he hoped that he would remain a counsellor. To some extent he did, but we shall see that his advice often fell on deaf ears.

It was a retirement packed with activity. As we have seen, the accusation of cowardice, levelled against Fastolf in 1429, was renewed when Talbot was released from captivity. This was a difficult charge to refute, since Talbot's career went from strength to strength, while Fastolf's was in decline, and there must have been more than one Garter Knight who sympathized with the case for the prosecution (Talbot being far from the only Englishman who was captured at Patay). In 1460 William Worcester made a claim for expenses, detailing the labour involved in helping his master with his lawsuits. Included in the bill is 100 shillings for expenses arising out of the Day of Patay ('la journée de Patay'). Worcester says there that he spent thirteen years on the case (1429–42), during which he collected testimony from the Duke of Bedford, Lord Scales and others. He also refers to the fact that in the spring of 1442 a tribunal of Garter Knights had finally been convened to deal with the matter, including the King, Cardinal Beaufort, the Duke of Gloucester, and Lords Fanhope and Hungerford. Two lawyers were also attached: Thomas Bekyngton, now Bishop of Bath and Wells, and Stephen Wilton, and judgment had at last been given for Fastolf. A triumphant conclusion, it seems; but we would never know it from the laconic way in which the servant records the outcome.[3]

Throughout the 1440s, Sir John continued to bombard the men in government with advice, telling them how they should govern occupied France, and urging that the advice of those who wanted to make peace be ignored. In 1907 the Reverend Duthie described him as a man who 'foamed at the pen', but Fastolf did not confine himself to writing. He still served on committees, in particular on commissions of the peace for Norfolk in March 1444 and July 1445, and all through the period when the towns of Normandy and Gascony were falling to Charles VII: in December 1447, May 1448, October 1450 and March 1452. He continued to serve in this way at least once a year between 1453 and 1458. On 1 August 1450 he was appointed to a commission of oyer and terminer held in relation to disturbances in Norfolk and Suffolk. Fastolf's committee work does not seem to have diminished when his wife died in 1445. It only came to an end about a year before his own death in 1459.[4]

The Surrender of Maine

There were further negotiations with the French at Gravelines near Calais in 1439 but the English Council was now divided as to whether to make concessions: Cardinal Beaufort was in favour of giving ground but the Duke of Gloucester was against. In taking a hard line, Gloucester voiced the opinions of many old soldiers who had fought in France and, predictably, Fastolf was in agreement with him. In earlier years Sir John had declined to assist Stephen Scrope when the latter wanted to join Gloucester's service, but the objection had been personal. By 1440, there were few differences between Fastolf and the Duke, politically or personally. At the end of his military career, Fastolf served as Gloucester's lieutenant for the Channel Islands and even travelled there on the Duke's behalf. When Gloucester died, he acted as an administrator of his goods.[5]

The conference at Gravelines did not bring peace, or even a truce (though it did lead to a commercial agreement between England and Burgundy), but in 1440 Henry VI decided to release the Duke of Orléans from his long imprisonment in England, and he determined to do so without any quid pro quo. Charles was the son of Louis of Orléans, murdered by the Burgundians in 1407, and the son-in-law of the Count of Armagnac. He would have been the natural leader of the Orleanist or Armagnac faction in France, had he not been captured at Agincourt in 1415. He had now spent twenty-five years in England and had become a significant poet, but he was out of touch with what was going on in France. Yet Henry and his ministers hoped that, if he were released, he could persuade his fellow countrymen to come to terms.

Fastolf was strongly opposed to the idea of releasing the Duke of Orléans, at least on an unconditional basis. He had fought the Duke's half-brother Dunois at the siege of Orléans, and he knew how important the prisoner was to the French, for he had listened to their demands for his release at Auxerre, in 1432. He would also have been aware of Henry V's strong views on the subject. From Sir John's point of view, the Duke was an important bargaining point, to be held in reserve, not thrown away: he is listed in Basset's Chronicle as the first and most important of the prisoners taken at Agincourt. Fastolf was far from alone in criticizing the new peace policy. Gloucester, excluded from the inner circle of government, also feared that the English position in France was being undermined. He protested loudly that it would be wrong to release Orléans and pointed out that the negotiations, at Arras in 1435 and at Gravelines in 1439, had only made the English position worse. Rather than abandon the royal claim to France, Gloucester declared that he was prepared to die for it.

Orléans was released nonetheless, and released unconditionally. Anticipating the adverse reaction this would produce, the Council arranged for the issue of a broadsheet in the King's name, justifying the decision which had been taken, and explaining the royal wish for peace. The war had been going on for a hundred years. Peace was necessary to promote Christian unity and avoid further schism in Mother Church. Even Edward III had not managed to make himself king of France, for all his many victories on the battlefield: he had settled for an 'easy part' of the kingdom at Brétigny in 1360. It was in any case impossible to conquer the whole of France: she was too 'ample, great, and so mighty in multitude of walled towns, castles and fortresses, in rivers and strong counties'. Even Henry V had become 'sadded of the war' at the end of his life. The war was draining the English kingdom, whereas the French were better able to bear the burden: they appeared to recover from their efforts 'without any or little cost or labour'. English hopes of building a new Normandy had been disappointed: the settlers were not willing to stay there in the face of increasing violence and resistance. In the last six or seven years, their numbers had dropped alarmingly: 'where there were 100 there are now 10, where there were 50 there are 5'.[6]

Six centuries later, and one hundred years after the Entente Cordiale, it is hard to disagree with these arguments. Yet, in Fastolf's mind, there was still all to play for, and pessimism seemed like defeatism. He continued to believe that God was on the side of the English, and he saw no reason to be intimidated by the size of France or the French armies. France was much larger than England, but not impossibly large – as Edward III and Henry V had shown. Even Shakespeare's 'hollow pampered jades of Asia' could manage 30 miles a day, which meant that the French kingdom could be traversed on horseback in less than a month. As to her large population, France was divided into many provinces, not all of which saw eye to eye with Paris, and her monarchs often had difficulty in concentrating the vast forces which were in theory at their command. In any event, the great authority Vegetius was clear that sheer numbers had never been decisive in ancient times: the Romans had prevailed by virtue of superior methods, particularly in training and discipline. Sir John had seen the truth of all this for himself, at Verneuil and Rouvray. Moreover he (and Gloucester) were undoubtedly right to question the wisdom of releasing Orléans in the early 1440s and surrendering Maine in the late

1440s. They were also right to suspect that each of these measures played into Charles VII's hands.

While the King pursued peace at the diplomatic level, Normandy still needed to be defended. In 1440 the Council reappointed the Duke of York as lieutenant in France, this time with the powers which Bedford had enjoyed as Regent. Fastolf did not come out of retirement, but he did form part of the Duke's 'discrete' (or inner) council, which advised on the conduct of the war. This body drew up a memorandum containing York's conditions for taking up office. Sea-captains should 'keep the mouth of the Seine', to ensure that Rouen was adequately supplied, facilitate raids on the French herring fishery at Dieppe, and interfere with the trade of Harfleur (which was in French hands between 1435 and 1440). Two thousand men should be deployed at sea to support any sieges which the Duke might undertake along the French coast. A long-list of siege-guns was included in York's demands.

The memorandum of 1440 contained some gloomy criticism. In particular, it made the point that many men who had been awarded land in France in return for military service had not in fact stayed, but had abandoned their posts, in some cases granting leases before coming home. Anyone reading the document would have had cause for concern about the future of Lancastrian France. Yet Fastolf was a practical man, familiar with Bedford's way of doing business, and he concentrated on the job in hand. He advised that York should be given the same powers as the Regent had enjoyed, including the power to replace absentees. Likewise, York and his heirs should be given a full indemnity in relation to his actions, so that none of them could be held personally liable if anything 'inconvenient' happened – 'be it battle, rebellion of the people, or otherwise'. Sir John clearly remembered the widespread revolts in Normandy in 1435, as well as the reverses suffered on the battlefield, and the accusations which might be levelled at a commander in the event of defeat.[7]

York took his time before he sailed for France, but he was a dynamic leader when he arrived. He and Talbot conducted a short campaign only a few miles north-west of Saint-Denis and Paris, and they succeeded in breaking up the French siege of Pontoise. They drove the French constable, Arthur of Richemont, back to the gates of Paris, although they were outnumbered two to one. Though they ran out of supplies and the French were soon able to retake Pontoise, it was a successful campaign. Interestingly, it seems to have followed the 'Fastolfian' plan described in the Memorandum of 1435, since it was essentially a small *chevauchée* which avoided both towns and costly sieges. However, unfortunately for the future of English rule in France, York was unable to repeat his initial success, though his second lieutenancy lasted five years.

None of Fastolf's writings – or none that survives – relates to the period between 1441 and 1448. However, on 4 March 1443 the Privy Council informed him that he was one of those appointed to receive money due to the Earl of

Somerset, in relation to a new expedition to France. This may sound like a minor role in what was a major military undertaking, but the decision indicates continuing confidence in Fastolf on the part of the Council. For his part, Fastolf may have been reluctant to play a more active role on this occasion, given that he was one of York's annuitants, and York was still in post in Rouen. Somerset's expedition was a separate venture, separately financed and did not find favour with the military establishment in Normandy. Yet the objectives of Somerset's new expedition must have been close to Fastolf's heart.[8]

This was not the same Somerset who was to become notorious, at the end of the decade, for presiding over the surrender of Rouen and Caen, but his elder brother, John Beaufort, nephew of both the Cardinal and of Thomas Beaufort, Duke of Exeter (Fastolf's old commander). A war hero, captured at Baugé in 1421 and held prisoner until 1438, John Beaufort had been Captain of Cherbourg, Avranches and Tombelaine (a fort built on a rock, opposite unconquered Mont-Saint-Michel). In 1439 he led a relief column to aid the garrison at Meaux. In 1440 he led a force of 100 men-at-arms and 2,000 archers from England, linked up with other troops in Normandy and raided the Santerre district, capturing Folleville and Lihons. He had gone on to help his younger brother Edmund in the recapture of Harfleur – news of which must have been music to Fastolf's ears. Fastolf had fought alongside many of the men who continued to serve in France after his retirement, and he must have known many of those associated with Beaufort. These included Osbern Mundeford, who had been with Sir John at Fresnay in the 1420s and helped reinforce Caen in 1433, but who subsequently joined Beaufort's retinue.[9]

Beaufort was created Duke of Somerset and enfeoffed with the Duchy of Anjou for seven years. One of his objectives was to conquer territory beyond the Loire (and thereby secure the English position in both duchies – Normandy and Aquitaine). The starting point for his expedition would be Maine, where Fastolf was a baron and knew the ground. Indeed, by 1443, there cannot have been many men with his experience. It may be more than a coincidence that a message, sent by Henry VI to the Duke of York about Somerset's expedition, has a distinctly Fastolfian ring to it. Henry referred to the fact that his adversary Charles VII had invaded Aquitaine that year and seemed unwilling to retreat until he had captured Bordeaux and Bayonne: on the contrary, he seemed 'disposed to come into Normandy'. The King tells York that this is why he has retained Somerset:

> The which with a great and mighty army shall pass the sea by a part of Normandy and so pass over the water of Loire into the ground occupied by the enemies and there use *most cruel and mortal war* that he can and may.[10] (My italics)

With hindsight the expedition of 1443 looks like a failure: John Beaufort died soon afterwards, possibly by his own hand. However, Fastolf may have been satisfied with the results at the time. The French had mounted raids into Normandy and Maine in 1439. The 1st Duke of Somerset did at least avert a French attack on Normandy and, during his raids into Maine and Anjou, he did succeed in recapturing Beaumont-le-Vicomte, using reinforcements from Fresnay. The property which Sir John still owned in Maine had been made more secure, and the strategy and tactics which he had advocated eight years before had been to some extent vindicated. It was only later that the wedge which the expedition of 1443 drove between Somerset and York caused a division to open up between Fastolf and the Somerset family.

Meanwhile, the King's mind became increasingly fixed on the idea of settling his father's quarrel with the Valois. The Earl of Suffolk, who was now chief minister, began a series of negotiations in France, in which Charles VII and his brother-in-law René of Anjou proceeded to run rings round the English team. It was agreed that Henry VI should marry René's daughter Margaret, and a two-year truce was negotiated at Tours in 1445. There was an implied promise, soon made express by Henry, that the province of Maine as a whole should be surrendered to the House of Anjou. Henry hoped that this gesture would bring about a full treaty of peace, but the hope was ill-founded. Once the promise to cede Maine had been made, it proved impossible to attach conditions – for example, that the English settlers in Maine should be allowed to stay, or be compensated for the loss of their lands and titles. When the expiry date for the Truce of Tours arrived, there were last-ditch attempts to persuade Charles VII to pay such compensation, but the French now replied blandly that this was for the English to decide. They had no knowledge or experience of such matters, or of English methods: 'It was not for them to interpret mandates, writs of execution, nor discharges of any of that party ... it belonged to [Henry VI] to cause his said promise to be performed.'[11]

Fastolf, and many like him, were frankly disgusted at the way in which the settlers in Maine were abandoned to their fate. They thought that the French had duped the English negotiators at Tours, but also that the royal councillors in England had been naive – indeed, bordering on criminally negligent. In this, they were possibly right. There are many historians who sympathize with Henry VI and Suffolk's policy but none who think that it was wisely implemented.

The process of withdrawal from Maine did not go at all well. There had been no consultation with the settlers, who now faced homelessness and ruin. Indeed, their situation was so dire that there was a good deal of resistance, and almost a mutiny in the English garrison at Le Mans. The captain there was Osbern Mundeford, a man who is frequently mentioned, among the brave, in Peter Basset's Chronicle. Fulk Eyton and Matthew Gough were delegated to receive the surrender, so that the place could be transferred on to the French, but Mundeford refused to co-operate in this process without direct orders from Somerset. Further negotiations with the French were interrupted by a group of English knights and squires, including Fastolf's proctor John Daubenay. These men demanded compensation even now, on behalf of those they represented. We may well see Fastolf's hand at work here, directly through Daubenay and indirectly through Mundeford, despite his apparent withdrawal from the immediate scene of the action.[12]

In a further agreement reached between English and French diplomats on 15 March 1448, special provision was included about the future of 'certain places which are disobedient'. The truce between English and French forces was to continue after Le Mans had been surrendered, but it would not apply to places which continued to offer resistance. These included Sillé-le-Guillaume, Fresnay-le-Vicomte and Beaumont – all places which Fastolf had either owned, or where he had once been captain. The garrison at Fresnay were so vehemently in favour of a policy of 'no surrender' that the place had to be exempted altogether from the agreement reached with Charles VII, and its ultimate fate is unknown. This diehard resistance again has a distinct Fastolfian flavour.[13]

During the winter of 1447–8, Charles VII's patience ran out, and a French army of between 6,000 and 7,000 men surrounded Le Mans. At first, Osbern Mundeford resisted and sallied forth at the head of his few hundred men. However, greatly outnumbered and outgunned, even he was compelled to surrender. He probably felt that he had managed to salvage some element of pride, in that his men were allowed to march away on honourable terms. Fastolf, however, was incensed. The French had recovered Le Mans, of which he had once been captain, and the whole County of Maine, where he had been governor, and they had done so virtually without striking a blow or firing a shot. No compensation was ever paid to the English settlers, either by the French or by Henry VI. Fastolf seems to have thought that he had been specifically promised an amount in respect of his barony at Sillé and La Suze, but nothing was paid for that. He reckoned that he had lost 2,500 marks by this act of negligence alone.[14]

In contrast to the shabby way in which the settlers had been treated, the 2nd Duke of Somerset was richly rewarded for his part in surrendering Maine. Yet, in March 1448, Fastolf broke his silence and produced a memorandum for the Duke, who had replaced York as lieutenant in Normandy. Why did he continue to be so helpful to men who were pursuing policies of which he thoroughly disapproved, and were paid handsomely for doing so? He must have been aware of the surrender of Le Mans, for Nicholas Molyneux, who was a servant of his, played a leading role in the negotiations which led up to it and signed the act of surrender. One explanation could be that Sir John continued to put country before personal advantage.

Fastolf now advised Somerset to maintain a good flow of supplies, spears, bows, arrows, axes, mauls and *ribauquins* (cannons) from England; to fortify the marches of Normandy and raise a navy; to appoint a good lieutenant for Aquitaine, and good men as captains, avoiding the 'covetous', 'oppressors' and 'extortioners'. He should also avoid having favourites on his council. This advice was particularly relevant at the time, because there had been a financial scandal in Normandy in 1446, when Sir Thomas Kyriell, Captain of Gisors, had been accused of embezzling his men's wages. Two inquiries were held, the first by Talbot (who was the Marshal in France) and Viscount Beaumont (the Constable in England), the second by Bishop Bekyngton (Fastolf's associate in 1432) and Lord Cromwell (who submitted the first 'Budget' to Parliament). It was discovered that the web of corruption extended more widely than anyone had suspected and possibly involved the Duke of York. Read in context, Fastolf's memorandum of 1448 was therefore more than a homily: he was trying to be practical, telling the new lieutenant how to avoid the irregularities which had recently plagued Lancastrian France. The question is whether anyone was listening.[15]

Fastolf also offered Somerset some advice of a more personal nature, which seems to have gone beyond the call of duty. In short, he told the Duke to 'mind his own back':

> First, it is thought right necessary, saving the good correction of you, my lord, and of your council, that you make sure of your true and steadfast alliance of your kind and steadfast friends in steadfast faith and love to the king's weal and the welfare of his realm, that they may in your absence, labour and acquit themselves truly unto you as nature, reason and truth will in support of the king's right and of your troth, if any charge in time coming might be imagined against you. And that you purvey [provide] yourself of wise and sad counsel in this realm of such as may, can or dare do for you in your absence.

Why was Fastolf so helpful to Somerset? Perhaps it was because he understood only too well the dilemmas faced by anyone who served the adult Henry VI. The King was not merely an inadequate ruler, he was an unreliable employer.[16] He had so little sense of purpose that he was liable to agree with whatever was suggested to him and, having listened to you, he might well listen to your opponents if you went abroad, even in his service. Henry was a disaster for the kingdom but he was also a problem for his own ministers. For whatever reason, it is remarkable that Fastolf was so sympathetic to Somerset in 1448, in view of the Duke's part in the surrender of Maine, and in the light of what happened next.

The Loss of Normandy

The English occupation of the Duchy of Normandy lasted thirty years but collapsed in less than two. William Worcester wrote:

> Of which Duchy, we have in the year of our Lord 1450 lost, as within the space of 15 months be put out wrongfully, through subtle workings conspired and wrought by the French party under the shadow and colour of a truce.

Worcester thus blamed French machinations. Other Englishmen too were unwilling to believe that the English had really been defeated, and thought that they had been 'stabbed in the back'. This led to internal revolt, but not to any successful attempt to recover what had been lost.

The surrender of Maine in the late 1440s meant that Normandy was once again in the front line. No peace treaty flowed from the agreement at Tours: English and French negotiators continued to meet from time to time, but extensions of the truce were all that was achieved. Meanwhile, as Worcester alleged, Charles VII did use the truce to prepare for war. In 1445, 1446 and 1448 he issued Ordinances which reorganized the French army, forming a permanent force out of the bands of 'Skinners' who had terrorized his domains for so long. This new standing army was composed of companies known as the Compagnies d'Ordonnance and they were led by a group of able captains, some of whom who had been fighting the English all their lives – Richemont, Dunois, Alençon and Poton de Xaintrailles. Meanwhile, John Bureau had revamped the French artillery train, and Jacques Coeur improved the coinage and rebuilt the royal finances, at a time when England repeatedly faced bankruptcy.

Monstrelet's description of Charles VII's troops would have made Fastolf green with envy:

> The king of France had placed his army on a most excellent establishment; and, as it was a novelty, it is worth describing. He had supplied all the men at arms and archers with good and secure equipment, namely the men at arms with cuirasses, greaves, light helmets and swords mounted with silver, as well as the lances which their pages bore; each man at arms had three horses, for himself, his page and his varlet, which last was armed with a light helmet, a brigandine, jacket or haubergeon, battle-axe or *guisearme*. Every man at arms had two archers on horseback, dressed in brigandines, greaves and light helmets, the greater part of which were ornamented with silver; or, wanting these, they had strong leather jackets and haubergeons. The soldiers, when on service, were always paid monthly; and under such strict discipline that none dared seize anything unpaid for, nor to make prisoners, or ransom man or beast, unless they belonged to the English or their friends.[17]

This 'new model army' would probably have outclassed any which the English could have sent against it; however, as it was, there was no standing army at all in England. Moreover, although there were probably sufficient men in the garrisons of Normandy to form a field army, this was not done in time. The memorandum which Fastolf prepared for Somerset in 1448 contained some advice on this point, but it was vague and brief: '[Find] you a certain number of men-at-arms to the field when you will require them, allowing for the need to man the borders and according to the availability of resources.' Sir John did not explain how the men were to be found for this field army, if the garrisons were to be kept up to strength. By 1449, the awful truth was that the defences of Normandy were falling apart from years of neglect.[18]

Some of the troops and settlers ejected from Maine in 1448, including Osbern Mundeford, took refuge on the western border of Normandy, and fortified or re-fortified Mortain and Saint-James-de-Beuvron, where Rempston had routed the French in the 1420s. Charles VII regarded this as a breach of international law, which forbade the occupation of border areas and the repair of key fortresses during a truce, but the crisis came in March 1449, when an Aragonese mercenary captain, François de Surienne, captured the Duke of Alençon's town and castle of Fougères, in the Duchy of Brittany. The Treaty of Tours had provided that, if a town or castle were taken after the truce began, it should be restored immediately, but de Surienne declined to do this. The Duke of Brittany appealed to Charles VII for help, which he agreed to provide on condition that the Bretons join him in expelling the English from Normandy. On 31 July Charles repudiated the Truce of Tours altogether.[19]

The English authorities blamed de Surienne for what happened, and pretended that he had acted on his own initiative, but this is frankly incredible. De Surienne had been a king's knight in 1435, as well as Constable of Porchester castle. He had served the English Crown in various theatres of war and was elected a Knight of the Garter in November 1447. He was still in the pay of the English. The conclusion is inescapable that the attack on Fougères was officially inspired, even if it was supposed to be a covert operation.[20]

De Surienne held on to Fougères for only five weeks (though there is a Tour Surienne there to this day). No help came from England or from English Normandy and he was eventually forced to surrender. He felt betrayed – and sent back his Garter – telling the world that the English government had planned the whole disgraceful episode. He revealed that, at the planning stage of the operation, he had informed Suffolk that he had no place near enough to Fougères from which to mount the attack. Suffolk had replied that, 'after several approaches' ('plusieurs ouvertures') he had managed to find a suitable base. The village of Condé-sur-Noireau, to the south of Caen in Lower Normandy, would suit his purpose ('serait bien propice').[21] This had been one of Fastolf's properties since Henry V's time – it is mentioned at a very early date in Basset's Chronicle – and it was evidently still thought to be of strategic value, despite the fact that it was over 60 miles away from Brittany. De Surienne's version of events has the ring of truth, and it tells us that Fastolf still owned Condé-sur-Noireau on the very eve of the French invasion, despite all the changes in English fortunes.

We cannot be sure that Sir John was a wholehearted supporter of the plan to raid Fougères. He may have been, but he may simply have succumbed to some kind of blackmail. De Surienne's memorandum is ambiguous on the point. He said that there were 'several approaches' made, before Fastolf agreed to the proposal. Did he mean that other people were approached, before the request to Fastolf was made, or that Fastolf needed to be asked several times? Given his prolonged disgrace with the brotherhood after Patay, Fastolf may have found it hard to refuse assistance to a fellow Garter Knight. In any event, it was virtually impossible to resist the Duke of Suffolk, who was the king's first minister and a power in his own right in East Anglia. In 1447, the Duke's officers had occupied two of Sir John's manors at Dedham in Essex. Suffolk's claim to these properties appears to have been entirely specious but Fastolf was quite unable to obtain any redress from the courts in the following three years: it was only after Suffolk's murder in 1450 that he was able to obtain justice. The politics of the situation may have been much the same in Normandy as they were at home.[22]

There is another reason for thinking that Fastolf may have been less than enthusiastic about the proposal for a raid on Fougères. Among the papers collected by William Worcester was a document prepared in French in 1449 and entitled *Suggestions for Questions to be asked of the Duke of Somerset, respecting his Misconduct in Normandy*. The authorship of this is uncertain but it is another of those papers which have a Fastolfian flavour. Among the questions to be put were the following: how much money did Somerset have from the capture of Fougères; why did he give de Surienne permission to take the town in the first place; and why was the latter unwilling to surrender on reasonable terms, when things went wrong? The botched raid featured large in the list of complaints levelled by York against Somerset the following year, and Worcester was very critical of it in the *Boke of Noblesse*, which was first composed in the 1450s. It looks very much as if Fastolf disliked de Surienne's project from the very beginning.

The author of the *Questions* raised other matters close to Fastolf's heart. Why had the Duchy been left so unprepared, on what turned out to be the eve of the French invasion? Why had Somerset 'ransomed and pillaged' his own officers? Why did he leave the fortresses without artillery and stores? What repairs had he made to fortifications? Why had he not made sure that the garrison troops had received their wages? Many of the Normans, as a result, had suffered such oppression that they had abandoned their homes and joined the partisans. The writer wanted all these matters looked into, but also suggested the need to strengthen the case against Somerset by questioning Lord Grey, 'master of the *bailli* of Rouen', who would have more information. (This displays a knowledge of the law, in that the writer knew the difference between assertion and evidence.) It would also be wise to speak to Osbern Mundeford to ask what had become of monies paid to him for onward transmission to Somerset. (The allegation – at the least the innuendo – was that money intended for the settlers of Maine had been diverted into Somerset's pockets.)[23]

When it came, the French 'recovery' of Normandy in 1449 was well planned and well executed. Indeed, Philippe Contamine has described it as one of the great successes of medieval strategy. The Valois took advantage of the fact that they had already nibbled away at the edges of the Duchy, by retaking Dieppe, Eu and Aumale in 1436, Louviers in 1440, Évreux in 1441, and Granville in 1442. They now launched a full attack from three sides with armies which may have been 30,000 strong. In the west the Duke of Brittany advanced up the Cotentin. The Counts of Eu and Saint-Pol attacked from Artois in the east. Dunois led the main French army from the south. Since Somerset was unable to form a field army, the invasion became another war of sieges (like Henry V's in 1417–19), though a bombardment was not always necessary. The English had taken six weeks to capture Harfleur in 1415, but it fell to a surprise attack in 1450. In 1417–19 the siege of Falaise had lasted two months; of Cherbourg, five months; of Rouen, six. In 1449–50 there was no siege at all of Dieppe, Harfleur and Évreux: they all fell to surprise attacks. In the words of one French historian, Normandy collapsed 'like a house of cards'. Some garrisons, with little reason to expect relief from England, failed to put up a fight at all: 'Having no trust of hasty succour and relief of an army to come in due time, [they] turned away from their allegiance and obedience, to your adverse party.'[24] In a note which was probably made at this time, Fastolf contrasted what had happened in Harfleur in 1416 with what happened there thirty-four years later in 1450. In the first year, when he and the Duke of Exeter had been in charge, 400 men had died from hunger, whereas in the second, 'I trow for hunger died few or none.' In other words the garrison of 1450 were not the men their fathers had been: they had simply given up.[25]

In August 1449 Fastolf prepared a further memorandum (written in Latin), advising how the English possessions in Normandy could be saved, even now that the enemy was at the gates.[26] This was addressed to the King, though we do not know that Henry ever saw it. Sir John's advice this time was quite startling. It would be necessary to raise 40,000 troops, 10,000 for Aquitaine and 30,000 for Normandy. The latter should be formed into four divisions: one for the Duchy itself, one for the Saint-Quentin area and the Vermandois, one for the area between Seine and Loire, the fourth for Brittany. They should sweep through the areas allotted to them, heading for Paris and Reims, the Loire, Tours and all points south – yes, even for the Langue d'Oc. They would need the prudence of Antenor and the strength of Hector, but it could be done. Indeed it must be done.

Fastolf knew full well that others would consider these proposals to be sheer fantasy ('excogitationes fantasticas'), not least because of the cost, but in his view the country could afford it. As governor of Maine, he had proved that expeditions could to some extent pay for themselves. We should not be afraid to follow the example of Venice, Genoa and Milan, which were spending enormous amounts on their armed forces. He also anticipated the objections of 'little Englanders', who thought that England would be better off without her overseas possessions. He took the classic position that it was better to fight the enemy on his own soil rather than to have to fight him in England – for the French would never be satisfied with

Normandy alone: they would want Calais, and then they would seek to invade. In any case, Fastolf argued, it was completely wrong to abandon the English settlers in Normandy, and if the worst happened and these men were expelled, they would undoubtedly cause trouble back home. Finally, though people would protest that even Henry V had never raised so large an army, the position had deteriorated considerably since his day. The French had been divided then, and many of them had been unused to war. Now they were united, experienced, and burning with desire to recover their homeland.

Had Fastolf lost touch with reality? Clearly not – he was always a rational man. Yet there was something unreal about the proposals he made in 1449. For one thing, the total number of men in the garrisons of Normandy after the Truce of Tours was never more than 6,000, but here he was, calling for a field army at least five times as large. In doing so, he showed that he was a political innocent. It may well have been true that, to match the numbers Charles VII was now putting in the field, armies of the size Fastolf called for were needed, but in practice nothing like this number could have been mustered in England in time, or indeed at all. The King could not 'live of his own' in budgetary terms, and the political class was unwilling to vote for more taxes. The fact that the Venetians, Genoese and Milanese might be willing to spend very large amounts on their defences was hardly the point. These Italians lived in commercially minded republics, with wholly different systems of government.

At the beginning of October 1449, the French surrounded Rouen, where the Duke of Somerset was in command. The town put up very little resistance, though it had possessed a formidable range of artillery in 1435.[27] The citizens opened negotiations with Charles VII. Somerset retired to the citadel, but surrendered at the end of the month. In exchange for safe passage out of the city, he agreed to surrender Harfleur, Caudebec, Tancarville, Honfleur, Arques and Montvilliers; to hand over hostages by way of surety (including the unfortunate Talbot); and to pay 50,000 *saluts d'or* in cash. On 10 December 1449 Charles VII entered the capital of Normandy in triumph. One of his first acts was to order a full investigation into the circumstances of Joan of Arc's trial and execution in 1431.

Back in England, Suffolk mustered an expeditionary force of 2,500 men and appointed Sir Thomas Kyriell to lead them. It was late in the year before the muster was held, and bad weather delayed the departure of the expedition. The troops were ill-disciplined and wrought havoc in several towns on the south coast of England. Worcester blamed this on the wrath of God, but also on the government's failure to pay the troops on time. Kyriell landed in Cherbourg in March 1450, but the French caught up with him on 15 April at Formigny – between Bayeux and Carentan – and annihilated his army. There were some stalwarts in Bayeux who attempted to make a 'last stand'. Interestingly, their leader was Matthew Gough, whose earlier adventures in Maine feature large in Basset's Chronicle, but even this veteran diehard, steeped in Fastolfian obstinacy, could only endure two weeks of bombardment. The fall of Bayeux, in May 1450, was a particularly miserable and humiliating affair for the English because it was accompanied by scenes of hundreds of women and children fleeing the town, as they made their way in carts to the port of Cherbourg.[28]

In June the French laid siege to Caen, where Somerset had taken refuge after the surrender of Rouen. According to Colonel Burne, Fastolf 'set about raising another army 3,000 strong' at this point, but the fact is that the 3,000 men were only an idea, not a reality. It is true that Sir John was at last invited to sit on the royal council, and he wrote one last memorandum, this time in English. He blamed the English defeat at Formigny on petty captains who had 'tarried' on the coast of Normandy and failed to push inland (not, as Burne seemed to think, on the inactivity of Kyriell himself). With characteristic belligerence, he called for yet another expedition to France. This time it need not consist of more than 3,000 men, but it must be sent quickly if it were to be of any use at all to Somerset. If it should arrive too late to help him in Caen – as Fastolf feared it might – then it should go to the aid of whatever enclave remained in English hands. While this was being done, a much larger army – a 'great puissance' – should be assembled, under a 'chieftain of noble and great estate'.[29]

In Normandy, Charles VII concentrated four divisions for the attack on Caen, with a total of perhaps 20,000 men. Somerset commanded only 3,000–4,000 Englishmen, and no further assistance arrived. Caen was bombarded for seventeen days, after which it too surrendered, on terms which allowed Somerset and his army to be evacuated via Ouistreham. A ransom of 300,000 *écus d'or* was agreed, and all the English artillery handed over. Falaise surrendered in July and the French, in the last act of the *recouvrement*, laid siege to Cherbourg. The captain, Thomas Gower, put up a brave fight, but the town was subjected to a tremendous bombardment, and it surrendered on 12 August 1450. On 19 August, James Gresham, who was John Paston's agent in London, reported that 'This Wednesday it was told that Cherbourg is gone, and we have now not a foot of land in Normandy, and men are afraid that Calais will very soon be besieged.'[30]

Fastolf thought that some soldiers in Normandy, notably Thomas Gower in Cherbourg, had done their duty, but he also thought that others, and principally the Duke of Somerset, had not. The loss of Normandy was total and ignominious, in an age when men cared a great deal about honour. The material damage was bad enough. It has been estimated that some 4,000 English refugees were created in Caen and 2,300 in Falaise, Domfront and Cherbourg. Many Englishmen lost their estates. According to Fastolf Paper 69 (an inventory compiled by William Worcester in 1459), Fastolf was among them: he lost several valuable estates which he had not been able to sell before the crash. French court records confirm that these included lands in Alençon, given to him as a reward for his services at Verneuil. The Duke of Bedford's widow saw her French income cut off entirely. The Duke of York lost counties and lordships important enough to be described as an apannage, and Somerset lost Harcourt and Mortain. The difference was that, when Somerset returned to England, he was appointed Constable of England and Captain of Calais, though it was he who had presided over the disaster. There was no compensation for other aristocrats like York, nor for loyal gentlemen like Fastolf, nor for the rank and file. All they got from Henry VI was sympathy.[31]

Why had Normandy failed to put up more of a fight? It is striking that the French victory at Formigny was won after the Duchy had been largely overrun, against a small expeditionary force which was attempting a 'comeback'. This was mainly because the English could not organize a field army in time, and partly because the garrisons had been run down, but there was surely another factor. In Henry V's day, morale had been high. Thirty years later, the English monarchy was weak, the aristocracy was divided and there were signs of popular discontent too. In 1439 the diplomats who prepared briefs for the English negotiators at Oye had asked, 'Whether the king had enough money, and whether the people of England were inclined to assist the king in continuing the war and whether he had enough allies outside England to help him recover his inheritance.'

At a lower level of society, the war in France had less appeal in the 1430s and 1440s than it had once had. Desertion was a problem as early as 1421, and in September 1430 the sheriff of Kent was ordered 'to arrest all … liege subjects who have left France for England without [the king's] special licence … leaving the realm of France without defence'.[32] In the *Boke of Noblesse*, Worcester deplored the fact that the sons of the gentry would rather qualify as lawyers than become soldiers. The historian Ralph Griffiths, who wrote the best biography of Henry VI, detected 'a lessening of enthusiasm – even a growing disillusion – for the war … among the political elite and merchant class in Parliament and elsewhere by the 1430s'.

Cade's Revolt

The loss of Normandy produced widespread unrest in England. Parliament, waxing indignant at the poor performance of the King's ministers, voted to impeach the Duke of Suffolk. Some Englishmen concluded that the only possible explanation for the wanton surrender of Maine, and the rapidity with which the French had recovered the Duchy, was treachery. Violent sentiments fuelled violent action. On 9 January 1450 the Bishop of Chichester was lynched by unpaid soldiers waiting in Portsmouth before crossing to France. The King banished Suffolk to save his life but, as the Duke tried to make his way abroad, he was captured by mutinous sailors and beheaded on the gunwale of a ship at Dover. His body was thrown on the beach, which may be the origin of the ballad 'Six Dukes Went A-Fishing', which is still sung today:

Six dukes went a-fishing,

Down by yon sea-side,
One of them spied a dead body,
Lain by the waterside.

As the song seems to demonstrate, there was little popular sympathy for Suffolk.

A full-scale rebellion broke out. The men who followed Jack Cade up to London in the spring of 1450 included many who agreed with Fastolf's criticisms of the government. They hated Suffolk, Somerset and all their cronies. The *Brut* chronicler tells us that many who did not actively take part in the rebellion still sympathized with Cade, until his followers turned to robbery and violence, but then 'the people's hearts fell from him & every thrifty man was afraid for to be served in like manner ... If he had not robbed, he might have gone far, before he was withstood.' Shakespeare portrays the rebels as a rabble: his Cade wants to kill all the lawyers, break open the prisons, burn down the Tower of London and introduce a form of communism. Modern historians, more sympathetic to the revolt, have shown that there was more to it than this. They emphasize the legitimacy of many of the rebels' grievances and demonstrate that not all the leaders were peasants, unlike those who had given their name to the Great Revolt of 1381. Yet there can be little doubt that Fastolf would have agreed with Shakespeare's noble squire Alexander Iden, that Cade was a 'monstrous traitor'. In *Henry VI*, Cade tries to hide in Iden's garden in Kent, once the rebel army has dispersed. In real life the rebels invaded Fastolf Place in Southwark, forcing Sir John to flee to the Tower of London, and they falsely detained his servant, John Payn.

Payn has left us a vivid account of his ordeal. When the rebel army first reached London in June, it camped on Blackheath and then marched on Southwark, where Cade lodged at the White Hart in the Borough High Street, on the approach to London Bridge. Fastolf had taken the precaution of stationing 'old soldiers of Normandy' in his house by the Thames. When the rebels drew near, he sent John Payn to find out what was going on, and Payn wrote about it fifteen years later, when he lodged a claim for expenses with Fastolf's executors:

My master Sir John Fastolf ... commanded your petitioner to take a man and two of the best horses that were in his stable to ride to the common people of Kent and to get a list of the reasons why they had come. And so I did, and as soon as I came to Blackheath the Captain [Jack Cade] made the rebels take me; and in order to save my master's horses, I made my companion ride off with both of them. And I was brought immediately before the Captain of Kent, and the Captain demanded of me what the reason for my coming there was and why I had made my companion slink off with the horses. I said that I had come to greet my wife's brothers and other friends and relations of mine who were there.

Fastolf Place

Shakespeare – who for some years lived near the Globe theatre – is remembered in Southwark Cathedral in stone, as is Falstaff in stained glass. There is no reference at all to Sir John Fastolf, though he lived in Southwark for many years after his return to England in 1439, acquired several properties in the borough, and built a fine town house there.

London Bridge, Borough High Street and Southwark Cathedral are still (more or less) in the same place as they were in the fifteenth century. The bridge was a magnet for travellers and horse-drawn traffic of all kinds, since it was the only one across the Thames in either the City of London or Westminster. Borough High Street was the site of dozens of inns and taverns, including the White Hart, where Jack Cade stayed when his rebel army occupied the capital in 1450, and the Boar's Head, which belonged to Fastolf (Falstaff's Boar's Head was in Eastcheap). In August 1459 just a few weeks before Sir John's death, his servant Henry Windsor wrote to John Paston, asking if he could take over as landlord:

> An [if] it please you to remember my master at your best leisure, whether his old promise shall stand as touching my preferring to the Boar's Head, in Southwark. Sir, I would have been at another place, and of my master's own motion he said that I should set up in the Boar's Head.

Before the Reformation, Southwark lay outside the jurisdiction of the City of London and was a haven for prostitutes. The borough had no theatres then, but it was famous for its 'stews', or brothels. However, there is no evidence that Fastolf was involved in this trade: the stews lay along Bankside, upstream of London Bridge, whereas he lived downstream in the parish of St Olave's. The mansion which he built was known as Fastolf Place (or 'Palace') and was at the end of Tooley Street, near its junction with Bermondsey Street. It had a large garden, a moat, and a wharf giving access to the Thames. In the early eighteenth century John Anstis, the Garter historian, wrote of 'a Royal Palace, as 'tis termed'.

Numerous excavations of the south bank of the Thames were conducted in the 1980s and 1990s, prior to the building of the new City Hall. The archaeologists discovered extensive remains of Edward II's palace, known as The Rosary, but there was virtually nothing left of Fastolf Place, which had been almost totally destroyed by subsequent building. However, enough was discovered to confirm what later drawings had already revealed: that it was a substantial manor house, with a moat and a wharf, and possibly fishponds, built around 1443. There were finds of pieces of revetment, a saddle, saddle wallets and two blankets: fragments of information which suggest that the comfort, even opulence, which Sir John enjoyed at Caister were also present in the capital, and that Southwark and Caister were the centres of his commercial life. City Hall, intriguing and even beautiful as it is, does not speak to us of the Late Middle Ages. Yet the view across the Thames does remind us of the day in 1450 when Fastolf fled from Jack Cade's rebels, to the safety of the Tower of London.

There was a man there who said to the Captain that I was one of Sir John Fastolf's men, and the two horses were Sir John Fastolf's; and then the Captain raised a cry of treason against me throughout the camp, and took me to four parts of the field with one of the Duke of Exeter's heralds in front of me in the duke's coat of arms, who made four *Oyez* at the four parts of the field. He proclaimed through the herald that I was sent there to spy, and to find out how powerful they were and what their equipment was like, by the greatest traitor that was in England or in France (so the Captain proclaimed at the time), one Sir John Fastolf, knight, who had [di]minished all the garrisons of Normandy and Mauns [Le Mans] and Maine and had caused the King to lose all his title and right of inheritance that he had beyond the sea.[33]

In view of what we know about Fastolf's attitude to government policy in the 1440s, it is richly ironic that the rebels should have regarded him, of all people, as one of the traitors who had sold the country short, but there was worse to come. Cade also thought that Fastolf's purpose in fortifying Fastolf Place could only have been 'to destroy the commons of Kent when that they came to Southwark'. Payn's lament continued:

He [Cade] said plainly, I should lose my head. And so I was taken at once and led to the Captain's tent, and an axe and a block were brought out, for my execution: and then Master Poynings, your brother-in-law, and other friends of mine came and stopped the Captain, and said a hundred or two would die if I died, and so my life was saved for the moment.

Then I was made to swear to the Captain and the common people that I would go to Southwark and equip myself as best I could and return to help them; that cost me more than 27 shillings that day, given to the common people.

Payn was a brave man. Instead of putting safety first, he returned to Southwark:

> So I came to my Master Fastolf and brought him the list of [the rebel] grievances and told him everything, advising him to put away his weapons and dismiss his soldiers. He did so, and he and all his household went to the Tower [of London], except for Bettes and one Matthew Brain.

But the rebels were not finished with the poor man:

> If I had not been with them, the common people would have burned [Fastolf's] place and all those of his tenants. This cost me, out of my own pocket, more than £4 in meat and drink. And despite this the Captain had me seized at the White Hart at Southwark, and commanded Lovelase to strip me of my equipment, which he did. He took a fine gown of grey woollen cloth, furred with fine beaver, and a pair of brigandines covered with blue velvet and gilt nails, with leg-armour; the value of the gown and brigandines was £8.

The rebels now broke into one of Fastolf's houses in Southwark – possibly Fastolf Place itself – and broke open his chest, taking away valuable bonds, a purse with five gold rings, money, 'a complete suit of Milan armour' and clothing. Payn himself was kept prisoner 'until the night of the battle at London Bridge':

> And then, at night, the Captain put me into the battle on the bridge, and I was wounded and hurt, almost mortally; I was in the battle for six hours and could not get out of it. And four times before then I was carried around through Kent and Sussex, and they wanted to cut off my head.

By extraordinary good fortune, the list of grievances which John Payn brought back after his meeting with Cade's rebels has survived, in a manuscript now in Magdalen College, Oxford. We can therefore say with confidence that there is nothing in them which Fastolf would have disagreed with, except the threat to stay in London until the rebels' demands were met. It is the methods used, rather than the substance of the complaints, which Fastolf could not stomach. Indeed, from a modern perspective, it is hard not to agree that the rebels had a point, when they said that 'the King has had false counsel, his lordship is lost, his merchandise is lost, his commons destroyed, the sea is lost, France is lost' (Article 10). The tone of the rebel complaints is moderate: 'We blame not all the lords, nor all that [have] been about the King's person, nor all gentlemen, nor all men of late, nor all bishops, nor all priests, but such as may be found guilty by a just and true enquiry by the law' (Article 13).

Like William Worcester in his *Boke of Noblesse*, the rebels blamed 'covetousness' for the nation's woes – the ruthless pursuit of self-interest at the expense of patriotism. The pity of it is that the best elements among Cade's followers were unable to control their followers, the protests degenerated into violent riots, and the riots were firmly put down. Yet the rebels believed, as almost everyone seems to have done, that God was on their side. The rebel manifesto concludes with an invocation in verse:

God be our guide and thou shall eke speed.[34]

The violence employed by the rebels totally alienated the ruling class. It is no surprise to learn that Fastolf continued to keep his London town house well stocked with munitions. In a letter of 8 August 1450 he wrote to Thomas Howes in Caister:

Buy me at least a five dozen longbows with suitable arrows, and also buy crossbow bolts of local manufacture, for the prices are dearer here than there. And don't listen to any talk of the price being fixed by law.[35]

The Loss of Aquitaine

The Lancastrian kings had long neglected Aquitaine: they worked on the assumption (which Fastolf seems to have shared) that the Gascons would remain loyal to the English king as Duke of Aquitaine, and that they could therefore take care of themselves. Henry V never sailed for Bordeaux to take the homage of his vassals, and he never led an army out of its gates. He concentrated his efforts in the north of France. Indeed he wrote to the men of Bordeaux in October 1414, to apologize for the fact that he had not sent them any reinforcements. The only assistance given in recent years had been that provided by Clarence and Dorset.[36]

The French mounted a series of attacks on Aquitaine in 1437–8, 1442–3 and finally in 1449–53, but the English were slow to respond. Henry VI's ministers planned to send reinforcements on several occasions, but not all of them arrived at their destination. The 1st Duke of Somerset's expedition of 1443 was diverted to Normandy. Two thousand men under John, Earl of Huntingdon did arrive in 1440, 500 in 1442, and 600 under Sir William Bonville in 1443, but these were not enough. After the Truce of Tours, the Crown sent no more help until it was too late. As for Fastolf, he offered the government no detailed advice about the defence of the southern Duchy, for all the ink that he spilt about Normandy. It was left to Gloucester to make the point that, if the Duke of Orléans were released in 1440, he might ally with the Count of Armagnac and cause trouble for the English in the south-west.[37]

Charles VII moved against Aquitaine in 1451, as soon as he had recovered Normandy, and English rule once again simply crumbled. On the face of it, this is surprising. There was no Lancastrian land-settlement in Gascony and there were no English colonists, but by and large the local nobility had been loyal and might have been expected to fight back, while their fortresses – Bordeaux, Fronsac, Beynac, Domme and Clermont-Dessus – were well supplied with up-to-date artillery. Yet, as the invading armies swept along, they met little resistance. At Cadillac, part of the town walls was demolished by the French gunners, but in many places the towns surrendered without a shot being fired; it was the threat of bombardment, not the cannonballs, which caused the strongholds to fall. Bergerac surrendered in November 1450, Bourg and the mighty Fronsac in June 1451. Bordeaux surrendered to Dunois without a fight at the end of that month. Once again, no field army was organized locally to oppose the Valois, and none could be sent from England in time.[38]

We can tell what Fastolf thought about events by looking at Worcester's *Boke of Noblesse*:

> Also another great army and expedition [was] doomed by default and the failure to arrange for timely payment in this year of Christ 1451 ... When it was ready to depart for Aquitaine, the army tarried upon the sea coasts of England almost a quarter of a year for their pay. And in the meantime, the city of Bordeaux was lost, because there was no prospect of relief.[39]

This was not the last chapter in the story of English Aquitaine. At least some of the Gascons resented the way in which the new Valois regime now treated them. In particular, the men of Bordeaux were made to pay a new tax for the cost of their own defence. Unlike the Normans, they had enjoyed three centuries of relatively loose English government, and the vintners and merchants among them feared for the future of their lucrative wine-trade. In 1452 they sent a secret delegation to England, offering to return to their former allegiance. (No such delegation ever arrived from Normandy.) The response was the sending of a new expeditionary force of 4,000–5,000 men, led by Talbot. This succeeded in recapturing Bordeaux in October 1452, but, although he had some success outside the town, Talbot soon ran out of luck. At Castillon, on 17 July 1453, he charged a fortified park outside the town, in which as many as 300 cannons were concealed. These had been assembled as siege-guns, but they proved to be formidable anti-personnel weapons. The English army was decimated and Talbot and his eldest son were both killed, in scenes recorded by Hall and Holinshed and dramatized by Shakespeare a century and a half later.

This loss of the English possessions in France (other than the Channel Islands and Calais) affected Englishmen and women of all classes deeply. In 1452 some of the former inhabitants of Maine made their voices heard when they petitioned Henry VI for relief. They complained that they had lost their lands, only to lose their moveables when Normandy was overrun. They were therefore reduced to utter penury. William Worcester included their protest in his collection of documents, which clearly points to Fastolf as their spokesman. Worcester even added a bitter postscript in his own hand:

> Note that this petition was not carried out nor granted, by occasion of which many soldiers died of grief, some were imprisoned for robbery and condemned to death as felons, and some are still rebels dwelling in the parts of France.[40]

We have always been taught that the Hundred Years' War ended in 1453, but the men of Fastolf's generation did not see it that way. The term 'Hundred Years' War' was invented in France and adopted in England in the nineteenth century. Though it is an extremely useful concept, no peace treaty was signed after the defeat at Castillon, and there was no outbreak of peace internationally. Indeed, there was not even a truce, either with the French or with their allies the Scots. Calais remained in English hands, as did the Channel Islands. The former had long been regarded as an English 'barbican' which must be held on to at all costs, and remained a base from which to mount future invasions. For his part, Charles VII continued to have designs against both England and Burgundy, and he lived until 1461. The English continued to spend heavily on defence. Fortescue included in his list of the Crown's regular charges the 'keeping' of the Scottish marches, the maintenance of the king's 'works' (which essentially meant fortifications), the keeping of the sea, the maintenance of a fleet, and the keeping of Calais. In 1452 there were rumours that Charles VII would attack Calais, as Duke Philip the Good had done after 1435. In August 1457 the French burnt Sandwich, while in 1458 and 1459 they threatened invasion. Charles VII's successor Louis XI operated throughout the 1460s on the basis that the English were likely to renew the war.[41]

Fastolf's county of Norfolk was in constant danger of raids, though it was objectively unlikely that the French would mount an invasion of East Anglia. In 1440 the vigilant Margaret Paston wrote to her husband to complain of the activities of certain Flemish sailors, 1,100 of whom had landed at Waxham, only a few miles north of Caister. In 1450 she reported that:

> There are many ships off Yarmouth and Cromer, who have done much harm and taken many Englishmen and put them in great distress and ransomed them for great sums. These enemies are so bold that they come ashore and play on Caister Sands and other places, so much at home as if they were Englishmen. People are very much afraid that they will do much harm this summer unless great preparations are made to resist them.

In 1456, at the age of seventy-six, Fastolf was appointed to a commission charged with ensuring that the Watchers of the Suffolk coast 'keep such watches to resist invasion by the king's enemies', while in the following year he was one of those responsible for the defence of Great Yarmouth and other ports nearby. There was clearly a risk that the French would make a landing, but there was also a threat from rival landowners, with whom he was constantly in dispute. His castle at Caister therefore remained an arsenal while being transformed into a mansion. In 1448 Margaret Paston, trapped in a most unenviable position in the disputed manor of Gresham, wrote a letter which contained eloquent comment on the shortcomings of the English longbow, when it came to defending one's house, and referred to Fastolf's abilities in the area of supply:

> Right worshipful husband, I commend myself to you and ask you to get some crossbows, and windlasses to wind them with, and crossbow bolts, for your houses here are so low that no one can shoot out of them with a longbow, however much we needed to. I expect you can get such things from Sir John Fastolf if you were to send to him. And I would like you to get two or three short pole-axes to keep indoors, and as many leather jackets, if you can.

Margaret's confidence that Caister was a ready source of munitions was justified. Nine years after Fastolf's death, William Worcester described it as 'a rich jewel for the whole country when needed, in time of war', adding that 'my master Fastolf would never have built it if it was going to come under the control of any sovereign who would oppress the country'. Caister Castle is now a ruin and the so-called 'Fastolf sword' in Norwich Castle is of dubious origin, but there is an inventory compiled in 1460 or 1461 which confirms that Sir John did have a substantial arsenal there:[42]

Two guns with eight chambers shooting a stone seven inches thick twenty inches compass.
Two lesser guns with eight chambers shooting a stone five inches thick, fifteen inches compass.
A serpentine with three chambers shooting a stone of ten inches compass.
Another serpentine, shooting a stone of seven inches compass.
Three fowlers shooting a stone of twelve inches compass.
Two short guns for ships with six chambers.
Two small serpentines to shoot lead pellets.
Four guns lying in stocks to shoot lead pellets.
Seven hand guns with other equipment belonging to the said guns.
Twenty-four shields of elm board, two of galain.
Eight old-fashioned suits of white armour.

Ten pairs of body armour, worn out. Fourteen horn jackets, worn out.

Ten bascinets, twenty-four sallets, six gorgets.

Sixteen lead hammers.

Nine bills and other pieces of armour and weapons, and zinc caps, and wire of little value.

Four great crossbows of steel, two of galain, four of yew.

Two habergeons, and a barrel to store them in.

We cannot be sure of the age and serviceability of this weaponry. Is this 'state of the art' artillery or a motley collection put together by an old man in his dotage, or a mixture of the two? The larger guns are all of a type which shot stones (whereas the smaller type used lead pellets), but stone cannonballs were becoming a little out of date. The Duke of Bedford had shot over 400 into the town of Lagny in 1431, but by 1460 the French were commonly using iron.[43]

The suits of armour are expressly described as 'old-fashioned' or 'worn out', indicating that the inventory was prepared at the end of a long life. By this time, refinements had been made in the manufacture of metal plate ('white armour'), though this was already a great improvement on the chainmail habergeon, of which Fastolf had two remaining. On the other hand, there are some signs that Fastolf had been keeping up when it came to helmets. The bascinet was suitable for jousting but it was too heavy, and the field of vision was too restricted, for the battlefield. The sallet was a great improvement, though it needed to be supplemented with a gorget worn round the neck. (There were many more sallets than bascinets in Sir John's armoury.) There are sixteen lead hammers listed, but no swords, and this is further evidence of change. With improvements in the quality of armour, a blow from a sword was less effective than it had once been, and men therefore took to using weapons designed to crush and pierce metal, rather than cut flesh. Most strikingly, there were no longbows listed at Caister: only crossbows, the best four made of steel, which was relatively expensive. Perhaps Margaret Paston had a point about the limitations of the English longbow in siege warfare.

Sir John continued to be interested in military and foreign affairs, even after Talbot's defeat and death at Castillon. In June 1454 William Worcester wrote that 'The Frenchmen have been before the Isles of Jersey and Guernsey, and a great navy of them, and 600 be taken and slain of them by men of the said true Isles.' In March 1458 Worcester informed his master of a threat which was even closer to home:

John Vincent of Bentley was in Sussex at the Priory of Lewes this last week, and he says that 60 sail were sailing before that coast of Frenchmen keeping the sea. The Lord Fauconberg is at Southampton with his navy. Edmond Clere of the King's household informed me that he heard of a soldier of Calais how Crowmere and Blakeney are much spoken of amongst the French.[44]

Charles VII was to become known to history as Charles le Victorieux. In the wake of his triumphs he held a series of treason trials. In 1458 Fastolf received an account of the proceedings brought against Jean II, Duke of Alençon, in Paris: the herald known as Fastolf Poursuivant prepared a seating-plan, showing the members of the court which tried the Duke, and sent it to his master. One can see why Fastolf might be interested in the fate of Alençon, for the two men's lives had been closely entwined. The Duke had been a youth of fifteen at the Battle of Verneuil, where Fastolf was one of his captors. The English had overrun his Duchy, and Fastolf had been made governor of the area and Captain of Alençon, as well as acquiring land there. Once he had obtained his release, the Duke joined Joan of Arc and fought the English on the Loire and on the Sarthe, near his former estates. In the mid-1440s, he allied himself with the new Dauphin (later Louis XI) and quarrelled with Charles VII, taking part in the noble revolt known as the Praguerie, but by 1449 he appeared to be reconciled once more with Charles VII. One might have expected an uneventful end to his story.

Not so. Alençon resented the fact that Charles VII failed to restore his fief of Fougères when François de Surienne surrendered it after his raid in 1449. He maintained a treasonous correspondence with the English and the Burgundians. Despite having participated in the French recovery of Normandy, he kept in touch with the court of Henry VI, and with the Duke of York. In the mid-1450s, he conspired with the English to re-invade Normandy, even proposing that he would deliver certain castles to them if they did, but the plot came to light and Alençon was arrested. Fastolf naturally wanted to know what became of his old adversary. The very existence of the report of this trial confirms that he did not regard the war as over. It should be possible for the English to go back to Normandy one day, if only there were leaders who were up to the job. In that event, there might be people in France as well as in England who would be willing to help.[45]

Chapter 8

'The Old Vulture'

Fastolf's name is sometimes mentioned alongside those of other Englishmen who fought and lived by war during the Hundred Years' War: Sir Robert Knowles, Sir John Chandos, Sir Hugh Calveley and Sir John Hawkwood, but these four all lived in the fourteenth century. English strategy took a different direction in the fifteenth. The gains of war (or what people generally refer to as plunder) were still an important way of maintaining an army, but the conquest of a large part of Northern France brought responsibility, as well as temptation. In Normandy and Maine English soldiers became office-holders and landowners; they did not merely pass through. They enjoyed the profits but they were also obliged to govern and to behave properly towards the French who stayed behind. The free and easy ways of the *chevauchée*, which had been essential to Hawkwood's way of life, had to be abandoned in Fastolf's day. At the same time, Hawkwood was a freelance, whereas Fastolf spent his whole life in the service of the king. He has been described as a vulture, but it is a strange kind of vulture which settles down to farming.[1]

Fastolf was an English gentleman. The term has become debased, but in the fifteenth century it meant that he was a member of a distinct social class. While he was wealthy – and a baron of France – he was not a nobleman in England. This was more than just a matter of status, for he never enjoyed a truly aristocratic lifestyle. He owned two mansions, at Southwark and Caister, but he did not progress from one great house to another, as the king and the aristocrats did. Rich as he was, his peacetime retinue numbered around thirty, whereas the great lords numbered their retainers in hundreds. From the vantage point of the twenty-first century, we can see that Sir John was a member of the 'rising' gentry, but he was entirely unaware of this and of its long-term political consequences. He built up his wealth for the reasons that most men do, if they can. He was childless but he learned to live with this, and he remained ambitious to the last. Despite his desire to found a chantry college, he would not have agreed with François Villon (*c*.1431–63), that it is better to be alive and poor than dead and rich:

Mieux vaut vivre sous gros bureau
Pauvre, qu'avoir été seigneur
Et pourrir sous riche tombeau.

The Building of Caister Castle

Fastolf did not come from a poor family. His mother had given him Caister and the manor of Repps two years before she died in 1406, and he also owned tenements in Great Yarmouth. However, it was his marriage to the wealthy widow Millicent Scrope in 1409 which was the making of him. She was the second daughter and co-heiress of Robert, Lord Tiptoft, and her first husband had been Sir Stephen Scrope, Fastolf's commander in Ireland. She brought land to the value of £240 a year to the marriage, including the Tiptoft manors of Castle Combe and Bathampton in Wiltshire, Oxenton in Gloucestershire and several properties in Somerset and Yorkshire. Fastolf settled £100 a year on her for her own use, but in fact she enjoyed a higher social status than her new husband. Her father had been a nobleman and, when he died in Aquitaine in 1372, she had inherited the right to bear the Tiptoft arms. She also became a ward of Richard le Scrope, 1st Lord of Bolton and married his third son, by whom she had three children. By his marriage to Millicent, Fastolf acquired the right to impale her arms with his: both sets were put on display at Castle Combe and later at Caister.[2]

Fastolf became very wealthy and eventually rebuilt his family home at Caister Hall. Though it looks like a fortress, the new castle was meant to be a sumptuous residence. It had two halls, one for the winter and one for the summer. There were facilities for lighting, heating and washing, while the private rooms had latrines or 'joined stools'. There were feather beds – and not just in Fastolf's bedroom. Even the cook slept under a coverlet decorated with roses and the heads of bloodhounds. There were cushions, pillows, expensive clothes, gaming boards, a set of chessmen and an astrolabe for entertainment and instruction. There was high-quality window glass from Norwich and a prominent display of the Fastolfs' coats of arms, together with his personal motto, *Me fau[n]t faire* ('I must be [up and] doing'). On one side of the oriel window in the Great Hall there were finely sculpted reliefs.

In the 1950s McFarlane wrote of Fastolf moving from Southwark to Caister in 1458. More recently, Helen Castor gives the date as 1454, but Anthony Smith has pointed out that the relevant question is whether Sir John ever 'moved house' at all, at least in the modern sense. He never sold Fastolf Place in Southwark and he owned other properties apart from these two – not least in Norwich. On the other hand, by 1454 Fastolf was an old man by any standards. Unable to attend the annual meeting of the Garter in Windsor, he often complained about his health in the years which followed. It does seem that he spent increasing amounts of time at Caister in the late 1450s and he was certainly there in February 1456, when John Bocking wrote to him with news of political events in London.[3]

Residence in Norfolk strengthened Fastolf's friendship with his much younger neighbour, John Paston (1421–66). The two men had supported each other in a common struggle with the Suffolk clan, and they continued to do so after Suffolk's murder in 1450. Since he had no children of his own and, after the death of his wife in 1445, seems to have had no thought of remarrying, Fastolf's mind turned to the idea of founding a chantry college at Caister, but this was not a straightforward matter, not least because a licence in mortmain was required from the Crown before land could be given to the Church. Paston was legally trained and could help to negotiate the appropriate fee. The older man came to see Paston as his 'truest kinsman and friend', almost as a son. They discussed marriage alliances between Fastolf's relatives and the Paston family, though no such union ever took place.[4]

Surviving accounts show that Caister Castle was built between 1432 and 1446, and William Worcester estimated that around £6,046 was spent on building it. There was an Inner and an Outer Court, with over fifty rooms, including state apartments and living quarters, a chapel, twenty-eight bedrooms with thirty-nine beds, a wardrobe, two halls, a kitchen, larder, cellar and pantry, and a heated room known as a 'stew'. Outside there were stables, bakehouses, a brewhouse and a garden with a permanent gardener. Worcester measured the Great Hall as '38 of my paces long, which make 59 feet, and 16 paces, or 28 feet, wide', and he described the castle as a whole as 'a rich jewell'. It was regarded with envy by the wealthy, especially since it was known that Fastolf had no heir. He received several approaches from people who wanted to buy it. After one embarrassing enquiry in 1456, he wrote to John Paston:

> Cousin, I pray you, in as much as my lady of York has been here, and seriously tried to persuade me to sell Caister to her, that you try to find a way to expedite a licence of mortmain for me in relation to my property, as you and I have discussed before, the purpose being the foundation of a college.

Fastolf's new mansion was modern, stylish and much in demand.[5]

A licence to crenellate Caister had been obtained, and its battlements were not merely decorative. There were wet moats around the Outer and the Inner Court, and the Great Tower had five storeys and stood 90 feet high, commanding an outlook over the coast. There were gunports as well as arrow-slits, drawbridges and machicolations, which served to protect a wall-walk for sentries. A relatively new feature was that the building was almost entirely of brick, though stone from Caen was used for many decorative features, and there were gargoyles. Norfolk is not naturally endowed with stone and Fastolf constructed brick-kilns at Caister, and bricks (and tiles) from there were used at Caister, Blickling, Hellesdon and St Benet's Abbey.[6]

At one time it was thought that Caister was modelled on the moated castles (*Wasserburgen*) of the lower Rhine, and that German craftsmen working in East Anglia may have helped to build it. On the other hand, there was a persistent legend that it was built with the ransom of a Frenchman – possibly the Duke of Alençon – and closely resembled a French château. It seems more likely that a variety of influences were in fact at work. Fastolf had seen many castles during the course of his military career – in Ireland, Aquitaine and several parts of northern France. The ruinous state of the building makes it difficult to cite Caister as an example of any particular school of architecture, though it was built when the Perpendicular was predominant in Church building.

A castle requires a garrison to defend it. On 15 March 1458, five years after Talbot had been killed at Castillon, John Bocking wrote to Sir John about a French attack on the coast near Great Yarmouth:

> My lord of Canterbury told me that the French appeared in front of you, and that you fired many guns, and he told all the Lords about it. I requested him to ask the Council to re-supply the town of Yarmouth with artillery and guns and gunpowder, and he said that he would.

In 1469, ten years after Fastolf's death, the garrison still included one man, Davey Cook, who is known to have served Sir John.

Caister is now a mere shell, and we struggle to appreciate how sumptuous and colourful the interior was, but Fastolf was a man who had seen the richly decorated *hôtels* of the great French aristocrats, and had the money to copy their ways, on a smaller scale. The walls at Caister were hung with tapestries, in all probability imported from the Duke of Burgundy's domains in Flanders, but they depicted episodes from military history as well as domestic, religious and hunting scenes. One such showed the nine 'Conquerors' or 'Worthies': Hector of Troy, Alexander the Great, Julius Caesar, the biblical heroes – Joshua, David and Judas Maccabeus – King Arthur, the Emperor Charlemagne, and Godfrey of Bouillon the Crusader. Another showed a 'Morysh' or 'Morysc' dance – one of the earliest references to Morris dancing yet found.[7] A third, hung in a conspicuous place on the south-west side of the Great Hall, showed the siege of a town.

There is a puzzle with regard to the last of these tapestries. It is tempting to think that the event shown was the siege of Falaise in 1417–18, because Fastolf was present at the time. However, it is much more likely that what was depicted was the Roman siege of Phalist (or ancient Florence), cited in William Worcester's *Boke of Noblesse*, and that the tapestry was intended to illustrate the virtue of the generals of ancient times, rather than an episode in the Hundred Years' War. Whichever it was, the tapestry was certainly an example of conspicuous consumption.

We should always remember Fastolf's age, and his widowed status, at the end of his life. This probably explains why he was not over-anxious to show his new house to prying eyes. He demonstrated a startling degree of false modesty when he wrote to John Paston in 1456, attempting to forestall another embarrassing visit from the Duchess of York:

> And cousin, if ye may understand that my lady of York be disposed to come to this poor place, I pray you heartily that ye will recommend me to

her noble ladyship and tell her how it is with me, so that I may be excused for this time, for it would be a great heaviness to me to understand [entertain?] her ladyship here and I might not receive her as I ought.

There is a legend that Fastolf was a member of the heretical sect known as the Lollards, but this is no more than a myth, which confuses him with Sir John Oldcastle (who was executed for rebellion and heresy). In fact, there is no evidence at all that Fastolf was critical of the Church. He was not one of the 'Lollard Knights' who flourished openly in the thirty or so years between Wycliffe's death in 1384 and Oldcastle's Rising in 1414, and after that date Lollardy was confined to the lower orders. There is no sign that he ever owned Lollard books, or protected those who preached heresy, and his will contains none of the hallmarks of Lollard belief. On the contrary, there is every sign of religious orthodoxy.[8] Sir John was a devoted follower of the ultra-orthodox Henry V. He gave generously to the parish church at Castle Combe (where the font, West Tower and unusual clock all date from the late fifteenth century). He was a benefactor of the regular clergy and a patron of St Benet's Abbey, where he was buried. The chapel of St John at Caister Castle is now a mere shell, but it is clear from the documents that it had all the accoutrements of Catholic worship, and Fastolf's adherence to traditional belief comes across strongly in his conversations with Friar Brackley (recorded in the Paston Letters) and in the orthodox confession which he made two weeks before his death. Despite the secrecy of the confessional, we know that he urged the priest in very specific terms:

> I require you before God, as you shall answer at the dreadful day of doom, that you record how I am in the faith of the Church steadfast as any Christian man may be; and, if through feebleness any word escape me that were against the faith, that you answer for me at the dreadful day of doom that it is my intent to die a Christian man.[9]

Fastolf demonstrated his religious orthodoxy in another way, through the strength of his intention to found a chantry college. The building of chantries was a product of the quintessentially Catholic belief in Purgatory and Fastolf referred repeatedly to the pain and anguish he expected to suffer there. If he had had his way, Caister Castle would have become a place where holy men sang a continuous round of masses in an attempt to reduce his time in Purgatory. One of his last instructions to his chief executor John Paston was that, if the latter found himself unable to found the chantry college, he 'should pull down the said mansion and every stone and stick thereof' rather than allow someone else to enjoy it. This reflects both his disillusionment with the present, and an entirely conventional hope (and fear) with regard to the afterlife.[10]

The Profits of War

Desmond Seward called Fastolf an 'old vulture'. The insult implies that Sir John spent his time in France picking over the dead carcass of the territories he invaded, whereas the reality was that he had to fight very hard all his life. 'Wily old bird' would certainly have been an appropriate description, since there is little doubt that he made handsome profits and some wise decisions about investment. This was demonstrated over fifty years ago by McFarlane in his seminal article 'The investment of Sir John Fastolf's profits of war', though his general theory, that Fastolf was typical of his age, proved much more controversial. Perhaps the more important question, politically, was not whether men like Fastolf made a profit, but whether they became dependent on the war for their living.[11]

Fastolf featured in the *Sunday Times* all-time 'rich list' of 2007. There is a lengthy inventory of his possessions, compiled in October 1448, which tells us that he had £4,640 11s 8d of gold and silver coins and plate (with over £2,000 deposited for safe keeping at St Benet's Abbey). The inventory also refers to a considerable collection of jewellery, brooches and precious stones, gold cups and silver candlesticks. Some of the jewels were not his own, however, but had been pledged by the Duke of York for 600 marks, including 'a great diamond in a white rose', and 'a ragged staff with various precious stones given to the king by the assent and commandment of [the Archbishop] of Canterbury'.[12]

One visible and obvious sign of wealth was the number of servants which a man maintained in his household, and the account roll prepared by Sir John's steward John Rafman for the year 1431–2 shows that there were twenty-nine such folk at Caister Castle. Rafman distinguished between the *generosi*, or gentlefolk, and the *valetti*, or servants. The former included Dame Millicent and two of her female relations, five gentlemen and gentlewomen, twelve yeomen and nine grooms. There was a cook, a butler ('pincerna'), three boys, a gardener, a fisherman (or perhaps more accurately, water-bailiff?) and a man employed to look after the swans ('custos cygnorum'). At a higher level, there was Thomas Howes, parson of Castle Combe, Wiltshire, who lived at Caister from 1450 and was described in the late 1450s as 'chaplain and menial servant', and a receiver-general, John Kirtling, who was also a clerk in holy orders and whom Fastolf called 'my right trusty chaplain and servant domestical thirty winter and more'. In 1452 Sir John referred to 'those that have been my riding servants'. These were the surveyors and auditors, whose job was to travel about, check up on the work done by others and report back to their master. Some of them had served with him in France, including Nicholas Molyneux and John Winter (who had sworn to be brothers-in-arms). Molyneux even married one of Fastolf's sisters.[13]

McFarlane had no doubt that it was the profits which Fastolf made in France that were the source of his landed wealth in East Anglia, and that his wages and winnings enabled him to progress from being a squire worth £46 a year to a landowner with a rent-roll of over £1,450 per annum. It is also clear that Fastolf was a lucky man: he was never captured and never had to pay a ransom. He was so wealthy that he could afford to lose some of his lands, first in Maine and then in Normandy, without facing total ruin. At the same time, he had the good sense to sell some of his French estates while the going was good and he could still get ten years' purchase for them.[14]

Some of the wealth which Fastolf brought back was moveable. Though it is difficult to trace the origin of individual objects, it is very probable that he acquired some items when he was the Grand Master and later as one of Bedford's executors. These included tapestries and books and at least one piece of jewellery – an 'ouche' (or brooch), in the form of a tree-root, which was one of Bedford's heraldic devices.[15] However, he also earned a substantial salary and most of the payments he received were in the form of cash. Some time after 1450, his servants calculated that the Crown owed him a little over £11,000 – a very substantial sum, though not as much (if Worcester can be believed) as the 20,000 marks he had won at Verneuil.

McFarlane once remarked that Fastolf and his kind spent a quarter of a century 'sucking France dry'. His receipts from the Crown were certainly substantial. In 1432 he was paid £3,276 *livres tournois* in respect of the captaincies of Caen, Falaise, Alençon and Meulan, while in 1434 he earned £1,000 for six months' tenure as governor of Maine and Anjou. He was paid £4,231 1s 11d for guarding Fresnay for two months in 1435, and a further £2,931 5s 2d for the same duty the following year. However, these were gross receipts, and included the wages and bonuses ('vadia et regarda') he had to pay his retainers, as well as his own. The flow of cash was sometimes interrupted altogether by the administration's more urgent need to pay for other military operations. In any event, Fastolf was only paid if he presented his troops at a muster or review, a process which involved an independent inspection. Moreover, the surviving *quittances* show him repeatedly declaring that he has not made any profit 'in taking prisoners, horses, cattle, as booty [*en butins*] or otherwise'. In one case they do show an abatement of £42 15s *livres tournois*, on account of certain 'omissions and faults' for which he openly accepts responsibility; but the three sets of accounts which date from 1441 in relation to Paris, Meulan and France show no deduction for gains of war. The same documents confirm that Fastolf sometimes had to wait a very long time – in these three cases, twenty years – before he was paid. One of them refers to Fastolf's claim that he had suffered a very great deterioration in his financial position as a result of being made to wait so long ('in magnam deterioracionem bonorum et catallorum suorum').[16]

The profits of war included ransoms, where the balance of payments was usually in favour of the English, and where it was sometimes possible to 'hit the jackpot' (as the Black Prince had done when he captured the King of France). However, important prisoners were customarily released on parole and they did not always honour their obligations. The most important person ever captured by Fastolf was the Duke of Alençon, at Verneuil, but it is very doubtful if Fastolf made as much money from this as is sometimes supposed. Alençon was only fifteen at the time and Fastolf was only one of two captors, the other being Lord Willoughby. The ransom was claimed by the Crown, and the Duke of Bedford took the prisoner to Rouen. Fastolf certainly thought that he had been short-changed and was still filing claims about it years afterwards.[17]

Nevertheless, the creation of Lancastrian France brought new opportunities which had not been open to Englishmen in the fourteenth century: they were able to acquire estates in France, as well as booty and ransoms. As we have seen, Fastolf became a landowner there at an early date and acquired more property as the English conquest expanded. He was granted Frileuse near Harfleur in the months after its capture in 1415, and four lordships in the *pays de Caux* in 1419 – Bec-Crespin (now Saint-Martin-du-Bec), Aurichier, Gausseville and Criquetot-l'Esneval. After the conquest of Maine he became the baron of Sillé-le-Guillaume and La Suze in Maine, and at some date after 1419 he must have acquired Condé-sur-Noireau in southern Normandy. Most of these lordships were granted as a reward for military service by Henry V or Bedford, but others were ceded in lieu of money owing, and some were purchased. At one point Sir John owned so much land abroad that he needed two households and two accounting systems – one for England and one for France. In the 1430s he administered his English estates through a body which, had he been a baron of England, would have been called a baronial council. This met in Norwich every Michaelmas. It seems likely that he adopted similar procedures in France.[18]

On 8 July 1423, Henry VI's council, sitting in Mantes on the Seine, granted Fastolf an estate in Picardy. The deed in question states that, in consideration of his loyal service, the expenditure he has incurred and the missions he has undertaken, Sir John is given the *chastellerie* of Breteuil-en-Beauvais, and all other possessions of Jean de Montmorency 'our rebel', whether they be in the *pays de Beauvais* or elsewhere in the kingdom of France. The grant is of an entailed estate, made for the benefit of Fastolf and his direct heirs – 'en droit ligne'. The disadvantages of an entail must have been apparent to anyone with an understanding of the law – and Fastolf was a man of the world – but they were spelt out for him in 1431. A judgment in Rouen that year shows that Sir John had also been given an entailed estate in Harfleur, but had purported to make it over to one Robert Spello. Spello had borrowed money from Fastolf but had defaulted on the debt; Fastolf had then repossessed the property in Harfleur. He was initially successful in obtaining judgment, but in 1431 this was set aside, since the court held that an entail could not be sold or passed on to another person. Fastolf's claim against Spello was based on a false premise.

Entails were highly inconvenient for many people – and not just for childless couples like the Fastolfs. In England, conveyancers eventually devised various ways of 'breaking' them, and it is interesting that Fastolf managed to achieve much the same thing in practice in France. The evidence for this consists of two deeds relating to his Norman properties, each dated December 1433. Ten years have now gone by since the grant of Breteuil made in 1423, years in which Fastolf and the English have known both triumph and disaster. This time the king, or his council, sits at Penshurst Place in Kent. The land is again conveyed for loyal service, but the terms are far more generous. The first deed, of 23 December 1433, relates to all Sir John's lands in Normandy except Aurichier and Angerville. The draftsman recites that the properties in question have been conveyed to him as entails, but the king now wishes to enlarge the gift ('amplier les dons'). From now on, Sir John will be able to pass the property on to his heirs in general, not merely from son to son, and he will even be able to sell it, provided that the purchasers are English from England ('pourvu qu'il soient natifs de notre royaume d'Angleterre et non autres'). A second deed, made after Christmas in relation to Aurichier and Angerville, likewise adjusts the tenure, but does not expressly include the restriction to true-born Englishmen.[19]

Much of Fastolf's French property was in areas vulnerable to enemy attack and, as we have seen, there was even a peasant rebellion in the *pays de Caux* in 1435. This took the English by surprise, as Sir John Fortescue later explained:

> There were never poorer people in that land, than were the commons of
> the country of Caux in our time, which was then almost barren for lack of
> farmers; as it now well appears by the new husbandry that is done there,
> namely in digging and uprooting of trees, bushes and groves, grown while
> we were lords of the country. And yet the said commons of Caux made a
> marvellous great rising, and took our towns, castles, and fortresses, and
> slew our captains and soldiers, at such a time as we had but few men of war
> lying in that country.[20]

The Norman rebellion reduced the value of Fastolf's holdings of land in the *pays de Caux* from £200 to £8, but he had already started to take his profit by selling French land – sometimes for as much as ten years' purchase, but if necessary at a loss. By December 1433, he was engaged in selling Aurichier and Angerville (which perhaps explains the enlargement of tenure). This was followed by the sale of other property in the *bailliages* of Caen and Alençon, though a valuation prepared in 1445 still showed him as the owner of ten castles, fifteen *manoirs* and an inn in Rouen, and his French possessions were still worth £401. He did not manage to sell all his property in northern France in good time, as is shown by the plummeting value of his barony at Sillé, where his income fell by four-fifths; and he still owned some French land when the victorious army of Charles VII swept through Normandy.[21]

Fastolf was not the owner of a great territorial estate in England before he went to France, but he eventually acquired land in many counties. The annual value of his English estates at Michaelmas 1445 was more than £1,061. His career had been given a considerable boost by his marriage in 1409 but between 1415 and 1445 he laid out a total of £13,855, or £460 a year, which can only have derived from the profits he made in France. This made him, in the opinion of the eighteenth-century Norfolk antiquarian Francis Blomefield, 'The Greatest Man of That Age', with no fewer than twenty-eight estates in East Anglia alone. Caister was the principal mansion, but it was not the only one. He laid out money on building works at Hellesdon, Cotton, Dedham and Yarmouth, at the same time as building a new choir-aisle on the south side of the abbey church of St Benet's. He bought a house in Norwich, later known as 'Fastolf's' and bought Blickling Hall (though he later sold that to Anne Boleyn's father).[22]

When Fastolf returned to England in 1439 he also acquired several properties in Southwark on the south bank of the Thames. In 1442 he rented, and in 1446 bought, a property called 'Dunnleyisplace', after the Dunley family which had once lived there. This consisted of houses, gardens and two watermills, but he pulled these down and built a mansion, surrounded by walls and a moat. The new house was called Fastolf Place and was situated at the end of Tooley Street, adjoining the Thames, in the parish of St Olave's and directly opposite the Tower of London. Fastolf also built thirty-nine tenements in Bermondsey Street and Horseleydown Lane in the 1440s. In the last two decades of his life, he lived at Fastolf Place and had a wharf there which he used for transporting men and goods up and down the Thames and round the coast to Norfolk. There was another wharf nearby called 'the Bukheed' (Buck's Head?). A little distance away, he acquired the Boar's Head on the east side of Borough High Street, in the parish of St Mary Magdalen, for £200. This was just south of London Bridge and seems to have been a beerhouse and an inn – one of dozens serving visitors to the capital.[23]

The administration of a great estate required skills in management and Sir John would have acquired these when he was Bedford's Maître d'Hôtel. His tone was often brusque, as one would expect of a man who had commanded troops on the battlefield. On 15 October 1450 he wrote to rebuke Thomas Howes:

> And again, I ask you, parson, to arrange that my household supplies be sent here as I wrote to you. And reeds, herrings and other new provisions have [already] been sent to London by cart from Yarmouth; but if you had remembered, you might have sent one or two casks, to please me.

In her study of medieval Southwark, Martha Carlin concluded that the thirty-nine tenements which Fastolf owned in Bermondsey Street and Horseleydown Lane were 'money-losers', though it is unclear whether this was a result of bad management or simply because rents were depressed at the time. Some problems were personal as well as financial. In May 1450 Sir John complained to Thomas Howes:

The Feathered Angels of Blickling Hall

When the owners of Blickling Hall in Norfolk wanted to improve their mansion house in the 1730s, they purchased some items from the sale of a hall at Oxnead, and it was probably around this time that they also acquired the sculptures of Sir John Fastolf's coat of arms which can now be seen in the Brown Drawing Room. Sir Nikolaus Pevsner, and the National Trust guidebook to Blickling, clearly state that these came from Oxnead, but in his book on the Order of the Garter of 1724, John Anstis wrote that the carvings could still be seen at Caister Castle 'on an arch over a bow window on the inside of the ruins'. If that is so, the Fastolf arms must have been transferred directly from Caister to Blickling, without finding an intermediate home. Whatever their provenance, they were clearly thought fine enough for a grand eighteenth-century mansion, though they celebrated values far removed from Whig ideology.

The coats of arms at Blickling are the key to understanding Fastolf, because this is how he intended to be seen at Caister. We see his own coat of arms to the right and the same arms (impaled with his wife's) to the left. The emblems include a great helm, crest and tattered mantle, and garter belt. Altogether, this is a spectacular display.

The message at Blickling is both personal and social: it tells the world that Fastolf was a member of an elite military order, equal in some ways to the greatest of aristocrats, but there is also a strong religious theme. Fastolf's arms are supported by four feathered angels, each with four wings. These are not Roman emperors or Greek gods: they are cherubim. Despite the prevailing belief in Purgatory, their mission was clearly to bear the Fastolfs and their heraldic achievements upwards to Paradise. They are highly unusual, but very similar to the two creatures who appear in the spandrels over the West door of Norwich Cathedral.

I often hear many strange reports in relation to the governance of my property at Caister and other places, about the management of my estate, of my wine cellar there, the keeping of my wardrobe and clothes, the profit made from my rabbit warren at Hellesdon etc., and the improvement of my land; and I heartily pray you, in accordance with the trust I have in you, to help me to reform matters; and, don't allow anyone of bad character to live at my place at Caister, but only well-behaved hard-working people – this is your responsibility.[24]

Fastolf was interested in business and commerce as well as the land. In a period of fifty years, his enterprise turned the lower village at Castle Combe into a thriving centre for the making of cloth. William Worcester wrote of the purchase of the equivalent of forty broadcloths a year there between 1415 and 1440, and concluded that his master's expenditure was 'one of the principal causes of the augmentation and store of the said town and of the new buildings raised in it'. Some clothiers, though villeins by birth and status, were thought to have become very rich. When William Haynes died in 1435, it was at first declared that his goods and chattels were worth a startling 3,000 marks, or £2,000. An inquest of local men revised this down to 300 marks – but this was still a tidy sum. William's widow, Margery Haynes, inherited his property, married again and in 1440 she had two foreign servants working for her – William 'Frenshman' and Morgan 'Frenshman'.[25]

Sir John was very far from being the stereotypical absentee landlord. Though there is no evidence that he ever visited Castle Combe, he was a great benefactor to the manor there: he purchased the right to hold a weekly market and a three-day annual fair, as well as buying exemption from the effects of *prise* (the right of the Crown to take animals for the King's use). At the same time, he kept strict control of his finances: his tenants had to pay an economic price for a licence to inherit their properties, or to marry anyone outside the manor of Castle Combe. He was also a strict disciplinarian, in Castle Combe as well as in France. In 1444 a new Ordinance was made appointing two wardens of the craft of dyers and fullers, and two of the craft of weavers. The Ordinance dealt with the organization of the common pastures in the village and other economic matters, but also maintained social control: drunkenness was to be curbed, by insisting that taverns close at 8 o'clock in winter and 9 o'clock in summer, and the villagers must not play at dice or 'tables'.[26]

In the late 1430s Fastolf made a profit of £300 by buying grain in Norfolk and selling it at Colchester and other places in Essex, while in 1446 there were some 7,800 sheep grazing his East Anglian manors. Anthony Smith discovered that he leased out two mills in Southwark, which appear to have more than repaid his investment. Jessie Crosland tells us that, when he returned from France in the late 1430s, he needed six ships to bring home his moveable possessions.[27] There was a barge-house at Caister as well as a wharf at Southwark. In 1443 the King granted him the right, for life, of using two 'plate'-ships, a cog, a 'farecost' and two ballingers in connection with building work, without let or hindrance from royal officials (presumably this exempted him from the obligation to pay internal customs duties or tolls). Reference was made to the transport of grouting, timber, stones and lead ('grana, maeremium, petras, plumbum'), but two conditions were imposed. He must not abuse the privilege by using the ships in question to engage in the export trade, and he must make them available to the Crown, if they were needed for an expedition to France. The 'Fastolf fleet'– as Helen Castor has called it – plied between Great Yarmouth and London, but also went as far as Newcastle, Boston and other ports on the east coast. On one occasion a cargo of fish was loaded at Cley and conveyed onwards for sale in France, but there was also a trade in grain, malt, wool and cloth. The Fastolf Papers contain at least one set of accounts which relates entirely to the expense of repairing ships ('reparatio navum'), while there is also a letter extant, written by Sir Thomas Kyriell as Lieutenant of Calais on 14 October 1441, confirming the sale to Fastolf by his master-mariner of a ship called the *Bonaventure*.[28]

On 12 January 1449 Thomas Howes replies to Fastolf about a complaint that he has failed to employ ten or eleven Dutch 'shipmen' to man a certain barge (or 'plate') belonging to his master. Howes concedes that he has not taken on the foreign sailors, but defends himself by saying that he has employed experienced Englishmen, who have manned the barge before. He has spoken to a Dutch captain about the job, but this man was unwilling to take responsibility for the barge during the winter. When it comes to another of Fastolf's ships, Howes is unsure whether it will be more profitable to rent this out or use it directly. He puts the options to his master and asks him to decide.

The shipping business was risky, even in peacetime: we can see how relieved Fastolf was when a ship completed a voyage. On 7 March 1450 he writes from London to say that both his ships have arrived home safely, 'blessed be God', while on 3 January 1451 he says, 'My ship with its supplies has arrived tonight, though she has been a long time coming.' In a typically waspish postscript to a letter written at the end of the month, he tells the long-suffering Howes that he has not always been so fortunate:

> And as to grain and malt to be sent hither, I pray you that it come in a secure vessel and accompanied by another vessel, on a fair wind, for you know well that I have suffered great losses in my ships and grain in recent times, and so you must manage the business more prudently in the future.[29]

Ships needed to be fitted out with artillery, not least because of the danger of piracy. At the time of Fastolf's death in 1459, a captain who had worked for him had to render an account of his stores, including the 'guns of iron or brass' which he kept on board ship. It was also recorded that Fastolf owned

> Two good little ships called the *Margate* and the *Blythe* of 40 tons each, well fitted out and equipped with tackle for sea-going voyages – under the keeping of the said John Rus – and three or four other small vessels besides, as a ballinger, a plate [sic] ship made in Holland, a great keel vessel to carry bulk cargoes of corn and malt, and a large barge, with another small vessel called a pont, for fishing herring.[30]

Fastolf often had money on deposit with agents, pending the completion of various land deals. As early as 26 January 1426 he sent 2,000 marks sterling to Sir William Breton, then *bailli* of Caen, to be forwarded to John Wells and John Kirtling, in connection with the purchase of Davington in Kent and Akethorpe near Lowestoft. Wells was a London merchant and alderman who commonly paid 5 per cent, despite the Church's objections to usury. On occasions, Fastolf also sent money home via Jean Sac ('Maître Jean de Paris'), who was both his banker and lawyer.[31]

When considering whether Fastolf was really an 'old vulture', we should not forget his liability for taxes. There seems to be little or no evidence relating to direct or indirect taxation, but the Lancastrian kings relied very heavily on loans and Sir John certainly lent money to Henry VI's government. Compared to the Crown's chief creditor, Cardinal Beaufort (who lent thousands), the amounts he advanced were small, but they were by no means insignificant: £1,000 in September 1436, 1,000 marks in February 1437, £100 in 1449, 400 marks in 1450, £400 in 1452. These loans were recorded in 1455 and, for all we know, they may represent the tip of an iceberg, but even looking at these dates alone, we can draw one conclusion. Fastolf continued to lend money to the Crown long after 1429, which has long been seen as a turning-point in the French war, and he continued to lend to a regime which he no longer fully approved of after 1439, though he continued to advise it. Of course, pressure may have been put upon him to do so, just as pressure may have been applied to secure the use of his estate at Condé-sur-Noireau for the raid on Fougères, but McFarlane demonstrated that the Lancastrians did not, in general, force their subjects to lend them money, if only because they lacked the means to do so.

Fastolf's loans to Henry VI are good evidence of his continuing devotion to duty, especially when we realize that by 1455 none of the money had been repaid. At the same time, Sir John was a businessman and expected a return on his money. The point of drawing up the list was to make a claim, and he expected to receive a good rate of interest, though medieval accounts are deliberately obscure about this. The idea of giving generously, with no thought of reward, might appeal to William Worcester – he recommended it as the solution to England's woes in the *Boke of Noblesse* – but this was the advice of a scholar, and, however learned he may have been, Fastolf was a practical man.[32]

Warfare by Litigation

One of the things which Fastolf had in common with Falstaff was the law. In *Henry IV* Part II, the fat knight is shown in Gloucestershire, reminiscing with Justice Shallow about their riotous youth at the Inns of Court – though the Justice is more interested in hearing about the streetwalker Jane Nightwork than he is about anything legal. His prototype Fastolf was constantly in court, both in France and in England.

The French cases of which records have survived relate to his military activities in the 1420s and 1430s, particularly in Paris. The first case shows that might was not always right, even in occupied France. The English in France were obliged by the Treaty of Troyes to use the French courts, but in a case in the municipal court of Paris in the early 1420s, involving a boat of grain arrested at the Port de l'École-Saint-Germain, Fastolf's opponents challenged his right to be heard. Sir John's lawyer refuted this by pointing out what should have been obvious to everyone – that he not only owned land in Normandy but was Captain of the Bastille, and an important office-holder. The argument was accepted by the Provost of the Merchants, but the need to justify his standing before the court at all demonstrates that the English were subject to the rule of law, and it was French law which applied.[33]

The second case involved military operations in the Valois district close to Paris. With its enormous population, the French capital needed to import a wide range of commodities from surrounding areas, but the Dauphinists constantly attacked the food convoys, whether they travelled to Paris by land or along the river. The Provost of the Merchants demanded that something be done to remedy the insecurity and, in 1423, the Grand Conseil ordered Fastolf to take action. He marched into the Valois and, within the space of a few days, took the fortress of Passy and a minor fort called La Folie, capturing the commander Guillaume Remon (popularly known as the Marjolaine), who agreed to pay a ransom of 20,000 gold *saluts*. However, when the Dauphinists recaptured Compiègne, the Regent released Remon, paraded him under the walls of the town with a halter round his neck, and threatened to hang him if the garrison refused to surrender. Surrender they did but, while Fastolf might otherwise have welcomed that news, the Marjolaine's release represented a serious financial loss. The amount Remon owed to Fastolf for his ransom had become, to say the least, difficult to collect, but the situation was worse than this. It transpired that Remon had previously taken several prisoners himself, including the merchants Henry de Lidan and Denis Sauvage, as well as the lords of Passy-en-Valois and La Folie. Under the law of arms, Fastolf had become entitled to these ransoms too, since they were owed to Remon, but Remon's unconditional release ruined everything. The conflict between public good and private profit, inherent in the medieval method of paying the army, was laid bare.

Fastolf was not a man to write off a debt. Unlike Remon, Sauvage and de Lidan were still in his power and, although they were probably friends to the Anglo-Burgundian cause, he arranged for them to be locked up again, de Lidan in the Bastille, Sauvage in the Châtelet. He filed suit in the Paris Parlement, claiming what he was owed from them, but he does not seem to have been successful in this. The case dragged on for years and may not have come to judgment when Paris fell to the Valois in 1436. In the end Fastolf petitioned the Crown for a remedy, claiming 4,000 marks from it in the mid-1440s, and may have accepted a grant of land by way of settlement. It must seem to us that he was a Shylock, determined to have his pound of flesh, but in Fastolf's view he was only pursuing what was legally his, as Henry V had done so single-mindedly before him.[34]

Sir John continued to regard litigation as a kind of warfare, even after he returned to England. He referred to his opponents in East Anglia as his 'adversaries', and in some cases the hostility was real as well as nominal, because those on the other side of the case were his political enemies too. The law was an arena where he could exercise his knowledge of human nature and tactics and where victory might be hoped for, though defeat sometimes had to be endured.

Fastolf's litigiousness has been seen as one aspect of a mean and cantankerous character. His servant Henry Windsor famously remarked, 'Cruel and vengible he hath been ever, and for the most part without pity and mercy.' He was certainly persistent in pursuit of what he judged to be his rights and he probably did have a harsh attitude towards those who had let him down. McFarlane showed that he caused as many as 50 per cent of the men he had once employed to be thrown into jail for debt, sometimes for periods as long as two years. Others were made to pay swingeing fines. Nicholas Bocking's complaint about his master ran to twenty clauses, one of which related to the alleged failure to repay a sum of 13s 4d. Bocking had given this sum to a French prisoner of war who 'had nothing in his purse', but Fastolf did not approve.[35]

Yet there was a kinder side to Fastolf's nature. In 1950 McFarlane wrote to a friend that his activities had been 'interpreted too unfavourably, thanks to the tales told by his servants after his death. He may have been a beast but at least there was justice about his beastliness, and I'm far from sure that he was a beast at all.'[36] Sir John gave generously to charity and, in one draft of his will, he directed that his 'menial' servants should be paid and maintained for six months after his death, to enable them to find alternative employment. There were other occasions when he went out of his way to help his old comrades. When John Rafman, his steward in 1431–2, was in trouble, Fastolf reminded him that he had once 'paid for his finance and ransom 100 marks and quitted him out of prison in France, where all the masters and friends that ever he had may not have done it, for it was not the guise or custom of men-at-arms to requite every prisoner that is taken'.[37]

Fastolf was probably no more litigious than the average English landowner. G L Harriss has written that 'the phenomenal growth' of litigiousness in the late medieval period was essentially a reflection of a more equal society, where more people had something to litigate about – something which might equally be said about Shakespeare's England, or the late twentieth century. Sir John was a strong character, but the practising lawyer encounters men like him every day. The volume of evidence which survives about his affairs does make him appear litigious, but he was probably not so different from Ralph, Lord Cromwell, who has also been characterized as a 'ruthless protector of his own interests', or his great rival Talbot, whose biographer described him as 'violent and quarrelsome'.[38]

Litigation was almost inevitable when land changed hands or when someone died, because the law was still developing. There was a much wider variety of legal estates and interests in land than exists nowadays. The conveyancing process involved a bewildering variety of laborious searches and title had to be investigated by perusing original handwritten documents, kept in private muniment rooms. There were at least two types of court available: those which applied the common law and those which applied the newer Equity. A different result might be achieved, according to where the case was decided: common law did not recognize trusts (or 'uses') of land, whereas Equity did. Delay resulted from the duplication, though the newer body of law sometimes delivered a more just result. Four hundred years later, in *Bleak House*, Dickens wrote about 'questions which Law sent to Equity and Equity sent to Law', but the problem was already there in Fastolf's day, when there was a greater temptation to resort to violence in order to resolve a dispute. Fastolf was much troubled by the uncertainty of the law in his last years, as he sought to dispose of his estate in the absence of an heir and while 'the vultures gathered'.[39]

Sir John cannot have been an easy client for his lawyers to have, because he was not content to leave the law to them, even when proceedings had been begun. He thought he knew best and was always hectoring them, telling them to be quicker about it, to look further into the matter in hand, to argue more forcefully, to make sure that no relevant piece of evidence was overlooked. At the same time he sometimes wanted to correct their drafting and reduce the length of their submissions. He saw that, in constructing a legal argument, less is often more. On 8 August 1450 he wrote to instruct Thomas Greene to 'see and correct' a pleading. 'Make every matter shorter,' he commanded, 'and it can be to understand of the matter not less.'[40]

It is Sir John's manipulation of judges and juries which is most difficult for us to understand. His letters repeatedly refer to the need to 'labour' the jury (which meant influencing the process of selection). In 1451 he instructed Howes to 'labour to the sheriff for the return of such panels as will speak for me, and not be shamed ... entreat the sheriff as well as ye can by reasonable rewards, rather than fail'. He also spent regular sums in entertaining and 'informing' the jury once it had been empanelled. This does not look right, but we have to at least realize that the machinery of justice worked differently in the fifteenth century.

Fastolf was a contemporary of Sir John Fortescue, the lawyer and legal theorist who wrote the treatise *In Praise of the Laws of England* (*De Laudibus Legum Angliae*) between 1468 and 1471. For Fortescue, England was a greatly superior country to France, and one of the key features of this superiority was the prevalence of trial by jury, but it is clear from the treatise that the English jury did not perform the same function as it does now. Nowadays, it adjudicates impartially on the evidence presented to it, and for that reason members of the jury are not supposed to know the witnesses. In the fifteenth century the opposite was the case: the jury was primarily a method of proof and jurymen were supposed to be acquainted with the

Norwich and the Cult of St George

It is a myth that the early fifteenth century was a time of economic stagnation everywhere, following the loss of a large part of the population in the Black Death and subsequent plagues. Norwich was booming, to judge by the amount of building work in progress. Many of the fifty-seven parish churches were being renovated and enlarged, and this was also the period when the city fathers built the Guildhall, the market cross and the New Mills, following the grant of Norwich's Charter by Henry IV.

Fastolf was often in Norwich, though the sources tend to show him at Southwark and Caister. His council met there, he had a house there, and this was where he attended the meetings of the Guild of St George, a kind of club where he could combine religious observance with business and pleasure. St George was commemorated in many of the parish churches and in the cathedral, where Sir Thomas Erpingham, who fought at Agincourt (and helped pay for the rebuilding of St Andrew's Church and the Erpingham Gate) was buried in 1428. The Guild had been founded in 1385 but was only incorporated in 1417, and it is thought that Fastolf may have co-operated with Erpingham in obtaining its charter from Henry V. It existed to celebrate St George's Day, with processions and festivities. One of the inventories of the Guild's possessions refers to a silver gilt statue of angel, said to contain an arm belonging to the Saint, which was kept in the Cathedral's Reliquary.

With its Norman keep, its Cathedral, Bishop's Palace and numerous clergy, its wharves and its boatmen, its 'hospitals', Guildhall and merchants, its law courts and lawyers, Norwich was a bustling county town. It must also have had a considerable cultural influence on the surrounding area. Stained glass, which was made for the Cathedral and the parish churches in the city, also appeared at Caister, and in the Fastolf Chapel at St Benet's. The feathered angels which appear in the spandrels over the West door of the Cathedral are remarkably similar to those which could once be seen over the fireplace at Caister and can still be seen at Blickling Hall. Over St Ethelbert's Gate in the Cathedral close, there is a man with a spear, boldly lunging at a mythical beast, who appears in an identical attitude on a wall at the abbey gatehouse at St Benet's. These are almost certainly, in all cases, representations of a pedestrian St George, and his dragon.

Norwich was a focal point of Fastolf's later life. Yet his private correspondence suggests that in his last years, and especially after his wife died, he lived a frugal and parsimonious life and lacked a sense of humour. It also suggests that he fell out with the men of Norwich, for in 1451 he wrote, somewhat petulantly, to Thomas Howes and John Berney that: 'There was no city in England that I loved and trusted most upon, till they did so unkindly to me and against truth in the Lady Bardolph's matter, where I never gave them cause.'

(With thanks to Dr Tim Pestell of Norwich Castle Museum and the Norfolk Archaeological Trust, for the information about St Benet's Abbey.)

facts of a case before the trial began.[41] In the light of this, Fastolf's expenditure on 'informing' juries was not corrupt. He was doing his best to ensure that the jury was in a position to return a true verdict, and his behaviour was absolutely normal for the time.

Likewise, it must seem to us that Sir John's dealings with the judiciary were quite improper. At the end of October 1457 he wrote to Justice Yelverton about a case involving the faithful Thomas Howes, who had been sued by John Andrews. Addressing the Justice as his 'right trusty brother' – which, in a sense, he was, since both men belonged to the Guild of St George at Norwich – Fastolf thanked him for his 'good support in all matters herebefore', and asked for further assistance:

> The parson Sir Thomas is about to come up before you and the other royal judges, at the cruel and hasty suit of Andrews and his affinity; [but] I trust to God that by your good help these proceedings, which that have been commenced so eagerly by him ... will be seen for what they are, and that perjury – which is so prevalent nowadays – will be duly punished.

Fastolf also wrote to his stepson Stephen Scrope, copying the letter to John Paston and John Bocking, and asked him to do what he could to influence the outcome of the trial, by speaking to Sir Richard Bingham, who was also a judge (as well as Scrope's father-in-law). Fastolf can even be shown to have paid a bribe to Sir John Fortescue, the author of *In Praise of the Laws of England*. The payment is recorded at the end of a long list of legal expenses in document 42 in the Fastolf Papers:

> Item, given as a reward to the Chief Justice of the Lord King through William Worcester the servant of Sir John Fastolf ... one gold and crimson-coloured velvet robe, in order that the said Judge should be more favourable with regard to the case of Thomas Howes, when he was imprisoned in the King's Bench
>
> £6 13s 4d[42]

In view of this evidence, can Fastolf be taken seriously when he complains about others who are accused of 'maintaining' juries and bribing judges? He certainly thinks that he is different: in his own mind he always stays within the law, while others step outside it. Is this mere hypocrisy? In 1955 McFarlane wrote to a former pupil that

> If you read the Paston Letters you notice that all the correspondents assume, even when desperate measures are being debated, that they are being denied justice, that getting at the sheriff and the jury is only necessary to secure that right will win; they never doubt the justice of their own cause.

The only way in which Fastolf's conduct may have been at all unusual was in his readiness to resort to the courts rather than use main force when he could have done. In his *War in the Middle Ages*, Philippe Contamine explained how medieval society gradually turned from war to law as a means of resolving disputes, and Fastolf could be said to have made that transition in a single lifetime. There seems to be no hard evidence that he ever took the law into his own hands in England, though he had the wherewithal to do so – in the form of friends, retainers, weapons and a defensible castle.[43]

Chapter 9

The War of the Dukes, 1447–59

With his great wealth, his many estates and his splendid new mansion at Caister, one might have expected Fastolf to play an important part in local and even in national politics in his last years. Yet the reality was that he held only minor office. This may have owed something to his alleged 'flight' from the battlefield at Patay, which cast a long shadow, but it was mostly due to his unpopularity with the dominant faction at court. He rarely enjoyed the favour of Henry VI and his favourites, though he hesitated to oppose them openly.

Fastolf's exclusion from office did not help his finances. In the early 1450s, William Worcester helped his master prepare an account of the amounts he claimed from the Crown. Two lists were finalized, each containing claims of several different types. In the first of these, Fastolf claimed 1,000 marks advanced in February, and another £1,000 advanced in September, 1437; £100 for the Queen's coronation in 1445 and a further £233 6s 8d for Kyriell's expedition of 1450; £100 for an expedition of Thomas Daniel's to Brittany; and an unspecified sum to 'speed and help' Talbot's last expedition to Aquitaine. He claimed 5,000 marks for the 'great and horrible extortions' suffered at the hands of the Duke of Suffolk; 2,500 marks for the barony of Sillé-le-Guillaume and La Suze, surrendered by the Crown in the late 1440s; 4,000 marks in respect of the prisoner Guillaume Remon; another 4,000 marks in respect of the balance of the ransom of the Duke of Alençon, captured at Verneuil in 1424; and 4,599 marks 5s 6d owed by the Duke of Bedford's estate.[1]

It will be seen that some of the debts claimed in this first list were already very old, but in the second list Fastolf went right back to 1412 and claimed £227 15s 3d in relation to his period of service as Deputy Constable of Bordeaux and further sums in relation to Clarence's expedition of that year as a whole. £133 6s 8d was still due in relation to service performed as Lieutenant of Harfleur in 1416, £42 for 'keeping and victualling' the Bastille in Paris and £89 10s 4d for keeping Meulan, both of which amounts related to 1421–2. The sting was in the tail: he claimed 5,082 marks 13s 3d in relation to his captaincies of Alençon, Fresnay, Verneuil and Honfleur.

Fastolf would not have submitted these claims if he had no hope of recovering the sums in question, yet he was clearly a sad and disappointed old man:

Since the last coming over of the said Fastolf into this realm, by the space of fifteen years and more, he hath borne great costs, charges and expenses, attending upon the king's highness and the lords of his council, as he hath had in commandment and was his part for to do. For this, and for all the service that he hath done for the right noble prince, king Henry the fourth, grandfather to our sovereign lord that now is, and to the most victorious prince and king his father, whose souls God assoil, and also to our said sovereign lord, he hath had neither fee, nor wages, reward, nor recompense in this his realm of England.

The Myth of the Roses

It was Shakespeare who immortalized the idea of a war between two sides, with each adopting a rose as an emblem, though he based his plots once again on the works of earlier Tudor writers. His Duke of York aims for the throne from the moment he appears on stage. The reality is that York was twice made Protector but did not claim the Crown until 1460, the year after Fastolf's death. There were power struggles all through Henry VI's long reign, but the conflicts were more about the king's minority, and then his incompetence – and the loss of the Lancastrian empire in France – than about dynastic ambition. The scene in *Henry VI* Act II in which York, Warwick, Suffolk and Somerset pluck white and red roses in the Temple Gardens may be wonderful drama, but it is bad history.[2]

It is tempting to think that men took sides before they really did, and indeed that there were two 'sides' when there were several or, in another sense, none at all. There can generally be only two sides on a battlefield, and there was only one king on the English throne, and, in the end, the Yorkist dynasty did indeed supplant the Lancastrian, but in the 1450s gentlemen like Fastolf did not line up to fight for the White Rose or the Red. What they did was to struggle to maintain their power and influence, usually as members of groups linked to the great aristocrats. At this late stage of Fastolf's life, he had little or no influence at court, but he was concerned for his own position in East Anglia, where there were certainly more than two sides. The Dukes of Norfolk and Oxford were each powerful there, in addition to York and Suffolk.

Henry VI was a baby when his father died, so that his uncles were the natural power-brokers for more than fifteen years. They did not always see eye to eye and the Duke of Gloucester had clashed with Cardinal Beaufort in the mid-1420s. The problem was not solved when Henry purported to assume personal control of government in 1437, because he was (by any standards) inadequate as a ruler; but the legitimacy of the Lancastrian dynasty was never in question so far as Fastolf was concerned. He had fought for Henry IV and Henry V and he had served all three of Henry V's brothers: Clarence, Bedford and Gloucester. He had also advised Exeter and the Dukes of Somerset, all members of the Beaufort family. He continued to serve Henry VI until the end of his life. There may have been moments when he sympathized with York's complaints, but we have to remember his age when the power struggle turned into civil war. At the time of the First Battle of St Albans in 1455, he was seventy-five – old enough to be York's father. He was never a committed 'Yorkist'. As McFarlane pointed out, it would be rash to predict which side he would have taken when full civil war broke out, after his death.

Henry VI was too much of a saint to be the effective ruler of a militaristic society. Many historians would go further, and say that he was 'inane' when he was not insane, but Englishmen were not free to criticize him. It was commonly believed that the King was divinely appointed. Shakespeare's words in *Hamlet* were as accurate for the fifteenth century as they were for his own day:

> There's such divinity doth hedge a king,
> That treason can but peep to what it would …

If Fastolf was secretly critical of Henry VI, he never said so. Criticism had to be reserved for the king's ministers.

Fastolf was one of York's advisers during the Duke's second Lieutenancy in France in the early 1440s, though he was heavily involved at the time in his own business affairs in Southwark and East Anglia. He was a member of the Duke's 'discrete' (or inner) council in 1441 and acted as the Duke's 'feoffee' (trustee) in land deals the same year. He continued to be one of York's advisers between May 1445 and June 1448 and was granted an annuity of £20 a year 'for his noble and praiseworthy service and for his good counsel'. The relevant indenture is not extant, but if another of York's which does survive is anything to go by, this required 'true and faithful' service to the Duke – and for life – 'against all earthly creatures of what estate pre-eminence or condition so ever they be', except for the king and his issue.[3]

When York returned from Ireland in September 1450, he caused Somerset to be indicted on a whole list of charges. He alleged that he had reduced the strength of the garrisons in France (something which Cade's rebels accused Fastolf of); that his villainy had caused the loss of Normandy and Aquitaine; and that, even now, he was plotting to 'sell' Calais to the French. Finally, Somerset had supposedly kept 72,000 francs in compensation, when it had been earmarked for the settlers in Maine. Fastolf would have agreed with these charges, and it is even possible that he helped to frame them. York and Fastolf each had ample reason to be critical of Suffolk and especially Somerset, who had supplanted them in Normandy. Both championed the cause of the dispossessed in Maine, and both were substantial losers by the French recovery of Normandy. There were remarkable similarities between the document entitled *Suggestions for Questions to be asked of the Duke of Somerset, respecting his Misconduct in Normandy*, which was probably prepared by

Fastolf in 1449, and the terms of an offer, made by York in 1450, to assist the King in bringing those who were 'openly noised of treason' to justice. Contact between York and Fastolf at this time is recorded in the Duke's household accounts.[4]

York was asset-rich – he owned land in twenty counties – but he sometimes had a problem with cash flow, and his financial position deteriorated considerably when the Crown neglected to pay him for his services in France and Ireland. In December 1452 Sir John lent him money on the security of some items of jewellery. On this or on another occasion, the Duke left two valuable items with Fastolf as a pledge, against a loan of £437. These precious items were described in 1461, when Edward IV redeemed the loan from Fastolf's executors:

> an ouche [a jewelled clasp] of gold set with a great pointed diamond set upon a rose, enamelled white, and an ouche of gold in the fashion of a ragged staff [the Earl of Warwick's badge] with two images of a man and woman garnished with a ruby, a diamond, and a great pearl.[5]

If Fastolf was close to York, his relationship with Suffolk turned sour in the 1430s. It had not always been so. They had been comrades in arms and Suffolk's early career was heroic. He lost a father at Harfleur and a brother at Agincourt, and had taken part in the difficult siege of Cherbourg in 1419. He was elected Knight of the Garter in 1421 and was a commander of the English forces at Orléans in 1428–9. When he was captured at Jargeau, Fastolf helped him to pay his enormous ransom of £20,000, by purchasing his estate at Cotton in East Anglia from him. Yet, strangely, it was this transaction which seems to have caused the two men to fall out – perhaps because Suffolk, like Talbot, resented the fact that he had been taken prisoner when Fastolf had avoided this fate. Perhaps Suffolk also resented having to sell the property where he had been born to someone he may have regarded as an upstart. We shall never really know, but there is little doubt about the enmity which developed in the 1440s.[6]

Suffolk returned to England several years before Fastolf and forged an alliance at court with Cardinal Beaufort (the advocate of peace), while his henchmen became well ensconced in East Anglia. His contacts with the French took an interesting turn. He acted as a custodian of the Duke of Orléans and remained friends with his own former captor, Dunois. As we have noted, he went to Tours in the 1440s to negotiate the marriage of the King with Margaret of Anjou. With the deaths of Gloucester and the Cardinal in 1447, he became the power behind the throne. Fastolf was never a member of Suffolk's inner council: he was closely associated with all three of his critics and opponents; York, Gloucester and Norfolk.[7]

Suffolk's years in power witnessed an almost total loss of the English possessions in northern France, and he took much of the blame. On 28 January 1450 he was arrested, imprisoned in the Tower of London and banished, but the ship on which he left the country was intercepted and he was butchered by the crew of the *Nicholas of the Tower*. The account of this murder in Sir Arthur Quiller-Couch's 1925 anthology of English prose is entitled 'Suffolk dies by Pirates', but it seems more likely that the pirates were ordinary English sailors, determined to take their revenge for the military debacle. The murder was widely celebrated in verse and popular song, and we can be sure that Fastolf would not have been sorry to see the end of Suffolk's 'reign'. However, he would have been very distressed by the breakdown of law and order, just as he was by the chaos created by Cade's Revolt.

There is good evidence that Fastolf's association with the Duke of York became too close for comfort in the early 1450s. There is a gap in his otherwise voluminous correspondence between September 1451 and July 1454, but during that time, on 19 August 1452, he conveyed all his land to trustees, in expectation of a long journey ('viage') – which he never in fact made – while at the same time making a will. What was going on here? The best guess is that he intended to make a journey to visit King Henry, with the idea of declaring his loyalty. On the eve of his intended departure, he wrote:

> If I am unable to undertake this journey, because of illness or the weak state of my body or for any other unfortunate reason, and therefore am unable to state my case, as – God knows – I wish and desire to do above all other things on earth, then [I wish] my said lords [feoffees] to incessantly try to convince the king's highness and his noble counsel that, according to the evidence ['by my records and proofs'] I may be openly declared, considered and adjudged to be a truly loyal servant of the Crown ['the king's true liegeman'], and that I have always been such, since I attained the age of discretion, having been educated, both at the courts and in the wars, of [the king] and those princes of blessed memory, his ancestors.[8]

The political background to this mysterious and probably abortive 'voyage' in the summer of 1452 was that the Duke of York had attempted to bully the King by an 'armed demonstration' at Dartford in Kent the previous February, but Henry VI had called his bluff. York had been arrested and compelled to swear that he would never rebel again. In July and August, Henry was touring the West Country with commissions of oyer et terminer, suppressing disorder and dissent. It seems likely that Fastolf wanted to try to make his peace with the King.

Fastolf was right to be fearful, for accusations of treason were in the air. In 1451 his old comrade in France, Sir William Oldhall, was twice accused of it and felt compelled to take sanctuary in St Martin's-le-Grand in London. Two years later, Oldhall was the subject of an Act of Attainder, by which he would have forfeited all his estates. Some properties were exempted from this harsh treatment, including a group of three London tenements held in trust for the knight, and Fastolf was one of Oldhall's feoffees. It was not uncommon for men to be prosecuted for little more than guilt by association, and looking across the Channel, as he was accustomed to do, Fastolf might have noticed that Charles VII had just imprisoned his chief financier Jacques Coeur, on fantastic charges, so that he could get his hands on his wealth.[9]

Fastolf came under direct attack in 1453, when a parliament was summoned to Reading. A man called Robert Collinson, who had also accused Ralph, Lord Cromwell, alleged that Fastolf and Lord Grey of Ruthin had been involved in plotting the events preceding York's demonstration at Dartford. The two men were summoned before the Council to answer for their conduct. It was at this time, on 6 September 1453, that Sir John was required to enter into a recognisance for good behaviour in the sum of £1,000, though it was later recorded that the obligation was cancelled: 'for that [Fastolf] did so appear before the lords of the council on 6 November … and made his excuse, wherefore he was by them reckoned as excused, and dismissed from further appearance'.[10]

This was a good outcome for Fastolf, but it must have been (to say the least) unpleasant to fall under suspicion of treason. Two members of his wife's family had been executed for the crime – Archbishop Richard Scrope of York in the early years of Henry IV's reign, and Lord Scrope of Masham in the early years of Henry V's. Fastolf may also have reflected on the sad contrast between himself and Talbot at this time. While he was embroiled in domestic faction and concentrating on clearing his name at home, Talbot was engaged in a last desperate campaign to save Aquitaine.

The first pitched battle in the 'Wars of the Roses' took place at St Albans in 1455. It was really no more than a skirmish (the armies were small and the total number of dead was no more than about sixty), but the fact that the supporters of the King and of the Duke of York fought each other at all, and on the streets of an English town, was a startling development, while at least three great lords were numbered among the dead, including the Duke of Somerset. There are no fewer than five reports of 'First St Albans', and one of these is the so-called *Fastolf Relation*.

The *Fastolf Relation* appears to have been written by Sir John's herald Fastolf Poursuivant, though it was saved for posterity by the ever-faithful William Worcester, who (some time after 1461) inscribed a title on the first page: *Le Primer Jorney Seynt Albans*.[11] Written entirely in French, the report tells us that Fastolf still employed a herald in 1455, just as he had in France a generation previously. It was his *poursuivant*'s job to accompany and assist Mowbray Herald, who served the Duke of Norfolk. It also demonstrates Fastolf's continuing interest in politics, in what was to prove the last decade of his life. He had, so to speak, a reporter on the case, but the *Fastolf Relation* contains no description of the fighting. It deals only with the verbal skirmishing which took place between the heralds representing York and the King, before battle was commenced. On the other hand, while almost all other accounts of the battle are written from a Yorkist perspective, the *Fastolf*

Relation is remarkably even-handed. As C A J Armstrong wrote in 1960, 'Few things are more remarkable about this source than the absence of party feeling and violent denunciation which bulk so large in the *Stow Relation*.' Fastolf Poursuivant was certainly not commissioned to write Yorkist propaganda – of which plenty was to be written in the 1460s: he must have been asked to file an impartial and objective account.

Yet Fastolf clearly had a good deal of sympathy for York. After the Battle of St Albans was over, he wrote to John Paston: 'I trust to God that, as the world is going now, this will all go well, with your help.' There is also evidence that Fastolf benefited from what turned out to be a Yorkist victory. Throughout the 1450s, he was involved in a series of proceedings relating to the wardship of Thomas Fastolf, son of John Fastolf of Nacton, in which his adversaries were Philip Wentworth and John Andrew (associates of the late Duke of Suffolk). He made no headway in this litigation before First St Albans but afterwards it was concluded to his satisfaction. It was at this time too that he seems to have hoped for better luck at national level, in relation to his claims for financial redress.[12]

Fastolf may have shared York's fate, in that he was never truly reconciled with Henry VI and his court. He went on lending money to the Crown in the early 1450s, including sums to help finance Kyriell's expedition to Normandy and Talbot's to Aquitaine; but he absented himself from Garter meetings between 1454 and the year of his death. Admittedly, this absence could be explained by illness and old age: in 1454 it was expressly recorded that he was 'so very old and weak that he could neither go [walk] nor ride without very great danger of his health', and Anstis wrote that 'his attendance was afterwards excused', impliedly for similar reasons, but there may well have been more to it than this. Garter records show that Fastolf was in fact 'left to the sentence of the statutes' in 1455, because he did not send an excuse at all. In any event his illness could have been diplomatic as well as real. It is worth remembering that Garter meetings were royal occasions, at which the King or his deputy always presided, and in 1454 the Duke of York did not attend 'because he thought that the King was angry with him'. Fastolf may have had reasons other than ill health for following York's example.[13]

Strife in East Anglia

William de la Pole, Duke of Suffolk (1396–1450) is still a controversial figure. So far as Fastolf and his friends the Pastons were concerned, the Duke's agents in East Anglia, Sir Thomas Tuddenham, Nicholas Appleyard, John Heydon, Philip Wentworth and John Andrew, were criminals, and the Duke was at the least negligent in his handling of the nation's affairs. On 7 September 1450 Fastolf wrote:

> I often suffered damage at the hands of the Duke of Suffolk's officers in Lothingland [the hinterland of Lowestoft], on account of their great and

exorbitant exactions, in the distraining of my belongings and in other ways; and I suffered the same treatment in various other places in Norfolk and Suffolk, both at Cotton and at the hands of Cossey's officers, and in the same way, though I cannot list all the items in my schedule of damage.

Fastolf had at least two main reasons for disliking Suffolk: the Duke had presided over the loss of Normandy, and he had persecuted him in East Anglia, causing him to lose estates there too. John Heydon was initially despised because he was of low birth: Thomas Howes said he was 'come up of poverty'; he too was accused of 'exactions' – forcible entry, damage to property, bribery of juries, and giving false evidence. Tuddenham was said to be an adulterer, but also a 'common extortioner' who had terrorized Swaffham with 'terrible menaces'. In 1450 Fastolf claimed that he had suffered this kind of oppression for thirteen years, though he once said it was seventeen. A list of twenty-two other individuals who had suffered in the same way was drawn up. Though he did not use the term, Sir John was a victim of the worst excesses of 'bastard feudalism'.[14]

Most historians who have studied the matter agree with Fastolf that Suffolk's 'rule' in East Anglia was corrupt and oppressive. Professor Jacob described John Heydon as a 'professional desperado', while Colin Richmond called his associates a kind of Mafia. One gets much the same impression from Anthony Smith's work on the subject. From the military point of view, Colonel Burne even took 'satisfaction' in Suffolk's murder. On the other hand, there is a benign view of the Duke, taken by Kingsford in the early twentieth century and more recently by Helen Castor. On this view Suffolk was little different from any other member of the landowning classes, but he made better use of his traditional powerbase (which was the de la Pole inheritance), while also exploiting his control of the Duchy of Lancaster estates, which had come to the Crown in 1399. The two schools of thought disagree about the chronology and the interpretation to be put on events. The former blames Suffolk for the strife which undoubtedly occurred and agrees with Fastolf that the trouble began around 1437. The latter thinks that, if Suffolk was guilty of oppression, it was only from about 1447 (three years before his murder): before that date his agents were acting on their own account. They were not Suffolk's 'henchmen' so much as independent contractors. If Fastolf felt persecuted, this was in part psychological: 'he nursed a growing conviction that he was the victim of a *vendetta*.'[15]

The argument that Suffolk was not responsible for the actions of his subordinates in East Anglia appears to defy the laws of political gravity, in an age when aristocrats like Suffolk were still much more powerful than gentlemen like Fastolf. It may well be that Thomas Daniel was a maverick, but the argument appears much weaker in the cases of Tuddenham and Heydon. In addition, there is a sense in which, even if his agents were acting as independent contractors rather than servants, Suffolk was still responsible for their actions, because he failed to rein them in when he could have done. In any event, it made little difference from Fastolf's point of view whether the guilty men were told what to do by Suffolk. What mattered to him was the degree and duration of the oppression he suffered at their hands, and his helplessness in the face of it. He certainly thought that he was oppressed, and from around 1437 onwards. All sides agree that, in some instances, Suffolk deliberately put pressure on Fastolf in East Anglia because of political differences about the conduct of the war in France.

Traditional landowners have always resented the pretensions of 'new money', but there is a debate as to who was the parvenu in East Anglia – Fastolf or Suffolk. Sir John had been born in East Anglia and was an erstwhile member of the de la Pole retinue; he inherited land at Caister and his roots were firmly in Norfolk. One can see why he would have regarded men like Tuddenham and Heydon as upstarts, but it is also true that, when Fastolf returned to England in 1439, he had been away from home too long to be able to compete with Suffolk on his home territory. The Duke had returned nine years earlier and Sir John never caught up. He was never a sheriff, nor a Member of Parliament, as several of Suffolk's men were; and he sat on the royal council for a few short months only, between April and July 1450. Other men had done their 'networking' in his absence. In the eyes of his opponents, he could be made to seem the *arriviste*.

In his groundbreaking doctoral thesis and subsequent work, Anthony Smith examined the relationship between Fastolf's fortunes in the law courts and the power exercised by Suffolk and his agents in East Anglia, and he found that Fastolf could only make headway, locally or nationally, when the Duke of Suffolk's regime collapsed in 1449–50. This suggests very strongly that Sir John's complaint of persecution was fully justified. It was only in these years that Sir John was appointed to public office on a scale commensurate with his status and experience and that his advice even stood a chance of being listened to. However, his moment of power soon passed.[16]

Fastolf certainly had enemies in East Anglia in the 1440s and 1450s. He may also have been running short of friends. Sir Henry Inglose died in 1451. Thomas, Lord Scales, who had fought with him in Maine in the 1420s and had once addressed him as 'father', was no longer a friend in England twenty years later. Likewise, Osbern Mundeford had been among the most prominent of those who had resisted the surrender of Maine, but served on a jury at Walsingham which acquitted Fastolf's opponents. Perhaps it is relevant here too that, in the 1450s, Fastolf was in his seventies, an age when men do not easily make new friends. The Pastons were now his loyal supporters, and John Paston did indeed become a close friend, but he, like Fastolf, was of the gentry rather than the aristocracy, and he too had to suffer Suffolk's oppression.

The persecution which Fastolf and his few friends suffered in the 1440s did not abate significantly when Suffolk was murdered in 1450. The Duke's formidable widow, Alice Chaucer, survived her husband for twenty-five years. Lord Scales assumed the leadership of the de la Pole affinity alongside her, and they quickly re-established political control in East Anglia. Anthony Smith has shown how Scales denied access to vital documents when Sir John was in dispute with Hickling Priory.[17] Nationally, Somerset picked up the reins of government which Suffolk had released. As late as 1455, when Suffolk had been dead five years, Fastolf was still complaining that he:

> hath been vexed and troubled since he last came into this land [1439] by the might and power of the Duke ... and by the labour of his council [counsel?] and servants in diverse ways, as in great oppressions, grievous and outrageous amercements and many great horrible extortions.[18]

There was at least one concerted attempt to put an end to the oppression. An oyer and terminer commission was appointed in 1450 to look into the disorders in Norfolk and Suffolk, and Fastolf worked hard to bring this about and see that suitable men were appointed as commissioners. He thought he was acting in the public interest as well as his own. On 20 December 1450 he wrote to Thomas Howes that, if the commission was not successful, 'the poor people and all the great part of both shires' would be 'destroyed'.[19] Yet the tactic did not succeed. Despite the support of Justice Yelverton, some of the judges appointed to the commission of oyer and terminer were not sympathetic. As Fastolf wrote despairingly on 9 May 1451, they were apparently not willing to listen:

> When the counsel for the city of Norwich, for the town of Swaffham, for you, for my Master Inglose, for Paston and many other plaintiffs had asserted and declared both in writing and in their speeches before the judges, the offences at law, the judges, by their wilfulness, could not find it in their heart to pay the least attention, not even a nod or a wink, but scorned it. God reform such partiality!

The presiding judge, Chief Justice Prysot, was 'pro-Suffolk' and 'anti-Fastolf'. He knew that if the oyer and terminer proceedings were held at Norwich, a favourable outcome – from the point of view of Tuddenham, Heydon and their cronies – could not be guaranteed. He therefore adjourned the case to Walsingham:

> And the said Tuddenham, Heydon and other oppressors of their set came down there with, so I understand, 400 or more horsemen. Considering how their supporters had gathered there at their request, it was very dangerous and frightening for any of the plaintiffs to appear; and not one of the plaintiffs or complainants was there, except for your trusty and faithful supporter, John Paston.[20]

Despite his long years of service to the Lancastrian dynasty, Fastolf was treated as an outsider during the last ten years of his life. Perhaps it is in this light that we should see his continued employment of a private herald, or *poursuivant*, to carry messages, act as a reporter and deal with other matters relating to the law of arms. He had employed a man called Laurent de Fougères for this purpose in the 1420s. (The fellow had used the intriguing name of 'Secret'. He had been removed from office for some unspecified misdemeanour in 1431 but reinstated the following year.) As we have seen, he employed a herald called Fastolf Poursuivant to report on the First Battle of St Albans in 1455 and the trial of the Duke of Alençon in Vendôme in 1458. Some of his contemporaries might have thought that this was somewhat presumptuous, given that he was only a knight in England, but from Fastolf's point of view, he was only continuing to use the services of an official he had found useful when he was Bedford's Grand Master.[21]

Despite all his travails, Fastolf continued to use the law to obtain redress for his grievances, though his adversaries sometimes behaved as if they were above it. In 1454 he expressly told Thomas Howes: 'I instructed you not to do anything which would be against the law, nor work unlawfully against right and truth.' Though he had the wealth and the weaponry to do so, he never reacted with violence.[22] It is true that there were sometimes threats of 'direct action' by his associates. When Margaret Paston was holding out in Gresham against Lord Moleyns's men in the late 1440s, she wrote to her husband that she 'supposed' that Fastolf could be relied on to supply some crossbows, but there is no evidence that he ever used these in civil conflicts, either in his own cause or hers. Likewise, in December 1450, a courtier with East Anglian connections reported to the Lord Chancellor that, if Tuddenham and Heydon were to be pardoned – or even if steps were taken to remove the court proceedings against them to London – the authorities could expect trouble:

> London should within a short time have as much to do as it had to keep London Bridge when the Captain [Jack Cade] came thither, for … there were 5,000 men and more up in Norfolk who were ready to rise, if the oyer and terminer did not proceed.[23]

Yet the threat of violence never materialized, and it is inconceivable that Fastolf would ever have appeared in arms against his sovereign and the lawful authorities, as Sir John Oldcastle and Jack Cade, and for that matter his old commander York, had all done.

Chapter 10

The Legacy

In the last years of his life, Fastolf moved into the third and final area of activity described by Stephen Scrope in the dedication of his translation of the *Epistle to Othea* – the one in which a man should concentrate on 'spiritual and ghostly deeds'. He spent a great deal of his time planning the foundation of a chantry college: in fact, this became something of an obsession, though it was entirely typical, in an age which was superstitious as well as intensely religious. Some of the chroniclers had noted that, when Joan of Arc summoned the English captains to leave her country, she threatened them with dire consequences if they did not obey her commands. They recorded that Sir William Glasdale drowned in the Loire, that the Earl of Suffolk was murdered at Dover, and that Talbot had been killed at Castillon. No sudden end awaited Fastolf: he died in his bed at Caister on 5 November 1459, at the age of seventy-nine or eighty, after 158 days of 'hectic' fever.[1]

What had the old man achieved? Unlike Talbot, he was never ennobled in England and he founded no dynasty. He was the quintessential gentleman: his house at Southwark was a 'place', not a palace, and the castle at Caister was a mansion, not a base of aristocratic power. Talbot was long remembered by his heirs, while his effigy may still be seen in Whitchurch in Shropshire, the cast courts at the Victoria and Albert Museum and the Beauchamp chapel at Warwick (where he appears as a mourner). By contrast, we cannot look on the face or the figure of Sir John Fastolf. He was buried alongside his wife at St Benet's Abbey, but his grave was neglected, the abbey church became ruinous soon after the dissolution of the monasteries, and even the ruins were pulled down by 1585.[2] No trace of the Fastolf tombs remains. James Parker's nineteenth-century portrait of Fastolf in the National Portrait Gallery is no more than a guess as to what the knight might have looked like.

The castle at Caister survived a long and bitter series of lawsuits, and even violent capture (though not by the French), but it was abandoned by the Pastons in 1599 and is now a mere shadow of its former splendour, though the Great Tower retains its original height. In 1465 Thomas Howes erected a stained glass window in the parish church at Pulham Market in Norfolk, which showed Fastolf in gilt armour, with crest and escutcheons. The inscription read, 'Pray for the soul of Sir

John Fastolf, who achieved many good things during his life', but the window had disappeared by 1919, when Wylie wrote his monumental books about the French wars.[3] Nothing at all remains of Fastolf Place in Southwark, and with the exception of the Tower of London and the castle of Caen, the other strongholds he was associated with – Ombrière and Fronsac, Rouen, the Bastille of Paris and the forts of the Calais Pale – have also crumbled away. There is a marked contrast here with the fine castles at Fresnay-sur-Sarthe and Sillé-le-Guillaume, at Beaugency and at Meung-sur-Loire, which were built by French lords after the English had departed. They demonstrate that it was they who came off best.

A sorry tale; and yet much has survived, if one knows where to find it. The lower village of Castle Combe has retained much of its medieval aspect and (to the modern eye) its charm. Above all, Magdalen College, Oxford, is a fitting tribute to Sir John. He never intended to endow it – his aim was to found a chantry college for the benefit of his soul, not to promote education – but, by a quirk of history, Fastolf is remembered there. A Fastolf Society has recently been founded to commemorate his role as benefactor, and Magdalen is now a home to both the Fastolf Papers and the McFarlane Library, named after the man who did most to explain their significance.

Perhaps the most enduring of Fastolf's legacies is archival and literary. Because he was a meticulous estate manager and employed efficient servants, a vast amount of documentation was generated and much of it has survived, for the benefit of the student and the historian, not only in the McFarlane Library but in the British Library, the National Archives at Kew, and in Norwich – enough to repay years of study. This is highly unusual for the period.[4] As for his books, Sir John has achieved a degree of notoriety as the author of the Memorandum of 1435, but he was also a collector and patron.

Fastolf's Books

Henry Windsor wrote that Worcester was 'as glad to obtain a good book of French or of Poetry as his master Fastolfe was to purchase a fair manor', and this seems to be the reason why Sir John is often condemned as a dilettante. It seems to have influenced Thomas Amyot in the nineteenth century and Jessie Crosland and H S Bennett in the twentieth. Bennett stated baldly that Fastolf was not a reader: he collected books because it was 'the right thing to do', not because he loved them, but this is unwarranted as well as unfair.[5]

It is true that Fastolf was not a collector of books on the same scale as the Dukes of Bedford and Gloucester, or for that matter the Duke of Burgundy or Charles of Orléans, who managed to preserve his library even while he was imprisoned in England. However, the list of titles which he owned has caused some to call him a 'proto-humanist'. As Master of Bedford's Household and one of the Duke's executors for France, he had ample opportunity to collect French books, and we

St Benet's Abbey

Thanks to William Worcester, Fastolf was given a magnificent funeral, with military honours, including eighteen banners and fifty-two pennants displaying his coat of arms, together with images of Mary, the Trinity, St Nicholas (patron saint of sailors) and St George (the first soldier-saint). His body was taken for burial – probably by barge – to the abbey church of St Benet's of Holme, next to the River Bure. In Fastolf's day the river was a busy thoroughfare, while access by the causeway was circuitous.

St Benet's was a community of Benedictine monks, who offered up a daily round of prayer and devotion. It was a place where travellers could stay, in the Abbey's Hospital. The fishponds provided a constant source of food, and the abbey played an important role in commerce and trade, not least as a kind of bank. At the time of his death Fastolf had deposited a large amount of cash there – far more than he had at Caister Castle. Sir John wanted to be laid to rest alongside his wife Millicent, in a chapel which he had paid handsomely for: this was situated in the new south aisle of the chancel and was known as 'Fastolf's Chapel'. He had given directions that his tomb be made of marble, inlaid with brasses, and placed before the altar of St Edmund, the Anglo-Saxon king of East Anglia who had been killed by the Danes. He expected the monks of St Benet's to remember him and to engage in a spiritual battle on his behalf, while he endured the pains of Purgatory.

Did he get what he wanted? So far as we can judge, the answer is no. There is good evidence that all was not well at St Benet's Abbey in the late fifteenth century. William Worcester gained a very unfavourable impression in 1472:

Filthy linen
Cabbage without salt
New ale
Stony bedding
A filthy stable
Sword–like hay
Stingy hospitality
A chilly fire in the chimney
The servants' wages amount to nothing
Therefore the guests will leave without farewell.
Fastolf their benefactor in gifts generous
Very soon forgotten by the monks.

know that he brought at least one manuscript home with him when he retired in 1439 (a French copy of the *Epistle of Othea*). At the time of his death he owned at least twenty-five books in all. They were all manuscripts – the printing revolution was yet to reach English shores – and it has been estimated that each was worth as much as a medium-sized farm, though none of them was as beautiful or as valuable as Bedford's *Book of Hours*.[6]

Many of these books were about war – but not about the recent war which Fastolf had himself been involved in: there was a life of Julius Caesar, Livy's histories of Rome, a volume by the Jewish historian Josephus, three prose chronicles, a rhymed *Brut* (a history of Britain), courtly romances including King Arthur, and Vegetius's treatise *The Art of War*. However, he also owned a 'great' Bible, incorporating Petrus Comestor's *Historia Scolastica*; a scientific encyclopaedia written by Bartholomew the Englishman; a French copy of a medical treatise by Aldobrandinus of Siena; Ptolomey's *Almagest* and four other books on astronomy and astrology; a number of religious works including *Vices and Virtues* and *The Meditations of St Bernard*; Aristotle on *Ethics* and *Problems*; two versions of works by Cicero – *On Old Age* and *On Friendship*; Justinian's *Institutes* – a fundamental textbook on Roman law; and a book by the Italian Pietro de' Crescenzi on gardening. Many of these works were stated to be 'French', meaning either that they were written in French, or acquired in France – it is difficult to be sure. So far as we know he owned none of the works of Chaucer, or of contemporary English poets.[7]

Fastolf was not just a collector: he sat at the centre of a small literary circle, and commissioned copies and translations from the members. He had the *Epistle to Othea* translated into English by Stephen Scrope in about 1440. In the dedication Scrope extols the virtues of John, Duke of Berry (1340–1416), but also praises the work which Sir John has done in Normandy, France and 'other strange regions':

> And God, who is sovereign chieftain and knight of all chivalry, has ever preserved and defended you in all your said labours of chivalry to this day, for which you are most especially obliged and bound to become his knight in your old age.

Scrope points out that the *Epistle* can be of great use, both in retirement and in the after-life:

> And also you shall find here in this said *Book of Chivalry*, how and in what manner you may well be called a knight who overcomes and conquers his spiritual enemies by taking care to defend his soul.[8]

Scrope prepared translations of other philosophical works for his stepfather. One such work was *The Dicts and Sayings of the Philosophers*, which he translated around 1450. The dedication of this work certainly indicates a French origin for the original, since it refers to Simon Morhier, the Provost of Paris at the time of the English occupation of the French capital:

> Here begins a book called in French *Les ditez de philesophurs* and in English *The doctrine of wisdom of the wise ancient philosophers*, as of Aristotle, Plato, Socrates, Ptolemy and such others, translated out of Latin into French for King Charles VI of France by [the] late provost of the city of Paris, and now translated out of the French tongue into the English tongue in the year of Christ 1450 for John Fastolf [Fostalfe] knight, for his contemplation and solace by Stephen Scrope, esquire, son in law [stepson] to the said Fastolf.

A striking feature of the *Dicts and Sayings* is the interest shown in the life of Alexander the Great, but this is a very medieval, and a very English, Alexander. He rides at the head of a 'host', leads the 'chivalry' against the pagans in the name of the one true God, and is accompanied by innumerable men of lower rank, who are described as 'varlets'. He listens to 'sermons', has 'Lieutenants' and a 'secretary', and his knights wear 'habergeons'. There are clearly parallels with the life of Henry V: Henry, like Alexander, had fought against great odds but succeeded in transforming the political landscape, though he died before reaching the age of thirty-five.

There are no fewer than nine English versions of the *Dicts and Sayings*, of which perhaps three emanate from Fastolf's circle. In one manuscript there are even marginal notes, indicating that discussions must have taken place between scribe and patron, when Fastolf thought that he had found philosophical support for his own views. In the margin opposite the saying of Pythagoras that 'a man should not enforce him in this world to make great buildings, nor great gettings, the which after his death is left to serve others, but he should enforce him to get and to win things that may profit him after his death', someone has written, 'à propos of an injunction not to make great buildings which others will inherit'. Surely, this is Fastolf, talking about Caister (and possibly realizing that his hopes for it may prove to be vain)? The passage certainly helps to explain why he would rather have seen his house pulled down than enjoyed by another man.[9]

We have been warned that the ownership of books does not prove that the owner read them, or had them read out to him, as was the common practice, but one is struck by the fact that Fastolf commissioned translations, from the Latin and the French. Why did he do that, if he was merely going to keep the manuscripts for show, or for the beauty of the occasional illustration? At the same time, some of his books remained in French: his Garter Statutes from the 1420s; the report of the First Battle of St Albans, commissioned in 1455; Basset's Chronicle, written in 1459. The signs are that he could read in that language as well as in English, though it is impossible to be sure.[10]

As for his own writings, the Reverend Duthie wrote that Fastolf 'foamed at the pen' when engaged in correspondence, and it is true that his letters are neither contemplative nor reflective. They were concerned with business and litigation, areas where a fine literary style is hardly required. When he wrote for public consumption, it was about war and diplomacy. What he wrote was scarcely literature, yet at least he wrote clearly, concisely and cogently. McFarlane concluded that he 'was able to express himself fluently on paper in practised and legible hand .... [he was] a good deal more than merely literate, for he controlled every detail of estate business from a distance and was perfectly at home in a discussion of accountancy or law'. There are dozens of letters, memoranda and accounts which confirm this.[11]

Fastolf was more than just a medieval Colonel Blimp. He had witnessed the culture and ceremonial of the Burgundian court at first hand. He liked fine art, if the evidence of his tapestries is anything to go by. He could probably converse as well as read in English and French. He was instrumental in bequeathing to us at least two works of lasting importance.

Peter Basset's Chronicle

In the last year of his life, Fastolf commissioned Peter Basset to write an account of the war in France. Basset was a man-at-arms who had been part of the Earl of Norfolk's retinue on the expedition of 1417 and served as a member of the garrison at Alençon – where Sir John was captain – between 1429 and 1437. According to the sixteenth-century historian John Bale, he was the author of a lost *Life* of Henry V. While working on the Fastolf commission he received some assistance from Christopher Hanson, a former archer who served in France in various capacities between 1427 and 1447, though he was said to be of German extraction – 'de patria Almayn'. (Hanson's adventures certainly feature in the chronicle.) A third man called Luket Nantron, who was a native of Paris and one of Fastolf's clerks, was involved, and William Worcester also lent a hand. The prominent position given to the escapades of Matthew Gough, particularly in and around Le Mans in 1426–7, suggest that he may have been an important source of information. The Chronicle was an attempt, perhaps, to make up for the dearth of books in England about the wars in France between 1415 and 1453.[12]

Basset's Chronicle has never been published. Colonel Burne, for one, seems to have been unaware of it, since he wrote that there was an 'absence of English chroniclers' for the 1420s, but in fact it survives in the College of Arms.[13] This seems appropriate, since it is full of lists of participants and casualties, possibly derived from records kept by the heralds, while the writers clearly share a taste for notable 'feats of arms'. The long title of the Chronicle, which is in Latin, makes a series of remarkable claims:

This is a book of deeds of arms performed during the conquest of the kingdom of France, the Duchy of Normandy, the Duchy of Alençon, the Duchy of Anjou and of Maine, with various other counties, [and] was compiled for the noble John Fastolf, baron of Sillé-le-Guillaume, by Peter Basset, man-at-arms of the English nation, who followed the profession of arms in France in the time of Henry V and under John, Duke of Bedford, Regent of the Kingdom of France and under various other principal lieutenants in the time of King Henry VI, in total for a period of thirty-five years.

In fact, of course, the English did not conquer the whole of France – they did not even conquer the whole of Anjou; and, if Peter Basset spent thirty-five years continuously in France, this would have been ten more than Fastolf himself. On the other hand, the Chronicle contains invaluable information, particularly about the years after the death of Henry V, long a neglected period.[14]

Benedicta Rowe called Basset's Chronicle 'a plain soldierly account', written for an audience which would take a 'bluff delight in adventure', but this underestimates the authors. It appears to be an accurate account of the events of 1415–29, by men who had personal experience of what they wrote about, and were anxious to record what had been achieved before memory (and interest?) faded. It contains no speeches made to the troops on the battlefield – this is an invention of later chroniclers and playwrights; but many passages are very exciting. If the chronicler undoubtedly exaggerates the size of the French armies (150,000 men at Agincourt!), he is probably about right when he tells us that Salisbury brought 7,000 men with him from England in 1428. Conveniently for Fastolf, the account stops immediately after the Battle of Rouvray, and before the Battle of Patay. It may have broken off because of Sir John's death, but this end-date did enable the writers to remain upbeat about the War. With some exceptions, the narrative is a success story, a stirring tale of a great national endeavour and of a conquest nearly achieved, against the odds. Yet the authors are not narrow chauvinists. They are interested in chivalry and the law of arms, and in the fate of the vanquished as well as the victorious.

Basset's Chronicle is important for what it relates, but also for what it does not relate. The story of Agincourt is told only briefly, confirming that in all probability Fastolf was not present. If he had been, we would surely have heard more about it here. Likewise the Chronicle tells us nothing about Fastolf's time in Jerusalem, Ireland or Aquitaine and it says nothing to confirm Fastolf's claim that he had been the first man 'over the side' when Henry V's army first disembarked in Normandy, but it does tell us about the French siege of Harfleur. Indeed, the text portrays Sir John as Exeter's lieutenant and gives an exciting account of the minor *chevauchées* conducted during the terrible winter of 1415–16. It takes us through the sieges of Caen and Rouen in the years 1417–19, and relates the outcome of the Battles of Baugé, Cravant, Verneuil and Rouvray.

Like Shakespeare's *Henry V* (written in the aftermath of the Spanish Armada), Basset's Chronicle aims to give its audience something to cheer about. It tells us how the English exploited Henry V's victory at Agincourt by conquering a large part of northern France, and how Henry's brothers carried the conquest forward. The chronicler may be unreliable when it comes to numbers, but the narrative is clear, that the English achieved much, with small forces against a larger enemy, and in record time. Despite the circumstances in which it was written, the Chronicle does not pay excessive attention to Fastolf's part in the proceedings. It is the account of patriotic Englishmen, proud of what was achieved by the army as whole.

Basset and Hanson must have witnessed some of the fighting they describe at first hand. They write with feeling about the 'treachery' of Andrew the Lombard at Baugé, and of Clarence's death there. Most moving of all is the death of Henry V:

> Weep, all you princes, lords, nobles, townsmen and people, and all you true and loyal subjects, for the loss and the death of so noble and victorious a prince, your protector and defender.[15]

Basset's Chronicle is a very English account of the war, yet it is written in French. Why produce an account of the deeds of the English in the enemy's language? McFarlane thought that it was the participation of Luket Nantron, who was French, which was decisive here. More recently it has been suggested that French was chosen because it was still the language of chivalry, and that the English had an abiding tendency throughout the Hundred Years' War to copy French fashion in all areas.[16]

Basset tells us stirring tales of the adventures of Matthew Gough in Le Mans and at Courcillon. He confirms what William Worcester also relates, that Sir John was made a knight banneret at Verneuil. He takes pleasure in telling us about Fastolf's success at Rouvray in 1429. On the other hand, Joan of Arc – whom he simply calls 'the Maid' – receives only the briefest of mentions. Whether by accident or design, there is no hint of the defeats and disappointments to come, or of the eventual loss of all that the English had fought for, in humiliating circumstances. The Chronicle is emphatically not part of 'the literature of defeat'.[17] On the contrary, it is about the 'good old days' when Sir John was in his prime. The irony was that it was used extensively by Edward Hall a century later, and that Hall paved the way for Shakespeare's destruction of Fastolf's good character.

The Wooden Cross

Thirty-five years after Fastolf's death, the Bishop of Norwich conducted an inspection of St Benet's Abbey. There were twenty-three monks in residence (including the abbot) and he questioned each in turn. He found more than a dozen irregularities, some more serious than others. Discipline was lax in the dormitory and in the choir; the monks were so burdened by their offices that they had no time for study and there was no schoolmaster; the Prior was often absent from recitations; the subcellarer did not prepare a meal each day for the novices, as he ought to, and the younger monks were insolent towards their elders. There were serious financial irregularities (the abbey's jewels had been pawned and the previous abbot had given a vicarage to a relative), but, with all these problems, the Visitor still thought the following worthy of note: 'There is no remembrance of any kind of Sir John Fastolf *in mortilogio*, though he was a great benefactor of this monastery.'

What does this mean? *In mortilogio* means little more than 'in the form of a memorial', so the criticism is somewhat vague. It probably means that, while Fastolf was buried at St Benet's, he did not get the marble tomb he had requested, though he had given precise directions in more than one draft of his will. It must certainly mean that there was no chapel named after him. It may even have meant that there was no inscription to record his benefactions to the monastery. At any rate it is clear that remembrance of the knight in the very place where he should have been remembered was not all it should have been.

St Benet's has the distinction of being the only monastery in England and Wales not to have been dissolved by Henry VIII, but this did not save it from the effects of the Reformation. The abbey was still abandoned in the 1530s, and rapidly fell into a ruinous state. Only the hospital of St James and the gatehouse remain today, yet the site is very beautiful. The ruins are approached along quiet footpaths and lie among the water and the reeds, with only windmills, church towers and farm buildings in view. The few stones which remain of the abbey church are a place of great tranquillity. The site of the high altar is marked by a wooden cross of Sandringham oak, given by the Queen in the 1980s and inscribed with the message 'Peace'. One is reminded of a line in one of Shakespeare's sonnets:

Bare ruined choirs where late the sweet birds sang.

St Benet's is still used, at times, as a place of worship. The great wooden cross reminds us that Fastolf was a kind of Christian as well as a soldier, and even the irreligious must feel that the old knight has at last found a resting place. Whether he would have recognized it as such is another matter.

The Boke of Noblesse

Unlike Basset's Chronicle, William Worcester's *Boke of Noblesse* was written in English. It was far from being a 'plain and soldierly' narrative and the writer was anything but 'bluff'. Worcester was an Oxford man, with many interests, including medicine, ornithology and astronomy.[18] In addition to being an exhortation to war, his book was philosophical: a hymn to Stoicism, peppered with classical allusions. It seems from internal evidence that there must have been a first version, written in the 1450s and addressed to Henry VI, but it is only the second version, presented to Edward IV between 1472 and 1475, which has survived. In each case, the author celebrated the military achievements of Henry V and Bedford and argued that, if only a fresh invasion of France were mounted, all would be well in England. The book has much to tell us about Fastolf, although, unlike the Beauchamp Pageant (written about Warwick, his master in Normandy in the late 1430s), it contains no illustrations.

Worcester had been brought up in Fastolf's household and Sir John had paid for him to study at Oxford. The range of his duties was vast. On some occasions, he was Fastolf's manservant, on other occasions effectively his solicitor. In the late 1430s, the faithful servant travelled to Normandy to collect evidence for a lawsuit involving the administration of the estate of Fastolf's nephew Robert Harling, and he returned there for several months after Bedford's death, when Sir John had become the Duke's executor. Later, he was involved in the complex business of administering Fastolf's own estates in England. He chased up rents and debts, advised on the conduct of litigation and investigated titles to land. He undertook frequent visits to London, East Anglia, Wiltshire and Bristol.

Worcester did not always feel appreciated. He complained that his master paid him only 'normal household wages' (not as much as he might have received as a clergyman with a good 'living'). At the same time, he was fond of Sir John and he was both conscientious and loyal. He served Fastolf from the late 1430s to 1459 and it was only after the knight's death that he devoted himself completely to the private study he so much enjoyed. In retirement he made the journeys which formed the basis for his *Itineraries*, a sort of historical guidebook to the counties of England, completed around 1480.[19]

Fastolf's patriotism, and chauvinism, burn bright in William Worcester's *Boke of Noblesse*. The French were to blame for the war and had been from the very beginning. It was they who started it, in Edward III's time, by confiscating the Duchy of Aquitaine. They had prolonged hostilities by denying Henry V his lawful inheritance, and they had frequently and regularly gone back on the solemn treaties they had signed. Fortunately, God was on our side. He had shown this time and again, at Crécy, Poitiers, Agincourt, and Verneuil. There was nothing morally wrong with the war, since it was a just one, fought in defence of the king's lawful rights. By 1450 it may have begun to seem as if God had deserted us, but the setbacks in Normandy and Aquitaine were merely temporary and the situation could be reversed, if only the English were true to themselves. The French would always remain hostile, so there was no point in negotiating with them. The foolish policy of appeasement, pursued by Suffolk in the 1440s, had inevitably failed. The only answer was to launch a further invasion.[20]

Worcester is at his most interesting when he is giving the reader the benefit of military experience which he can only have gleaned from Fastolf. Sometimes he relates conversations with Sir John, at others he refers to the old knight's account books. The most important advice was essentially the same as that given by Oliver Cromwell 200 years later: 'put your trust in God and keep your powder dry'. Fastolf had made sure that the towns and castles of which he was captain were adequately supplied; that his men were properly clothed; that a proper watch was maintained during a siege; that law and order was at all times maintained. A 'manly' (or prudent) man was of more value in war than a 'hardy' (or foolhardy) one, who rushed into battle and chose to rely on dash, or *élan* – as the French repeatedly did.[21]

In Worcester's view, it was essential that the garrisons and the army should be well equipped and paid on time. Steps should be taken to ensure that merchants and victuallers could come and go safely. We are reminded that these are matters which were dealt with in the proclamations issued by Henry V, and in the Ordinances issued by Bedford in 1423 (which Fastolf helped to draft and promulgate). Worcester even includes an example of Sir John's expertise in supply:

> I find by his books of his purveyors, how in every castle, fortress, and city or town he would have great providence of victuals of corn, of lard, and cattle, of stockfish and saltfish out of England, coming by ships. And that policy was one of the great causes that the Regent of France and the lords of the King's great council left him to have so many castles to keep that he led yearly 300 spears and bowmen. And also in similar wise purveyed yearly for livery white and red for hubes [jackets] for his soldiers, and for armour [and] weapons ready to a naked man that was able to do the king and the said Regent service.[22]

The *Boke of Noblesse* contains vivid flashbacks to the hardships endured at the French siege of Harfleur in 1415–16, admiration for Bedford's victory at Verneuil in 1424, and bitter criticism of the policies pursued by Henry VI's ministers in the 1440s and 1450s. The Crown is urged to settle its debts, especially those owing to 'those who have lost their lands, livelihood and goods in the wars'. The failure of Kyriell's expedition in 1450 is blamed on the fact that the troops were forced to wait too long on the coasts of Normandy, before advancing inland. Contrary to what was suggested by Colonel Burne, this was not Kyriell's fault:

A great cause was that the petty captains would not obey at the day of that journey at that sudden encounter to their chieftain, and tarried longer in his voyage after he was landed or he came to any stronghold was present.[23]

In a document of 1449, which contained questions to be put to Somerset, and which is thought to have been drafted by Worcester, the writer explained more fully why the English had lost Lancastrian Normandy. It was the dire consequence of a general failure to pay the troops:

> it became necessary for [English soldiers] to plunder the people and waste the country, and this to such an extent that there was no one who dared continue in the country who was not killed or plundered, and the poor country people were pillaged day and night, in such sort that some of them abandoned the country that they might go to the side of the French. As he [Somerset] would do no justice to the inhabitants, it followed that the whole country turned to the French.[24]

There is much here for historians of the Hundred Years' War, French and English, to ponder.

Some of the old soldiers who had marched on London with Jack Cade may simply have thought that the army had been 'stabbed in the back' – betrayed by Henry VI's ministers – rather than defeated in the field in a fair fight, but Worcester's analysis was more sophisticated. He was driven to the conclusion that the English had lost their lands in France because they had developed a 'hard covetous heart'.[25] They had become avaricious and corrupt. Individual captains had claimed expenses they were not entitled to. Englishmen who did not have anything at stake in Lancastrian Normandy had been unwilling to make sacrifices to support those who had done their duty in France. The 'Little Englanders' of the day had 'no consideration for the commonwealth, but rather to magnify and enrich [themselves] by singular covetousness'. In addition, the diplomats had been outwitted by their French counterparts: they had been naive to trust them at all, but had also made concessions which should never have been made. On this view, the English had not lost their estates in Normandy and Maine because of French military superiority. It had been a moral defeat for the nation as a whole, but the consolation was that England could rise again, provided she put her house in order.

Worcester was undoubtedly wrong in one respect. Like everyone in Fastolf's household, he grossly underestimated the French. This is clear from Basset's account of the English defeat at Baugé in 1421. According to his version of the event, the French and Scots won the battle because they did not fight fairly. The implication is that, where both sides do fight fairly, the English will always prevail; but this had not proved to be true at Orléans and Patay in 1429, nor at Formigny and Castillon in the 1450s. To judge by the books produced by his literary circle,

Fastolf never appreciated just how much the French had achieved in re-fashioning their artillery train and reorganizing their armies, nor did he give the French generals much credit for strategy, let alone recognize the courage shown by Joan of Arc and the French rank and file. All this is entirely understandable. A man who had fought at Verneuil and Rouvray, before the walls of Orléans and in Normandy was hardly likely to sing the praises of his enemies, and, if one wants to encourage one's own side to fight, one does not tell them that their weapons are useless; but the consequence is that both Basset's Chronicle and the *Boke of Noblesse* give a very one-sided view of the Hundred Years' War.[26]

Conclusion

Fastolf and the Hundred Years' War

The whole notion of a 'Hundred Years' War' has recently been called into question, and not merely because it lasted more than a hundred years. Ian Mortimer has suggested that there was 'no overarching theme' which connects at least three separate wars between England and France in the relevant period, and that 'the Hundred Years' War only has an integrity for the French'. The answer to this is that there was indeed an overarching theme (and one that made a great deal of sense to the aristocracy and gentry in England), which was the royal pursuit of inherited rights in the Duchies of Aquitaine and Normandy, and indeed the royal claim to the Crown of France. That was how the matter appeared to Henry V, and to Bedford and his Grand Master Fastolf. For obvious reasons, they never heard the expression 'the Hundred Years' War', but Henry V's was not a new war. Shakespeare was right in thinking that Henry knew enough history to feel that he was fighting for the same things as Edward III and the Black Prince, and the rest of the military class seems to have swung into line behind him. There were even men, like Sir Thomas Erpingham from Norfolk, who were old enough to remember John of Gaunt's expeditions and to fight at Agincourt. The expression 'Hundred Years' War' was indeed invented in the nineteenth century and in France, but the many historians on both sides of the Channel who have adopted it – Perroy, Fowler, Allmand, Curry and Sumption – knew what they were doing. The War was much more than a 'historiographical myth'.[1]

The War began as a feudal quarrel between the Kings of England and France about the fief of Aquitaine; by the time Henry V came to the throne in 1413 it had turned into a dynastic dispute, with the King of England claiming to be King of France as well; and it finally became a national struggle, as the English peoples learned to recognize themselves for what they were and (it has to be said) to heartily dislike each other. This was the nub of Perroy's classic *Hundred Years War*, and Fastolf's career is almost a re-capitulation of that story. He served in Aquitaine before he served in Normandy. He was closely involved in the events leading up to the Treaty of Troyes, when Henry V dropped the demand for territory in exchange for recognition as the heir to both kingdoms. Fastolf is the classic example of a gentleman who identified himself with the royal war of conquest, in pursuance of that claim. He reaped rich rewards from it, and became committed to it ideologically, as his Memorandum of 1435 shows. Henry V's war had become Fastolf's war. It was unfortunate for him that Henry VI ceased to share the commitment.

The history of the War between 1415 and 1453 poses certain obvious questions. How did the English manage to conquer so large a part of the much larger French kingdom? How did they manage to hold on so long in Normandy and Maine once the tide turned against them in 1429? Why was the French recovery of Normandy and Aquitaine so rapid in 1449–51? Perroy gave convincing answers as long ago as 1945. Fastolf's life, which spanned the entire period, can be used to test them out.

The success of English arms between 1415 and 1429 was remarkable, given the 'crushing disproportion' between the two countries, in terms of size, population and military potential. That success has long been explained in terms of the skill of English archers and the superiority of longbows over crossbows. Hence the famous victories won at Agincourt in 1415, Verneuil in 1424, and Rouvray in 1429. In his *History of the English Speaking Peoples* Sir Winston Churchill wrote that Fastolf deployed as much firepower at Rouvray as an eighteenth-century army armed with muskets, and yet one gets no sense from Basset's Chronicle that the English enjoyed any superiority in weaponry. One has the impression, instead, that they had to fight very hard all the way.

Good leadership and generalship clearly had an important part to play. Henry V was a charismatic but also an efficient leader, keen to use cannons as well as the trebuchet at sieges, though in some French and Scottish accounts he is described as an evil genius. Bedford, Exeter, Salisbury and Talbot were all very competent generals, though Bedford was not a natural field commander. Fastolf may have resembled his master in this respect: he won at Rouvray, but lost at Patay and this has inevitably cast a shadow over him. He is generally thought to have been too cautious, too reluctant to commit his forces to the charge.[2] On the other hand, his strong suit was logistics and supply: it was as Master of the Regent's Household, between 1422 and 1435, that he made his mark. He kept the Bastille safe in 1420–1 and he resupplied the siege army at Orléans (or perhaps, strictly speaking, at Meung) in February 1429. There must have been many other occasions we are ignorant of, when his men were grateful for his skill in that department. The battle at Rouvray did not become known as the Battle of the Herrings for nothing.

Efficiency was a key factor in the success of English arms. England had long been a relatively strong, centralized and well-run state, with a more efficient tax system than France. The royal administration was able to concentrate troops in the Channel ports, organize the shipping needed to transport them, keep the army in the field, and supply it – not least throughout the many sieges undertaken by Henry V. No previous historian has given Fastolf sufficient credit for the part he played in this. The conquest of a large part of northern France could not have been undertaken, or successfully concluded – and discipline could not have been maintained – without the services of officers like him.

Fastolf had a long life and a long career. Born some decades after the victories of Edward III and the Black Prince, he witnessed those of Henry V but he also lived to see the decline of English military supremacy. His career illustrates the increasing professionalization of the English army, before that decline set in. Many of the men who landed at Touques in Normandy in 1417 did not expect to stay in France for very long, but in fact stayed for decades. In March 1419, a soldier in the English army wrote home from Évreux to his friends: 'I ask that you pray for us that we may come home soon, out of this undesirable soldier's life, into the life of England.' On reading this letter, McFarlane remarked, 'Poor bugger, the war lasted another 33 years!' In Fastolf's case, the 'poor bugger' stayed in France for over twenty years, but did so willingly – as far as we can tell. Indentures of war were usually signed for comparatively short periods of time, but in practice they were more like perpetually renewable leases than fixed-term tenancies.[3]

Men like Fastolf had determination and staying-power. He first went to northern France in 1415 but he did not retire from active service until 1439. Though he was not in France continuously, he served Bedford, York and Warwick. His grit and determination are part of the reason English rule lasted far longer in Rouen than in Paris. It is not enough to say that the English were 'well dug in' in Normandy, or that there was a 'vast number of fortresses' there: the Lancastrian regime was more than just a military dictatorship. Fastolf's part in drawing up Bedford's Ordinances must be remembered, as well as his spirited defence of Caen. He was one of those men who helped the Regent in his attempt to achieve a kind of partnership with the indigenous Norman authorities; he was also someone who was prepared to risk his life and his livelihood in the cause. One of the reasons for the eventual collapse of the Lancastrian regime in France is that there were not more 'adventurers' like him.

The military situation in France changed with the lifting of the siege of Orléans. The English archer, who had proved so effective at Agincourt, Verneuil and Rouvray when protected by his stake or by wagons, was not so effective in siege warfare or when caught in the open at Patay. The French drove the invaders back from the Loire and made large inroads into the areas subject to Anglo-Burgundian control. Part of the English response was to counter-attack, as John Talbot did after his release from captivity in 1433, but it also involved holding on, grimly, in the areas which were still in English hands. This Fastolf continued to do, and he never gave up entirely. He did not sell all his possessions in France. He was a firm advocate of continuing to take the war to the French and he continued to give advice to that effect, as well as practical support with money. As late as 1449, he lent his estate at Condé-sur-Noireau to François de Surienne for the raid on Fougères (though the degree of his enthusiasm here is questionable).

Yet there was another side to the land settlement in Normandy and Maine, of which Fastolf was only dimly aware. Throughout the occupation, which in some places lasted from 1417 to 1450, the English lived on the profits they extracted from the French population. There is room for debate as to the extent of this exploitation, but no doubt that it took place. The army of occupation was obliged to live off the land because the English Parliament was reluctant, after the Treaty of Troyes, to pay for the war (though it sometimes had to). Bedford raised taxes from the Norman estates but there were many other levies, not least the local arrangements known as *pâtis* or *appâtis*, which stipulated the amounts which local communities had to pay in tribute. When Desmond Seward reproduced a photograph of Sillé-le-Guillaume, his caption read that this was the place from which 'English archers rode out to cow the local peasants and levy the protection money'. In fact there is no documentary evidence of the existence of a *pâtis* for Sillé, but it is overwhelmingly likely that there was one. We know that in the 1430s the system of charging the local population for the costs of the military occupation became centralized in Bedford's hands, and Fastolf was after all a Governor of Anjou and Maine.[4]

Perroy wrote that France was 'bled white', though he did not claim that the bleeding was done by the English alone: much damage was done by 'the Skinners' – the mercenary bands who feature so large in the Canon of Notre-Dame's litany of complaints. Even McFarlane, who thought that two or three examples did not make for a generalization, wrote that 'the English sucked France dry'. For all the fine words used by William Worcester in the *Boke of Noblesse*, the harsh truth is that men like Fastolf helped to expropriate many native landlords in Normandy and Maine, just as the Normans had expropriated the Anglo-Saxon ruling class after 1066. Those who would not swear allegiance to the new regime were made into internal émigrés, and Fastolf himself received numerous grants of land in occupied France. He was made captain of many other places, as at Fécamp, where his troops enjoyed the revenues of the ancient abbey and the monks had to do without. The army of occupation had to be fed somehow. Kenneth Fowler considered that the system of levying *appâtis* in Maine in the 1430s and 1440s was relatively benign, and 'a commentary on Bedford's clemency'. We are entitled to a degree of scepticism about this: the amounts extracted from local people may have been relatively small (compared to those paid in some areas in the fourteenth century), and perhaps they were no larger than the amounts payable in taxes to the Valois, but it would have been surprising if those who had to pay were in a position, or at all inclined, to make those comparisons.

The struggle became national, rather than merely feudal and royal. For the English, the Lancastrian land settlement became something to be preserved for its own sake, and an obstacle to peace. Among the French, the presence of English soldiers and settlers evoked resentment and even hatred, both among émigrés and those who stayed. The more efficient the English were in maintaining their garrisons, the more they alienated the very people whose allegiance they needed. The battle for revenue and supplies might be won, but it was at the expense of hearts and minds. Fastolf and Worcester never understood this. They saw that dishonesty in the collection of money, and irregularity in the keeping of accounts, was counter-productive, but they did not see that the entire system of governance produced resistance.

It was not just the exploitation which produced resentment. The English were also disliked because of who and what they were. Henry V may have thought that he was returning to Normandy to claim an ancient inheritance, but there was no residual kinship between the peoples of England and Normandy, nor even between the military aristocracies. Although Bedford and Fastolf sought to build on Norman feelings of separatism (as when they founded the University of Caen), too much time had elapsed since King John of England had lost Normandy in 1204 for there to be any genuine affinity between the two. Fastolf doubtless spoke fluent French, but the average English soldier did not, no more than the average Norman spoke English. Basset relates that when Sir Olivier Mauny was captured at Meaux, the King released him on condition that he travel to England, where he could learn to speak the language, but even when an Englishman and a Frenchman could make themselves understood, there was no basis for trust. Monstrelet tells us of an Englishman, Sir James de Harcourt, who pays a call on a Frenchman of the same name in 1418, greeting him as a long-lost cousin, but he only does so to lull him into a false sense of security, so that he can take him prisoner.[5]

There were large numbers of Normans who were never reconciled to English rule, and who always regarded it as alien. Perroy again: 'The iron hand of foreign soldiery led the country to ignore the benefits of orderly administration and the fairness of officials chosen from its own nationals.' With a pardonable degree of exaggeration, since his book was published in the year after D-Day 1944, he also claimed that, when the French did re-invade Normandy in 1449, 'the people welcomed them as liberators'. It is certainly true that many towns in the Duchy opened their gates to the Valois before any bombardment was necessary. On the other side of the coin, there is a good deal of Francophobia in Fastolf's private correspondence as well as in his secretary's *Boke of Noblesse*.

Yet we cannot explain the rapidity of the French *recouvrement* of Normandy solely by reference to hatred of the foreigner. The latter does not explain the recovery of Aquitaine, which was just as rapid, but where there were no English landowners or garrisons to speak of. There is no escaping the fact that the re-conquest of the two duchies was an impressive military achievement. A large part of the credit for this must go to the political and military reforms which Charles VII undertook in the 1440s, long after the brief career of Joan of Arc. Perroy wrote that 'one could scarcely imagine a prince less fitted to evoke enthusiasm' than Charles VII, yet the same monarch presided over a military revolution. The erstwhile Dauphin reformed the organs of central government; Jacques Coeur enabled him to put French finances on a new footing; the *compagnies d'ordonnance* provided the Crown with the first standing army in Western Europe; and Jean

Bureau was put in charge of artillery which finally put an end to the longbow's supremacy.

By 1449 there is no doubt that the French were militarily superior, though neither Fastolf nor Worcester knew it, or ever admitted it. Normandy and Aquitaine collapsed under the hammer blows delivered by the new French armies. The English army of occupation in Normandy crumbled before the onslaught because it was, in comparison, under-resourced and poorly led. There was no field army and the garrisons of Normandy had been run down – from a peak of about 6,000 men to possibly no more than 2,000. As far as we can judge, morale was low. Fastolf's advice, though plentiful, was ignored and his example was not followed. Relief armies were eventually sent to Normandy and Aquitaine, but in each it was a case of too little, too late, despite the brief success of Talbot's re-invasion of Aquitaine in 1452–3. Men might argue as to who was to blame for the defeats at Formigny near Bayeux (1451) and Castillon near Bordeaux (1453). For many, Suffolk and Somerset were the villains of the piece, but some of the more extreme followers of Jack Cade blamed Fastolf too: they even accused him of running down the garrisons in Normandy. This was totally unjust, because Fastolf was in retirement at the relevant dates.

Nothing is inevitable in history. It was not inevitable that the English attempt to conquer France should fail, but in the end numbers did count, despite all William Worcester's comforting references to Roman example. Fastolf's retinue in the 1420s consisted of only eighty men and this was typical of the very small numbers in English garrisons in the north of France. In 1449 Charles VII and his allies put several well-equipped armies into the field, each of them as large as the army which Henry V had led across the Channel in 1415 and 1417. Yet Fastolf was typical of the type of English captain who gave of his best, whatever the odds, despite the accusations levelled against him after Patay. One hundred and fifty years later, Shakespeare's portrait of him in *Henry VI* and the character of Falstaff in *Henry IV* were immediately popular, and quickly and indelibly entered the English mind, but they were not true to life. Though it is impossible to compete with the Bard, I hope I have shown that there was more to Sir John Fastolf than a fat rogue and a coward, and more to the Hundred Years' War than a theatrical production.[6]

Notes

Abbreviations used in the Notes

Allmand, *LN*	Christopher Allmand, *Lancastrian Normandy 1415–1450* (Oxford, Clarendon Press, 1983)
BC	Basset's Chronicle
Berry Herald	*Les Chroniques du Roi Charles VI, par Gilles le Bouvier*
Bib. Nat.	Bibliothèque nationale de France, manuscrits français
BL	British Library
BON	*The Boke of Noblesse*, by William Worcester (*c*.1450 and *c*.1475)
CCR	Calendar of Close Rolls
CPR	Calendar of Patent Rolls
Davis (ed.), *PL&P*	Davis, Norman (ed.), *Paston Letters and Papers of the Fifteenth Century*, Early English Text Society, 3 vols (Oxford University Press, 2004–5)
DKR	Report of the Deputy Keeper of Public Records
English Suits	*English Suits Before the Parlement of Paris*, ed. C T Allmand and C A J Armstong (Camden Fourth Series 26, London, 1982)
FP	Fastolf Papers (stored in the Muniment Tower, Magdalen College, Oxford)
Gairdner (ed.), *PL*	James Gairdner (ed.), *The Paston Letters* (Edinburgh, 1910)
GHQ	*Gesta Henrici Quinti, The Deeds of Henry V*, trans. and ed. Frank Taylor and John S Roskell (Oxford, Clarendon Press, 1975)
JBP	*Journal d'un bourgeois de Paris* (Lettres Gothiques, Libre de Poche, 1990)
Marin (ed.), *La Normandie*	Jean-Yves Marin (ed.), *La Normandie dans la guerre de Cent Ans 1346–1450* (Caen, Musée de Normandie et Rouen, Musée départemental, 1999–2000)
McFarlane, *EFC*	K B McFarlane, *England in the Fifteenth Century* (Hambledon Press, 1981)
Mémoires	*Mémoires concernant la Pucelle d'Orléans*, in *Nouvelle Collection des Mémoires pour servir à l'histoire de France*, ed. J F Michaud and J J F Poujoulat, vol. 3 (Paris, 1837)
ODNB	*Oxford Dictionary of National Biography*

Pernoud, *Trente Journées*   Régine Pernoud, *Trente Journées qui ont fait la France* (Gallimard, 1969)

PPC   *Proceedings and Ordinances of the Privy Council of England*, ed. Sir Harris Nicolas (1834)

Richmond, FS&P   Colin Richmond, 'Sir John Fastolf, the Duke of Suffolk and the Pastons', in Linda Clark, *The Fifteenth Century* (Woodbridge, Boydell Press, 2008)

Richmond, FW   Colin Richmond, 'Once again: Fastolf's will', in Keith Dockray and Peter Fleming (eds), *People, Places and Perspectives* (Stroud, Nonsuch, 2005)

RP   *Rotuli Parliamentorum* (The Rolls of Parliament), ed. John Strachey (London, 1767–77)

Smith, 'Fastolf'   Anthony Robert Smith, 'Aspects of the Career of Sir John Fastolf (1380–1459)' (unpublished PhD thesis, Oxford 1982)

TNA   The National Archives (at Kew)

Note: For other shortened references, please see the Bibliography.

Chapter 1: The Real Falstaff

1. Norman Davis, *Shakespeare Quarterly*, 28:4 (1977); G W Williams, *Shakespeare Quarterly*, 30:1 (1979); Rymer, *Foedera*, X.527 and 530 (1432) has three different versions; TNA C 1/52/90.
2. *Archaeologia*, 9 (1789), 261.
3. BL Sloane 4046, f66; Turner's *Tour of Normandy*.

Chapter 2: Early Travels and Campaigns, 1380–1413

1. *English Suits*, 263; *Expeditions to Prussia*, 234, 267, 280, 302; Christopher Tyerman, *England and the Crusades 1095–1588*, (Chicago, 1996), 304, 309. Fastolf's name does not appear in Rowena Archer's unpublished PhD thesis on the Mowbrays, but he was only a boy in 1392–3.
2. CPR Henry IV, 1399–1401, 507.
3. Stevenson (ed.), *Letters and Papers*, II, 2, Annals [759]; Richmond, FW, 79, n. 97, and his *The Paston Family in the Fifteenth Century: The First Phase*, (Cambridge University Press, 1990), 235, n. 121; *ODNB*, Michael de la Pole, 2nd Earl of Suffolk and Thomas of Lancaster, Duke of Clarence; CPR Henry IV, 1401–5, 496, 512 (Prince Thomas); 503 (Scrope, *History*).
4. Cosgrove, 581; *Annals of Loch Cé*, II, 123, 139; Sweetman, Chapter 5.
5. *The Annals of Loch Cé*, II, 123, 125; Curtis, 287–8.
6. Rymer, *Foedera* (1740 edition), vol. IV, part II, 18 ('Johannes Fastolfe'); J H Wylie, *History of England under Henry the Fourth* (Longmans, 1898), IV, 74n.
7. TNA E 101/185/6 no. 2 is Fastolf's order relating to Fronsac, given as 'Lieutenant for Sir William Farringdon, Constable of Bordeaux'. TNA E 101/186/2 no. 117 is an indenture describing the castle of Bordeaux and its contents. TNA PRO 31/8/135 item 7 A document 1 contains a transcript from the French records in Paris of the receipt of 19 October 1413. (The first paragraph says that when Clarence agreed the sum payable under the treaty he assigned and gave 1,365 écus to Fastolf, but the date

given for this – 10 April 1412 – cannot be right. BL Add Charters 1403 also relates to this transaction.) McFarlane, *EFC*, 178 n. 8, relying on FP 69 membrane 4, has Fastolf as constable of Bordeaux in Faryingdon's time in office only; but I prefer the account in Vale, *English Gascony*, 8, 67–8, Map I and Appendix II. See also his *Ancient Enemy*, 37, illustration 3, and 119, citing TNA E 28/28 nos. 125, 126.

8. CCR 1413–19, 173, membrane 1.
9. According to Fastolf Paper 69, Fastolf was Captain of both Soubise and Veyres in Gascony. Soubise is easily identified; but it is much more difficult to be sure about Veyres, since there are several places of that name; *Registres de la Jurade, 1414–1422*, 27.
10. Gairdner (ed.), *PL*, I, 364.
11. CCR 1413–19, 96 membrane 16d; *Calendar of Inquisitions, Miscellaneous, Chancery*, VII, 1399–1422 (London, HMSO, 1968), 615, p. 361.
12. Renouard, 413–17; *Registres de la Jurade*, 12.

Chapter 3: In the King's Name of England, 1413–22

1. Walter Bower, *Scotichronicon*, 119, 121; Perroy, 235; Burne, 124; Seward, 135.
2. For Fastolf as a king's squire in 1415 see McFarlane, *EFC*, 186 n. 50, citing Rymer, *Foedera*, IX, 270.
3. Rymer, *Foedera*, IX, 270; Curry, *Agincourt*, 61–2. TNA E 101/44/30 roll 2, membrane 7 is a muster roll which lists a John Fastolf, but it is difficult to be sure that this is our man: he appears here as a simple man-at-arms, without a retinue.
4. *English Suits*, Overton v Fastolf, 264.
5. *GHQ*, 23; Rymer, *Foedera*, IX, 329–30; Mason, 90; Stratford, 13.
6. *GHQ*, 35, 155; Dockray, 217.
7. *JBP*, 500 (Jargeau); Poulett Scrope repeated the story about René, found in the *Biographica Britannica* and Drayton's long poem *Poly-Olbion* of 1622. I am grateful to Margaret Kekewich for confirming that it has no basis in fact.
8. TNA E 101/44/30, roll 1 no. 1, membrane 10; TNA E 101/46/24, cited by Anne Curry in *The Battle of Agincourt: Sources and Interpretation* (Woodbridge, Boydell Press, 2000). Fastolf's is the 9th name on membrane 1 (though the database www.medievalsoldier.org. cites the 3rd membrane). Confusingly, there were two other John Fastolfs, of Nacton, and of Oulton (McFarlane, *EFC*, 183 n. 36), both of whom were also squires at the time. However, Fastolf of Nacton is thought to have died in the reign of Henry IV: Vernon Harcourt, *Transactions of the Royal Historical Society*, (1910), 59–60.
9. TNA E 101/47/39 membrane 1 (the list is very difficult to read but it is clearly headed *Milites* – knights – and there is no mistaking the name *Johan FFastolf*, which is the 13th name); *GHQ*, 59n.; 115n.
10. Curry, *Agincourt*, 85, 100; *GHQ*, 135–6 and n.; Strecche, *Chronicle*, 24; *Gesta Henrici Quinti*, English Historical Association (1850), p. 86n., citing Ms Arundel 48, College of Arms, f 324b.
11. *BON*, 15.
12. *GHQ*, 145; Curry, *Agincourt*, 81, citing *inter alia* E 101/47/39. The figure of thirty-five men also appears in FP 69, though Worcester records them as knights.
13. Oman, II, 387; BC 34r, 37v.

14. A shield divided into four quarters, coloured gold in two quarters and blue in the other two, with a red 'bend' or diagonal stripe running from top left to bottom right (looking at the shield from the observer's perspective), with three gold crosses on the stripe. In later records, the three crosslets are described as *crosses botonny Or*, and even as *escallops Argent*. I am grateful to Chester Herald at the College of Arms for this information.

15. Fastolf's name does not appear in the detailed accounts of these operations written by Léon Puiseux in the mid-nineteenth century, nor in the contemporary English poem about the siege of Rouen written by John Page. Hall, 98; Newhall, *English Conquest of Normandy*, 262, citing Bib. Nat., fr. 4485, 130; BC 38r.

16. *Norman Rolls* (ed. Hardy), I, 367–8; Newhall, *English Conquest of Normandy*, 249; Burne, 125–6.

17. DKR vol. 41, 745, membrane 13; McFarlane, *Nobility of Later Medieval England*, 80; Jean-Pierre Bernard, *Dépossession des seigneurs Normands en faveur des seigneurs Anglais ou pro-Anglais*, in www.histoire-généalogie.com.

18. Perroy, 262; M Howard, *The Franco-Prussian War* (Routledge, 2001), 285; Ditcham, Chapter 2; *JBP*, Introduction, 211.

19. Oman, II, 388; BC 39v, 41r; Stevenson (ed.), *Letters and Papers*, I, xxxv; Allmand, *The Hundred Years' War*, 63; Allmand, *Henry V*, 152–3; Dockray, 193. Régine Pernoud (*Trente Journées*) considered that the *bourgeois* was a clerk attached to the University of Paris.

20. DKR vol. 42, 390–1, membrane 19 dors.; Thomas de Elmham, *Vita et Gesta Henrici Quinti* (ed. T Hearne, 1727), 282–4. Three men are supposed to have diverted the attention of the Burgundian guards by pretending to arrange a duel, 'in the manner of noblemen' (*coeperunt, more procerum, facere contendere*), while the rest kept cover. Their leader deprived the gate-keeper of his keys and then let his comrades in.

21. The *compotus* is at TNA E 101/50/5. The contract was printed by J G Nichols in *Archaeologia*, 44:1 (1873); Thompson, 88 n. 4, 92–8 and Table 4; Allmand, *LN*, 158–9; Stevenson (ed.), *Letters and Papers*, I, xli n. 1. Adrian James of the Society of Antiquaries has informed me that there is no information as to the fate of the original. It was not unusual for the authorities to make provision about the value of the currency: see *Registres de la Jurade*, 271. See also Marin (ed.), *La Normandie*, 97 and FP 69; *Histoire et Images Médiévales*, 17 (2009), p. 41 (Franck Viltart, *Les Fonctions militaires de l'Hôtel Ducale*); *JBP*, 268, 278.

22. Monstrelet, *Chronicles*, I, 458; Fauquembergue, II, 17–18; Thompson, 158, 208, 212–13.

23. *BON*, 68–9 (Worcester, referring to Fastolf as 'mine author').

24. DKR vol. 42, 408 membrane 17 dors.; Newhall, *English Conquest of Normandy*, 248 n. 3; Thompson, 92, citing the primary source for the ligitation.

25. *JBP*, 282–5 and Map 7; le Cacheux (ed.), *Rouen au Temps de Jeanne d'Arc*, 52–3; Monstrelet, *Chronicles*, I, 455. FP 69 refers to Fastolf as Bedford's 'seneschal' rather than 'steward'.

26. Longnon, LXX.

27. BC 39v (which refers to Meulent); Bib. Nat., fr. 25766, 810 (which refers to 'Pont de Melanc'). It is easy to confuse Meulan and Melun – and Fastolf was present at both: Hall has 'Melans' and again 'Melaus'. I take both of these to be Meulan, because he later spells Melun as either 'Melune' or 'Molyn upon Seyne'. See also FP 69; BC 45r,

44v; Hall, 108; TNA E 101/50/24 (for Meaux).
28. BC 47r; Monstrelet, *Chronicles*, I, 492–5. I am grateful to Mme Tetard, archivist for Meulan for twenty-five years and now its historian, for information supplied.
29. Only the first of these medieval bridges remains, the second having been completely destroyed during the Second World War, and never rebuilt.
30. Waurin, V, Book 3, 11–16. Two sets of accounts survive in relation to Fastolf's captaincy of Meulan: TNA E 101/50/24 and E 101/50/25.
31. BC 57r.

Chapter 4: From Triumph to Disaster, 1422–9

1. Stevenson (ed.), *Letters and Papers*, II, Part 2, 434–5; *English Suits*, II, 29; see also BC 55v.
2. In my view this is Meulan in the Vexin (which had two bridges), not Pont-Audemer in Normandy, as the editor of Worcester's *Itineraries* suggests. Where Pont-Audemer appears in Stevenson's documents, it appears as Ponteaudemer: e.g. vol. I, 22.
3. BL Add Charters 7944 and 47305.
4. *BON*, 68; Carus-Wilson, 197–205. William Worcester uses the term 'hubes'. I assume this is an abbreviation for 'houppeland' – a type of jacket on display at the National Army Museum in Chelsea (February 2009). For the Norfolk connection see Harper-Bill (ed.), 76.
5. *JBP*, 355; Longnon, 44, 136; Spufford, 74–5.
6. Rowe, 'Discipline in the Norman garrisons', Appendix, document I, clause (6).
7. *English Suits*, 15, 273.
8. McFarlane, *EFC*, 180 n. 19.
9. Rowe, 'The Grand Conseil', 210–14; McFarlane, *Nobility of Later Medieval England*, 34–5; *Chronique du Mont-Saint-Michel*, II, pièces diverses, CLXII, 66; BL Add Charters 7944.
10. Newhall, 'Bedford's ordinances on the watch of September 1428'; Rowe, 'The Grand Conseil', Appendix VI; Curry, 'The first English standing army?', 204, 213 n. 61.
11. BC 47v.
12. BC 49v, 53v, 54r; Walter Bower, *Scotichronicon*.
13. Strickland and Hardy, 347.
14. *Itineraries*, 335; *BON*, 32, 44. The speech does not feature in Basset's Chronicle.
15. Monstrelet, *Chronicles*, I, Book II, Chapter XX, 510; Curry, 'The first English standing army?', 265; Stevenson (ed.), *Letters and Papers*, II, Part 2, 394, [550–1]; Newhall, *English Conquest of Normandy*, 44, citing BM Add Charters 7944. For the Scots see Brian Ditcham's thesis.
16. BC 55r; Hall, 126–7; Newhall, *English Conquest of Normandy*, 321, citing BM Arundel, 26 f 4.
17. Stevenson (ed.), *Letters and Papers*, II, 1, 38–42 and II, 2, 411, [535], [553]. In the introduction to *The Parliament Rolls*, X, 205, Anne Curry also states that Fastolf led the first assault on Maine, which began in early September 1424. This incident is also referred to in TNA PRO 31/8/135 documents 5 and 6 (dated at Rouen 17 and 18 October 1424).
18. Stevenson (ed.), *Letters and Papers*, II, 1, 44–50. The indenture is at TNA PRO 31/8/135 document 7, where the date is given as 17 November 1424, and where the

clerk makes a Pooteresque pun: he says the 'chieftains' who were required to be handed over to the Regent, if captured, were 'chieftains but not Christians'. Document 3 relates to the same indenture.

19. TNA PRO 31/8/135 documents 4, 8, 9 and 10.
20. BC 56v.
21. *BON*, 19. For Gough, see Rowe, 'A contemporary account of the Hundred Years' War' and the BC generally.
22. Anstis, 142, confirmed by Chester Herald in a letter to me of 11 March 2009.
23. Jacob, 244; Allmand, *LN*, 29, 30; Newhall, *English Conquest of Normandy*, 308, citing *Bibliothèque Nationale de France*, fr. 4485, pp. 262–3; fr. 26047 no. 200; Rowe, 'The Grand Conseil', 211; Stevenson (ed.), *Letters and Papers*, II, 2, [535], [555–7]; McFarlane, *EFC*, 188 n. 67, citing FP 69 membranes 5–7; Hall, 126–7.
24. BL Add Charters 47305: 'casque de profil surmonté d'un cimier; accosté de palmes, appuyé sur un collier d'ordre; portant sur la pointe droite de l'écu ci-dessous le quell écu est supporté par deux espèces d'aihles aux ailes ouvertes': TNA PRO 31/8/135 document 23, dated 14 January 1432. This transcript describes the seal, and there follow the words 'on lit autour fastolf johannis', together with a crude drawing of the shield itself.
25. Rymer, *Foedera*, X, 408, 472; *Dicts and Sayings*, 292n.; Allmand, *LN*, 289; Allmand, *Henry V*, 65; Berry Herald, 138; *RP*, IV, 423; Maurice Keen, 'The end of the Hundred Years' War', in *Nobles, Knights and Men-at-Arms*.
26. BC 58r; *JBP*, 224; *English Suits*, 302–3; Burne, 221.
27. BC 57r, 49v; TNA PRO 31/8/135 documents 12 and 13; Monstrelet, *Chronicles*, I, 536–7; BC 62v; *Chronique du Mont-Saint-Michel*, I, pièces diverses, LXXXVII, 257 (orders given by Richard, Earl of Warwick, relating to the muster and review of Fastolf's retinue at Pont d'Orson).
28. BC 60r, confirmed by the French account in *Mémoires*, 81.
29. Hall, 141; *English Suits*, introduction, 18, XVII and XIX; Pollard, 12–13; Williams, 155; Talbot, 83; Harriss, *Shaping the Nation*, 552–3. Michael K Jones gives a very different account of La Gravelle, saying that this was the scene of an important victory by Jean d'Harcourt, Count of Aumâle: Jones, 'The battle of Verneuil: towards a history of courage', *War in History*, 9 (2002), 379.
30. BC 44v.
31. BC 63r; *JBP*, 246; *Mémoires*, 84, 100.
32. BC 63r; Duparc (ed.), *Procès de Condamnation*, IV, 5; *Mémoires*, 86.
33. *Mémoires*, 84; Basin, cited by Vale, 'New techniques and old ideals', in Allmand (ed.), *War, Literature and Politics*, 63; BC 63v; *JBP*, 279 n. 70; Pernoud, *Trente Journées*, 11 and the map at pp. 90–1.
34. BC 64r; Pernoud, *Trente Journées*, 78, 98, 92. Pernoud also cites Surreau to the effect that Fastolf mustered at Chartres on 22 January 1429.
35. See J-P Bernard's articles, 'La bataille des Harengs', and 'Une journée au siège d'Orléans': www.histoire-généalogie.com. M. Bernard cites contemporary documents, in the form of indentures, musters and *quittances*. He makes the point that although the indentures might provide for payment of wages in sterling, the troops were actually paid in local currencies, such as *livres tournois*.
36. *JBP*, 197.

37. A Tuetey, *Journal d'un bourgeois de Paris* (Paris, Champion, 1881), 231 n. 2; Burne, 234, 244–5. I have examined Ms Fr d 10 (Bodleian Library, Oxford), which is an abbreviated version of the *Journal*; but this stops in 1429 and says nothing about the Battle of the Herrings.

38. Cagny, *Chroniques*, ed. H Moranvillé, Société de l'Histoire de France (Paris, 1902), 138. To add to the confusion, there is also a village called Terminiers, which lies next door to Rouvray-Sainte-Croix, which could well have been corrupted to 'Tomray' or 'Tommiray' or for that matter 'Tonmray', though scarcely to 'Tonmray-Saint-Denis'.

39. Pernoud, *Trente Journées*, 272.

40. BC 64v; Monstrelet, *Chronicles*, I, 549; Waurin, 255, 259. There are details of property transactions in the *Guides des Archives du Loiret* (Orléans, 1982) which suggest that Rouvray-Sainte-Croix was a medieval settlement.

41. Pernoud, *Trente Journées*, 8.

42. BC 65v: 'fit planter devant chacun archier un pal agu pour render la force des chevaux'.

43. Basin, I, 125; *Mémoires*, 87–8; Pernoud, *Trente Journées*, 100. 'Raidement' literally means 'stiffly' or 'tensely'. Strickland and Hardy, in *The Great Warbow*, translate this as 'thick and fast'; BC 65v; Waurin, 254–61.

44. Ditcham, 163.

45. Pernoud, *Trente Journées*, 100.

46. Girault, 12; Perroy, 283; Pernoud, *Trente Journées*, Chapter 7, 233, 263. In Luc Besson's film about Joan, *The Messenger*, the English captain tells her to 'go fuck herself'.

47. Duparc (ed.), *Procès de Condamnation*, IV, 6–7; Pernoud, *Trente Journées*, 207, 241–3, 251–2, 258, 261, 274.

48. *Mémoires*, 88; Basin, I, 121.

49. Pernoud, *Trente Journées*, 191; Burne, 242–3.

Chapter 5: Soldiering On, 1429–39

1. Duparc (ed.), *Procès de Condamnation*, IV, 5; Vale, *Ancient Enemy*, 96.

2. Duparc (ed.), *Procès de Condamnation*, I, 137–8; Pernoud, *Trente Journées*, 166.

3. *Mémoires*, 99.

4. Cochon, *Chronique Normande*, 308–9; Monstrelet, *Chronicles*, I, 561; Michel Sot et al., *Le moyen âge*.

5. *JBP*, 257, 265, 291–7; Pernoud, *Trente Journées*, 169.

6. Rymer, *Foedera*, X, 408. For the opinion of Dunois and Alençon see Duparc (ed.), *Procès de Condamnation*, IV, 2, 66.

7. Cochon, *Chronique Normande*, 299; *Mémoires*, 100; Pernoud, *Trente Journées*, 152.

8. *Mémoires*, 100.

9. Basin, I, 143; Berry Herald, 138; Cochon, *Chronique Normande*, 300. The French chroniclers are examined in detail by Collins in 'Sir John Fastolf, John Lord Talbot and the dispute over Patay'.

10. *Mémoires*, 100; Fowler, 134; Newhall, *Muster and Review*, 125 n. 279, citing Bib. Nat., fr. 4488, 514; also 126 n. 282, citing Bib. Nat., fr. 26052, 1134; Cochon, *Chronique Normande*, 300. For Pontoise, see TNA PRO 31/8/135 document 14.

11. Anstis, 139; Drake, *Archaeologia*, 9 (1789), 266.

12. *BON*, 46–7.
13. Marin (ed.), *La Normandie*, 124; Newhall, *Muster and Review*, 124–5. For Louviers, see TNA PRO 31/8/135 document 15.
14. Berry Herald, 137n.
15. TNA PRO 31/8/135 document 22.
16. *The Parliament Rolls*, X, 453.
17. Rymer, *Foedera*, X, 527 and 530–1; *ODNB*, Langdon (R G Davies); Bekyngton (Robert J Dunning); Keen, *Nobles, Knights and Men-at-Arms*, 231 (essay on Henry V's diplomacy). It seems that Fastolf was only included as one of the envoys to Auxerre at a late date, as a substitute for Sir Henry Bromflete.
18. Stevenson (ed.), *Letters and Papers*, II, 1, 252; Rose, 177.
19. Stevenson (ed.), *Letters and Papers*, II, 2, 431–3; Dickinson, 143 and n. 5.
20. Curry, 'The first English standing army?', 204–5.
21. Taylor, 69.
22. Vegetius, 116; Christine de Pisan, *The Book of Deeds of Arms and of Chivalry*, 78–9.
23. Fowler, 100; Froissart, *Chronicles of England, France, Spain*, II, 636; Burne, 23–4.
24. Stevenson (ed.), *Letters and Papers*, II, 2, [581]; Jacob, 263; Keen, *England in the Later Middle Ages*, 2nd edition (Routledge, 2003), 312; Christopher Allmand in Keen (ed.), *Medieval Warfare*, 264, 267; Pollard, 125.
25. Vale, 'Sir John Fastolf's report of 1435'; *BON*, 6–8, 24; Rowe, 'A contemporary account of the Hundred Years' War'; *PPC*, V, 260.
26. It is impossible to verify Fastolf's commercial activities in Calais, since the records of the Staple were almost entirely destroyed by the French after 1558, and those which did survive date only from King Edward IV's time: Rose, 40–1. Likewise, he only appears tangentially in David Grummitt's *The Calais Garrison* (Woodbridge, Boydell Press, 2008).
27. Dickinson, 24–5.
28. Stevenson (ed.), *Letters and Papers*, II, 1, Preface.
29. *Itineraries*, 353; Newhall, *Muster and Review*, 73 n. 147 citing BM Add Charters 6903. The latter, now BL Add Charters 6903, shows Fastolf as Captain of Caen in November 1436.
30. FP, 69; Pollard, 22; Stevenson (ed.), *Letters and Papers*, II, 1, 286–7; *Chronique du Mont-Saint-Michel*, II, pièces diverses, CLXI, 50–1; CLXXXI, 76–7; CLXXXVIII, 86–7; TNA PRO 31/8/135 document 31 (letters sent by Fastolf to England).
31. *BON*, Introduction, p. lvi (referred to as Royal MS 18 B, XXII f 44). The Beaumont here must be Beaumont-le-Richard in the *Vicomté* of Bayeux. See also FP 69.
32. *JBP*, 340–1.
33. Butler, Chapter 16; Stevenson (ed.), *Letters and Papers*, II, 1, xxv.
34. Allmand, *The Hundred Years' War*, 150; Thompson, 224–40; *JBP*, 364. Louis of Luxembourg is buried in Ely cathedral: *JBP*, 385 n. 19; Spufford, 135–8.
35. Johnson, 16–18; TNA C 8/703, 3334 A (an order to draw a proxy for Fastolf) and B (the appointment itself) – see also Rymer, *Foedera*, X, 642–3; Rowe, 'The Grand Conseil'.
36. Newhall, *Muster and Review*, 73, citing BM Add Charters 6905.
37. *ODNB* and *English Suits* (Oldhall); Pollard, 37, 48.
38. *ODNB* (Warwick); Worcester, *Itineraries*, 221; Stevenson (ed.), *Letters and Papers*, II, 1, lxvi no. VII; Johnson, 28–30; Pollard, 28, 49.

39. FP 69, membrane 6, cited incorrectly as membrane 5 by McFarlane *EFC*, 178 n. 9: Worcester writes in Latin 'and on the feast of Michaelmas in the 18th year of the reign he came to England from the aforesaid Islands'. The expenses cited are, however, set out in FP 26 membrane 6, item 4, beginning line 5. See also Stevenson (ed.), *Letters and Papers*, II, 1, 436 and [529]; DKR vol. 48, 317 membrane 5; and *PPC*, V, 5; Davis (ed.), *PL&P*, II, 93. Unfortunately there is no confirmation to be had in the Channel Islands of this voyage: the records held in The Greffe (the official archive of the States of Guernsey) begin in the sixteenth century; as do the records in the Lieutenant-Governor's collection in Jersey.

40. The list of bishops on display in the cathedral at Sées confirms what Fastolf said about this: the bishop in 1449 was Jean V de Perouse (1438–54); and he was indeed the third appointed since 1422. The cathedral was pillaged on at least three occasions down the centuries: during the Hundred Years' War, the Wars of Religion in the sixteenth century and the French Revolution.

41. Stevenson (ed.), *Letters and Papers*, I, 493–5.

Chapter 6: The Army of Occupation

1. DKR vol. 41, 708 membrane 40 dors.
2. Pernoud, *Trente Journées*, 235; Allmand, *The Hundred Years' War*, 50; Curry, 'The military ordinances of Henry V'.
3. Rowe, 'Discipline in the Norman garrisons'; *BON*, 31; *GHQ*, 69; Williams, *My Lord of Bedford*, 89; Curry, 'Sex and the soldier', 18–22.
4. Davis (ed.), *PL&P*, III, 954: 29–35.
5. *JBP*, 277.
6. Longnon, LXVIII. See also CXLVIII and CLXVII.
7. TNA PRO 31/8/135 document 18.
8. *Actes de la Chancellerie*, II, CCXXI, 231–3.
9. McFarlane, *EFC*, 127.
10. *JBP*, 151.
11. Curry, 'The first English standing army?', 211 n. 24; Newhall, *English Conquest of Normandy*, 308, citing Bib. Nat., fr. 4485, 262–3; fr. 26047, 200; Rowe, 'The Grand Conseil', 211; Stevenson (ed.), *Letters and Papers*, II, 2, [535], [555], [557].
12. *The Hundred Tales* (*Les Cent Nouvelles Nouvelles*), Tale 62: 'The Tale of the Lost Ring'. The wife arranged assignations while her husband was on watch.
13. *English Suits*, XIX, 225–6.
14. TNA PRO 31/8/135 document 25; Curry, 'The first English standing army?', 202; Allmand, *LN*.
15. McFarlane, *EFC*, 212; FP 69, membrane 5 (last entry).
16. Hastings Rashdall, *The Universities of Europe in the Middle Ages* (Oxford, 1936), II, 195; Anthony Black, *Council and Commune* (Burnes & Oates, 1979), 38; *Sources de l'histoire des universités françaises au moyen âge* (Université d'Orléans, 1978), 14.52; Rowe, 'The Grand Conseil', 233; Pernoud, *Trente Journées*, 72.
17. Juvénal des Ursins, 534–9; Fauquembergue, II, 125–6; Newhall, *English Conquest of Normandy*, 308, citing Bib. Nat., fr. 4485, 262–3 and fr. 26047, 200.
18. *Camden Miscellany*, 24 (1972), 130; *ODNB* (Fastolf); Allmand, *LN*, 189, 309, citing *Revue Historique et Archéologique du Maine*, 1 (1901), 113–81 and 3 (1878), 279–303;

http://fr.wikipedia.org (Ambroise de Loré); Juvénal des Ursins, 539; *Nouvelle Collection des Mémoires pour servir à l'histoire de France*, 81. For Fresnay as a personal possession of the Regent, see Rowe, 'Discipline in the Norman garrisons', 200 n. 1. For resistance fighters see Marin (ed.), *La Normandie*, 33 and 41. There is also a story in *Les Cent Nouvelles Nouvelles* involving a Burgundian who escaped hanging by the Armagnacs in Troyes, by playing the bagpipes until his comrades could arrive to rescue him: Tale 75, 'A Timely Tune'.

19. BC 45r; *JBP*, 205; Monstrelet, *Chronicles*, II, 152.
20. BC 57v; Hall, 127.
21. Rowe, 'John Duke of Bedford and the Norman brigands'; Marin (ed.), *La Normandie*, 52 (Jouet); Juvénal des Ursins, 534; *JBP*, 175–7, 187.
22. *JBP*, 216–17, 221, 277, 288, 308–11, 334.
23. Strecche, *Chronicle*, 43; Stevenson (ed.), *Letters and Papers*, I, 34; *JBP*, 189; Waurin, 8 (Paris), 187 (Normandy); *Actes de la Chancellerie*, II, CXCI, 121–7 (Verneuil); le Cacheux (ed.), *Rouen au Temps de Jeanne d'Arc*, 225; Marin (ed.), *La Normandie*, 53; *JBP*, 327–8; Scrope, *History*, 174; Allmand, *LN*, Chapter 6 and Epilogue.
24. Stevenson (ed.), *Letters and Papers*, II, 2, 434–5, [541–4]; TNA PRO 31/8/135 documents 19, 20 and 22; Marin (ed.), *La Normandie*, 24, 29, 33, 112–15; *JBP*, 445 (refers to the palace constructed by the English in Rouen); information kindly supplied by Jean-Marie Levesque.
25. F M Stenton, *The First Century of English Feudalism, 1066–1166*, 2nd edition (Oxford, Clarendon Press, 1961); Marin (ed.), *La Normandie*, 47. Some figures have been confirmed to me by J-M Levesque, of the Museum of Caen, for the year 1436; he cites Michel de Boüard, *Le Château de Caen*, 27, in turn citing Bib. Nat., fr. 26062, 3086.
26. Rowe, 'Discipline in the Norman garrisons', Appendix of documents.
27. Juvénal des Ursins, 561 (see also *JBP*, 162); *Chronique du Mont-Saint-Michel*, II, pièces diverses, CLXXII, 66–7.
28. *Actes de la Chancellerie*, vol. I, LXXIX, 218–20; *Chronique du Mont-Saint-Michel*, II, pièces diverses, CLX, 48–9.
29. BL Add Charters 7944 and 47305; Newhall, *Muster and Review*, 21–3; TNA PRO 31/8/135 document 17; FP 69.
30. Newhall, *Muster and Review*, 68–9, citing Arch. Nat. K 63, No. 1332 and Bib. Nat., P.O. 1101, Fastolf section 25366, 8.
31. BL Add Charters 11791, cited by Newhall, *Muster and Review*, 55, whose transcription I have adopted; Fowler, 134.
32. Fauquembergue, III, 59, 98, 140.
33. *English Suits*, XX, 263–4.
34. 'Autant à Bruges que à Gand': probably a figure of speech.
35. Allmand, *LN*, 208; *The Hundred Tales*, Tale 5.
36. Allmand, 'Documents relating to the Anglo-French negotiations of 1439'; *BON*, 72.
37. Monstrelet, *Chronicles*, II, 153; Waurin, V, 128; Hall, 156.
38. Don Pero de Niño, 115–30, 158–63; Richmond, FW, 79 n. 97; Monstrelet, *Chronicles*, I, 37n.
39. Brie (ed.), *The Brut*, II, 383.
40. Stevenson (ed.), *Letters and Papers*, I, 489; Gairdner (ed.), *PL*, I, 363; Richmond, FS&P, 86–8; TNA C 1/19/115.

41. Davis (ed.), *PL&P*, III, 968 and 1014; CPR Henry VI, 1446–52, 437.
42. Stevenson (ed.), *Letters and Papers*, II, 2, [594]; Allmand, *Henry V*, 89–90; Rodger, 142–52; Vale, *Ancient Enemy*, 18.

Chapter 7: The Fall of the Lancastrian Empire, 1439–53

1. Vaughan, 94.
2. Christine de Pisan, *Epistle of Othea*, ed. Bühler, 121 (Appendix A, Preface to L manuscript).
3. FP 72, membrane 8 (the roll is endorsed 'William Worcester's expenses after Fastolf's death); Jefferson, 365; Collins, 'Sir John Fastolf, John Lord Talbot and the dispute over Patay', 129; Monstrelet, *Chronicles*, I, 555.
4. CPR Henry VI, 1441–6, 474; 1446–52, 388, 592; 1452–61, 672. The deposition is mentioned in TNA SP 46/123/fo 7, 7d.
5. Davis (ed.), *PL&P*, III, 1039: 34–7; Griffiths, *The Reign of Henry VI*, 443–54; Smith, 'Fastolf', 118–20.
6. Stevenson (ed.), *Letters and Papers*, II, 2, 440–60.
7. Johnson, 37.
8. *PPC*, V, 233.
9. Curry, *The Hundred Years' War*, 71.
10. *PPC* V, 259–60.
11. Stevenson (ed.), *Letters and Papers*, II, 2, [674–5], [687–9]; Kekewich, *René of Anjou*, 8; Dunn, 'Margaret of Anjou, Queen Consort of Henry VI', 111, 113–14; Wolffe, 83n., 180; Griffiths, *The Reign of Henry VI*, 253, 486.
12. Stevenson (ed.), *Letters and Papers*, II, 2, [687–92]; *ODNB*, Mundeford; McFarlane, *EFC*, 153 (Gough).
13. Stevenson (ed.), *Letters and Papers*, II, 2, [715]; Griffiths, *The Reign of Henry VI*, 502, 503 and 541 n. 113, citing Stevenson (ed.), *Letters and Papers*, II, 2, 434, [549], [575] (Sillé); I, 494 and II, 2, [544] (Fresnay); II, 2, [704], [707]; *BON*, lvii, said to be Royal MS.18B.XXII.f.44 (Beaumont).
14. *Biographica Britannica*, V, 703 Note F refers to the surrender of the barony. In a wider claim for compensation prepared in 1455, Fastolf argued that he had been deprived of this by royal command.
15. Rowe, 'A contemporary account of the Hundred Years' War', citing Stevenson (ed.), *Letters and Papers* II, 2, [691]; Stevenson (ed.), *Letters and Papers*, II, 2, [592–4]; Abstract, 576. In Stevenson's edition, this document is erroneously headed 1440.
16. Watts, 252–3.
17. Fowler, 137; Monstrelet, *Chronicles*, II, 188; Contamine, 169.
18. Harriss, *Shaping the Nation*, 582; Griffiths, *The Reign of Henry VI*, 508; Stevenson (ed.), *Letters and Papers*, II, [594].
19. Monstrelet, *Chronicles*, II, 148–9 and 187; Rowe, 'A contemporary account of the Hundred Years' War', 81. Keen, 'The end of the Hundred Years' War', in *Nobles, Knights and Men-at-Arms*, 239; Stevenson (ed.), *Letters and Papers*, I, 211.
20. Stevenson (ed.), *Letters and Papers*, I, 474, 476 and 478; Collins, *The Order of the Garter*, Appendix III, 275.
21. Stevenson (ed.), *Letters and Papers*, I, 283.
22. *Camden Miscellany*, 24 (1972), 132; Stevenson (ed.), *Letters and Papers* I, 278–83; Hall,

80; Johnson, 72–3; Wolffe, 200–8; Griffiths, *The Reign of Henry VI*, 512; Smith, 'Litigation and politics', 67; Smith, 'Fastolf', 39, 218. The judgment of 1450 awarding Dedham to Fastolf is at TNA E 40/637.

23. Stevenson (ed.), *Letters and Papers*, II, 2, [718–22]; Michael K Jones, 'Somerset, York and the Wars of the Roses'; Stevenson (ed.), *Letters and Papers*, I, 243–64.

24. Marin (ed.), *La Normandie*, 24 and map 35 (André Plaisse, Anne Curry); *BON*, 74.

25. *GHQ* (1850 edition), 86n., citing Ms Arundel 48, College of Arms folio 324b.

26. Stevenson (ed.), *Letters and Papers*, II, 2, [723–30]. I attribute this memorandum to Fastolf because it is included in Worcester's collection, the language is Fastolfian, it presents the same argument as in the *BON*, and Fastolf's conduct in Maine is specifically applauded.

27. Marin (ed.), *La Normandie*, 128, citing *Bibliothèque municipale de Caen*, Ms Mancel 296 f 221.

28. *BON*, 33, 74; Stevenson (ed.), *Letters and Papers*, II, 2, [730–5]; Anne Curry, 'Soldiers' wives in the Hundred Years' War', in Coss and Tyerman (eds), *Soldiers, Nobles and Gentlemen*, 203.

29. Stevenson (ed.), *Letters and Papers*, II, 2, [595–7], [607], [630–1]; Burne, 323–4.

30. Stevenson (ed.), *Letters and Papers*, II, 2, [735–42, surrender of Falaise]; Marin (ed.), *La Normandie*, 24; Davis (ed.), *PL&P*, II, 455: 40–2.

31. Stevenson (ed.), *Letters and Papers*, II, Part 2, [619–34]; M A Hicks, 'The changing role of the Wydevilles in Yorkist politics to 1483', in Ross (ed.), *Patronage, Pedigree and Power*; Allmand, *LN*, 289.

32. CCR Henry VI, 1429–35, 70.

33. Goodman, 91; Griffiths, *The Reign of Henry VI*, 564, 686; Barber (ed.), *The Pastons*, 48–50; Jacob, 498; Carlin, *Medieval Southwark*.

34. Magdalen College Archives, Misc. 306, printed by Harvey, *Jack Cade's Rebellion*, 188–9.

35. Davis (ed.), *PL&P*, III, 983: 44–6.

36. *Registres de la Jurade*, 171.

37. Vale, *English Gascony*, 99, 114.

38. Vale, *Charles VII*, 121–4; Vale, 'New techniques and old ideals', 59, 62, 65.

39. *BON*, 42.

40. Griffiths, *The Reign of Henry VI*, 533; Stevenson (ed.), *Letters and Papers*, II, 2, [598–601]; Jacob, 507.

41. Fortescue, *On the Laws and Governance of England*, 96–7. Stevenson (ed.), *Letters and Papers*, I, 319, II, 2, 477–8, 493–4; Griffiths, *The Reign of Henry VI*, 815–16. For Calais, see Vale, *Ancient Enemy*, pp. ix, 16. For the notion of a Hundred Years' War see Fowler, 13.

42. CPR Henry VI, 1452–61, 344; Barber (ed.), *The Pastons*, 33, 98–101; Hawkyard, 53. I am grateful to Dr Tim Pestell, curator of Norwich Castle Museum, for the information about the Fastolf sword.

43. Keen, *Medieval Warfare*, 276; Contamine, 142, 197–8.

44. Davis (ed.), *PL&P*, II, 496: 17–19; 584: 12–17.

45. Paul Murray Kendall, *Louis XI* (Phoenix, 1971), 34; Cuttler; Allmand, *LN*, 265–6; Vale, *Charles VII*, 70–1, 155–7.

Chapter 8: 'The Old Vulture'

1. Fowler, 149; Seward; Keen, 'The end of the Hundred Years' War', in *Nobles, Knights and Men-at-Arms*; Monstrelet, *Chronicles*, 246.
2. FP 69; Scrope, *History*, 141, 171; McFarlane, *Nobility of Later Medieval England*, 83; McFarlane, *EFC*, 185 n. 48.
3. I owe this point to Anthony Smith. See also McFarlane, *EFC*, 203.
4. Barber (ed.), *The Pastons*, 66, 69; Griffiths, *The Reign of Henry VI*, 790; Haward, 170; Sandra Raban, *Mortmain Legislation and the English Church, 1279–1500* (Cambridge University Press, 1982), 69–70; K L Wood-Legh, *Perpetual Chantries in Britain* (Cambridge University Press, 1965), 44, 311.
5. McFarlane, *EFC*, 186 n. 55, citing FP membrane 5; Hawkyard, 41–3, 66; Worcester, *Itineraries*, 187; Richmond, FW, 192 n. 107, 195; Griffiths, *The Reign of Henry VI*, 591 (Norfolk); Castor, *Blood and Roses*, 126 (Southwark).
6. Davis (ed.), *PL&P*, III, 1036: 16–19; Marin (ed.), *La Normandie*, 113 (Richard Jones); Richmond, FW, 195; Smith, 'Fastolf', 37–8.
7. Amyot printed two inventories in 1827 (see *Archaeologia*, vol. 21). Morris dancing appears to be shown in the Burgundian tapestry shown in Brussels, *Bibliothèque royale de Belgique*, ms 6232–33 fo 148r.
8. See McFarlane, *Lancastrian Kings and Lollard Knights*, 139–221.
9. FP 85(2), cited by Hughes, 145 n. 177. I am most grateful to Dr Jeremy Catto for confirming that the form of the confession is more than conventional. See Richmond, FW, 69 for gifts to St Benet's.
10. Gairdner (ed.), *PL*, I, 445–60; Richmond, FS&P, 75; Norfolk Record Society, IX, 30 & 33 (for relics); Deedes, 202; Richmond, FS&P, 78; Smith, ' "My Confessors" '; Smith, 'Fastolf', 221.
11. *Transactions of the Royal Historical Society*, 5th Series, VII, 1957, reprinted in McFarlane, *EFC*; but see Allmand, The Hundred Years' War, 131.
12. Don Pero Niño, 103, 117; K B McFarlane, 'England and the Hundred Years War', *Past & Present*, 22 (1962); M M Postan, 'The costs of the Hundred Years War', *Past & Present*, 27 (1964); Beresford and Rubinstein, 'The richest of the rich', *Sunday Times* (7 October 2007); Hawkyard, 56n. Amyot's inventories are in *Archaeologia*, vol. 21 (1827); a later inventory of 1460–1 is printed by Barber (ed.), *The Pastons*, 98–100; Richmond, FW, 125 n. 71.
13. FP 47; McFarlane, *Nobility of Later Medieval England*, 110. These men may have worn badges, to indicate that they were retained by Fastolf. In *Notes & Queries* for 1948, H S London reproduced drawings of two of Fastolf's badges. One is in the shape of a (green) leaf, with an obscure object at the foot. The other is in the form of a (white) reel and pin, with a (green) cord and a (gold) tassel; Richmond, FS&P, 8; McFarlane, *EFC*, 192; TNA C 1/26/621; McFarlane, *EFC*, Chapter 8; Rowe, 'A contemporary account of the Hundred Years' War'.
14. McFarlane, *Nobility of Later Medieval England*, 35, 113n., 57, 92, 98, 183; Rowse, *Historians I Have Known*, 69. In his thesis, Anthony Smith was much more cautious about the profits made by Fastolf in France: he concluded that it was unlikely that he made a fair return overall, considering the many risks and losses incurred; but what counts as a 'fair return'?
15. Stratford, 52, 88, 103, 403. Stratford suggests that Fastolf's identity was disguised in

one document as 'Monsieur Legrant, maître d'hôtel'. I would venture to suggest that, if this was a disguise, it was a thin one.

16. McFarlane, *EFC*, 189; Seward, 223; TNA PRO 31/8/135 documents 23, 24, 28, 29, 30 and 32; E 101/50/5, E 101/50/24 and E 101/50/25 (the Latin quotation is taken from the last of these).

17. Crosland, 26–7; Davis (ed.), *PL&P*, III, 1027: 20.

18. FP 69 contains a very full list of Fastolf's French properties; DKR vol. 44, 577 membrane 4; (Frileuse); DKR vol. 41, 723 membrane 40 and 745 membrane 13 (the lordships in Caux); *Camden Miscellany*, 24 (1972), 132; *English Suits*, 292–3 (acquisitions in 1419 and 1423); Stevenson (ed.), *Letters and Papers*, I, 283; Smith, 'Fastolf', 44–5.

19. TNA Record Commission Transcripts Series II, PRO 31/8/135 item 7A, documents 2, 16, 26 and 27.

20. Fortescue, *Governance of England*, Chapter 13.

21. Much of this derives from McFarlane's interpretation of FP 69 in his seminal article 'The investment of Sir John Fastolf's profits of war' (1957), printed in McFarlane, *EFC*. See also *Camden Miscellany*, 24 (1972), 132; *English Suits*, 293 (sales of land). In 1907 le Cacheux printed documents which included a reference to a licence of December 1433 to sell Aurichier and Angerville. Intriguingly, there was said to be an investigation to see if the capital value of the two properties exceeded 15,600 saluts d'or, 'the sum allowed to the said Fastolf'; but I am unsure what this means: *Actes de la Chancellerie*, vol. II, 385.

22. TNA C 1/52/90 is a case which refers to messuages in Norwich called 'Fastolfes, late of Sir John Fastolf or Forstaff'.

23. Vale, *Ancient Enemy*, 15, 18–19; K H Vickers, *Humphrey, Duke of Gloucester* (London, 1907), 62, 248; Williams, *My Lord of Bedford*, 130; Gairdner (ed.), *PL*, I, 454 (the *Bukheed*). See also Martha Carlin's article 'Sir John Fastolf's Place, Southwark', and also the maps and text in her *Medieval Southwark*, 34–5, 52–5, 56n., 132 and 193n.; Richmond, FS&P, 96, 102; Adrian Proctor and Robert Taylor (eds), *The A to Z of Elizabethan London* (London Topographical Society Publications No. 122, 1979). Fastolf Place is discussed by Hughes, 114. See Inquisitions 38/39 Henry VI (160–1) no. 48 for beerhouses. For foreigners in London, Barron and Saul, 13.

24. Martha Carlin, *Medieval Southwark*, 132; Davis (ed.), *PL&P*, III, 982; Smith, addendum to Richmond, FS&P, 102.

25. Secondary sources cite TNA E 179/196/100 but I could not find the relevant entries.

26. Scrope, *History*, 199–203; Carus-Wilson, 197–205; *Victoria County History Wiltshire*, vol. 4, 129–33. My thanks to Maurice Keen for the last reference.

27. Smith, 'Fastolf', 40; Crosland, 35.

28. Rymer, *Foedera*, XI, 44–5; Castor, 103; FP 26; BL Add MSS 36988, fv (the master-mariner's name was John a Bekks).

29. Davis (ed.), *PL&P*, III, 965: 29–41; 978: 39; 1002: 53; 1005: 86–80.

30. Richmond, FW, 77.

31. McFarlane, *EFC*, 70, citing FP 9; Smith, 'Fastolf', 3; Armstrong, 'Sir John Fastolf and the law of arms', 47.

32. McFarlane, *EFC* (Loans to the Lancastrian kings), especially 71 n. 63, citing Gairdner (ed.), *PL*, I, 358–67; *BON*, 80–5.

33. Stevenson (ed.), *Letters and Papers*, I, xxxix; Thompson, 210, 219–20; 192–3, 197,

199.

34. BC 47v, 51v, 51r; *English Suits*, II, 28–43; TNA PRO 31/8/135 document 21; Armstrong, 'Sir John Fastolf and the law of arms'; Gairdner (ed.), *PL*, I, 358–67; Hall, 117; Thompson, 64, 88 n. 15.

35. Rose, 'Litigation and conflict in fifteenth-century East Anglia', 63; McFarlane, *Nobility of Later Medieval England*, 50; Richmond, FW, 88 n. 120.

36. McFarlane, *Letters to Friends*, 77.

37. Gairdner (ed.), *PL*, I, 456; McFarlane, *EFC*, 193n., citing FP 26.

38. McFarlane, *EFC*, xx–xxi; *English Suits*, 221–30, XIX, <u>Robert Stafford v Lord Talbot</u>. This suit is unusual in that it came to judgment, and the judgment has survived. The court held that Stafford had unjustly been deprived of La Ferté-Bernard, following its capture by the French in February 1428; and that Talbot, upon whom the Crown had conferred the property, was not, in modern parlance, the '*bona fide* purchaser for value' of the legal estate. It would seem that Talbot must have continued to litigate with Stafford while in captivity between 1429 and 1433; and Stafford certainly thought that he had been unscrupulous.

39. This is Smith's vivid phrase: postscript to Richmond, FS&P, 101. TNA C 1/12/268 relates to a case involving Fastolf where there was a 'false charge of forging deeds'.

40. Davis (ed.), *PL&P*, III, 983: 25.

41. Fortescue, *De Laudibus*, Chronology; introduction, p. cii.

42. Davis (ed.), *PL&P*, III, 1034: 4–9; 1035; *Norfolk Record Society*, 9 (1937), 12; FP 42, membrane 4, last entry.

43. McFarlane, *Letters to Friends*, 119; McFarlane, *EFC*, 217 n. 108; Fortescue, *De Laudibus*, Notes, 127, 129, 172, 206; Griffiths, *The Reign of Henry VI*, 573, 589; Rose, 'Litigation and conflict in fifteenth-century East Anglia', 59. There is a writ of *certiorari* in the Calendar of Inquisitions Miscellaneous, vol. VIII 1432–85 (Boydell Press, 2003), 54 which suggests that Fastolf may have been indirectly involved in 'direct action' at Deopham in 1432. Following a forcible entry made by others, the disputed property had been conveyed to him and Henry Inglose: they were said to have been 'enfeoffed for maintenance'; but it is difficult to know what to make of this.

Chapter 9: The War of the Dukes, 1447–59

1. Gairdner (ed.), *PL*, I, 358–67. The list must have been prepared before 1452, when Talbot set sail for Bordeaux: one draft contains the words 'to whom God grant good expedition'.

2. This is now conventional wisdom; but see Griffiths, 'The sense of dynasty in the reign of Henry VI'; Edmund Wright, 'The strange death of Sir John Mortimer', in Archer and Walker (eds), *Rulers and Ruled in Late Medieval England*; and Keen, *England in the Later Middle Ages*, 363.

3. Johnson, 16, 17, 25 148n., Appendices I and III, 231.

4. Vale, *English Gascony*, 141; Johnson, 113; Michael K Jones, 'Somerset, York and the Wars of the Roses', citing Hants Record Office 23M 58/57b (fragment of York's accounts).

5. Keen, *England in the Later Middle Ages*, 362, 355; Johnson, 16, 17, 25 148n., 231; Stevenson (ed.), *Letters and Papers*, II, 2, [585]; Ross, *Edward IV*, 263 (jewels – see also CPR Edward IV, 1461–7, 96); Griffiths, *The Reign of Henry VI*, 674, 704.

6. For Suffolk see *English Suits*, 306–7; Berry Herald, 138. For the Cotton affair see Smith, 'Fastolf'.

7. *ODNB* (Suffolk); Anthony Smith, 'Fastolf', 118–20; Richmond, FS&P, 82 n. 34, and Smith's addendum, 101. Jacob, 487; Dunn, 'Margaret of Anjou, Queen Consort of Henry VI', 134 n. 95.

8. H S Bennett, *Chaucer and the Fifteenth Century* (Oxford, Clarendon Press, 1948), 121; FP 47, which is two documents – one in English and the other in Latin – attached by a single seal. I confess that I would have found it impossible to read, let alone understand, these without Richmond's article, FS&P, esp. 74. See also Smith's learned postscript.

9. *RP*, V, 266a and 452b.

10. CCR 1447–54, 398 (1st Schedule); Smith, 'Fastolf', 153.

11. The report is reproduced as an appendix to Armstrong, 'Politics and the Battle of St Albans'.

12. Barber (ed.), *The Pastons*, 72; FP 48 and 49; Rose, 'Litigation and conflict in fifteenth-century East Anglia', 55 n. 8.

13. Anstis, especially 141. See also Diana Dunn, 'Margaret of Anjou, chivalry and the Order of the Garter', 49–51.

14. Davis (ed.), *PL&P*, III, 986: 15–19.

15. Richmond, FS&P, 81–2; Richmond, 'East Anglian politics and society', 185; Rose, 'Litigation and conflict in fifteenth-century East Anglia'; Watts, 219; Castor, *The King, the Crown and the Duchy of Lancaster*, 120–4, 145–55; Burne, 326–7.

16. Smith, 'Fastolf', 118–20.

17. *ODNB* (Scales); Smith, ' "My confessors" ', 69.

18. Rose, 'Litigation and conflict in fifteenth-century East Anglia', 62–5, 74; Griffiths, *The Reign of Henry VI*, 589.

19. Davis (ed.), *PL&P*, III, 996: 33–4.

20. Ibid., 1008: 22–7.

21. Armstrong, 'Politics and the Battle of St Albans', 4; G E Cokayne (ed.), *The Complete Peerage*, vol. 11 (London, 1949), Appendix C, esp. 102.

22. A conclusion which accords with that reached by Smith, 'Fastolf', 220.

23. Griffiths, *The Reign of Henry VI*, 131, 133, 136 (Talbot); 300–1.

Chapter 10: The Legacy

1. McFarlane, *EFC*, 203 n. 28, citing FP 72 membrane 7 and BL Sloane 4 fo 38v.

2. Pestell, 40.

3. Richmond, FW, 184–6.

4. Simon Payling, 'War and peace: military and administrative service among the English gentry in the reign of Henry VI', in Coss and Tyerman (eds), *Soldiers, Nobles and Gentlemen*, 245.

5. *BON*, p. li (note a) citing the Paston Letters; Bennett, *Chaucer and the Fifteenth Century*, 123, 125.

6. FP 43; McFarlane, *Nobility of Later Medieval England*, 237; McFarlane, *EFC*, 210, 218; Harriss, *Shaping the Nation*, 561; *ODNB* (Scrope); Hawkyard, 60–2; Wakelin, 103, 123; Stanley Gillam, *The Divinity School and Duke Humfrey's Library at Oxford* (Oxford, Clarendon Press, 1988), 2; Stratford, 52; Contamine, 210; Anne F Sutton

and Livia Visser-Fuchs, 'Choosing a book in late fifteenth-century England and the Low Countries', in Barron and Saul (eds), *England and the Low Countries*, 79.

7. Beadle, 99.
8. See Bühler's introduction to Scrope's translation, in the Early English Text Series, and Appendix A thereto; Chance's Preface and Introduction to her translation of Christine de Pisan's *Epistle*, pp. viii, 5; and Hughes.
9. *Dicts and Sayings*, pp. xxiv, xxxvii, 54.
10. For the Statutes see Jefferson in *EHR* (1994). I am grateful to Maurice Keen for this reference.
11. McFarlane, *Nobility of Later Medieval England*, 44.
12. Taylor, 66.
13. Burne, 219, 223; College of Arms, M9 ff 31–66v. The chronicle was rediscovered there in the 1920s by Benedicta Rowe. I am most grateful to Maurice Keen and to Jeremy Catto for allowing me to read a typescript. There is valuable comment on it in Anne Curry, *The Battle of Agincourt: Sources and Interpretations* (Woodbridge, Boydell Press, 2000).
14. Rowe, 'A contemporary account of the Hundred Years' War'. For Hanson and the surrender of Le Mans, see Stevenson (ed.), *Letters and Papers*, II, 2, [691].
15. BC 44v.
16. Rowe, 'A contemporary account of the Hundred Years' War'; McFarlane, *EFC*, 211; Curry, *The Battle of Agincourt: Sources and Interpretations*, 86; Taylor, 84.
17. Taylor, 84.
18. McFarlane, *EFC*, 222.
19. McFarlane, *EFC*, 203, citing FP 72, membrane 7; *JBP*, 340; McFarlane, *EFC*, 203, 201, n. 10.
20. *BON*, 28, 37.
21. Ibid., 64–5.
22. Ibid., 31, 68.
23. Ibid., 80–1, 42.
24. Stevenson (ed.), *Letters and Papers*, II, 2, [721].
25. *BON*, 29, 51, 72, 85; and Catherine Halsey's article on www.york.ac.uk: 'Reforming England's "harde covetouse hert".'
26. Worcester suggests a remedy in the *BON*, at pp. 80–5, which is that the Crown should rule justly, as St Louis had done in thirteenth-century France, and that the subject should be prepared to give money freely, by way of gift rather than loan.

Conclusion: Fastolf and the Hundred Years' War

1. See Ian Mortimer, 'What Hundred Years War?', *History Today* (October 2009).
2. Reid, 278.
3. Henry Ellis (ed.), *Original Letters Illustrative of English History* (2nd series: London, 1827), I, 76; McFarlane, *Letters to Friends*, 31.
4. Seward, 14, 225; Fowler, 171.
5. BC 45v; Monstrelet, *Chronicles*, I, 394.

Bibliography

Manuscript Sources

The National Archives (TNA)

Exchequer, Records of the Treasury of the Receipt
E 40/637

Exchequer, King's Remembrancer
E 101/44/30 roll 1 no.1
E 101/44/30 roll 2
E 101/46/24
E 101/47/39
E 101/50/4
E 101/50/5
E 101/50/24
E 101/50/25
E 101/185/6 no. 2
E 101/186/2 no. 117
E 101/322/37

Foreign Account Rolls
E 364/79

Alien subsidy roll for Wiltshire
E 179/196/100

Records of the Court of Chancery (also of the Wardrobe and Royal Household)
C 1/12/268
C 1/15/335
C 1/18/27
C 1/19/115
C 1/26/621
C 1/52/90
C 8/703, 3334A and B

Special collections: Court Rolls

SC 2/192/49

Record Commission Transcripts, Series II
PRO 31/8/135
SP 46/123/fo 7,7d

The British Library
BL Additional Charters 1403, 6903, 6905, 7944, 11791, 47305
BL Additional Manuscripts 24511 f 89, 36988 fv
Arundel 26f
Sloane 4046 f66

Magdalen College, Oxford
The Fastolf Papers 9, 26, 42, 47, 63, 64, 69, 72, 85(2)
Magdalen College Archives Misc. 306

The Bodleian Library, Oxford
Ms Fr. d 10 (an abbreviated version of the *Journal d'un bourgeois de Paris*)

The College of Arms
Ms M9 ff 31–66v (Basset's Chronicle)

Norfolk Record Office
Phi/612/7–8

Bibliothèque Nationale de France (Paris)
Manuscrit français 25766, pièce 810

Printed Primary Sources

Actes de la Chancellerie d'Henri VI Concernant La Normandie, ed. Paul le Cacheux (Rouen and Paris, 1907)

Allmand, C T, 'Documents relating to the Anglo-French negotiations of 1439', *Camden Miscellany*, 24 (1972)

The Annals of Loch Cé, ed. W M Hennessy (Longman & Co., 1871)

Armorial of the Peace of Arras, ed. Steen Clemmenson (Copenhagen, 2006)

Bailey, Mark, Maureen Jurkowski and Carol Rawcliffe (eds), *Poverty and Wealth: Sheep, Taxation and Charity in Late Medieval Norfolk* (Norfolk Record Society, volume 71, 2007)

Barber, Richard (ed.), *The Pastons: A Family in the Wars of the Roses* (London, Folio Society, 1981)

Basin, Thomas, *Histoire de Charles VII*, ed. and trans. C Samaran, 2 vols (Paris 1933)

The Beauchamp Pageant, ed. and intro. Alexandra Sinclair (Richard III and Yorkist History Trust, 2003)

Berry Herald, *Les Chroniques du Roi Charles VI, par Gilles le Bouvier*, ed. H Courteault and L Celier (Paris, 1979)

The Black Book of the Admiralty, ed. Sir Thomas Twiss (London, 1871)

Bower, Walter, *Scotichronicon*, vol. 8, Books 15 and 16, ed. D E R Watt (Aberdeen University Press, 1987)

Brie, F W D (ed.), *The Brut, or the Chronicles of England*, 2 vols, Early English Text Society, nos 131 and 136 (1906–8)

Calendar of Plea and Memoranda Rolls of the City of London 1413–1437 and 1437–1457 (Cambridge University Press, 1943 and 1954)

Christine de Pisan, *The Book of Deeds of Arms and of Chivalry*, ed. S Willard, trans. C C Willard (Pennsylvania State University Press, 1999)

——, *The Epistle of Othea*, trans. Stephen Scrope, ed. Curt F Bühler, Early English Text Society, no. 264 (London, Oxford University Press, 1970)

——, *Epistle of Othea to Hector*, trans. and intro. Jane Chance (Cambridge, D S Brewer, 1997)

Chronique du Mont-Saint-Michel (1343–1468), ed. Siméon Luce (Paris 1879)

Cochon, Pierre, *Chronique Normande de Pierre Cochon*, ed. Charles de Robillard de Beaurepaire (Rouen, 1870)

Davis, Norman (ed.), *The Paston Letters* (Oxford World's Classics, 1999)

——, *Paston Letters and Papers of the Fifteenth Century*, Early English Text Society, suppl. ser. 21 and 22, 3 vols (Oxford University Press, 2004–5)

The Dicts and Sayings of the Philosophers, trans. Stephen Scrope, William Worcetser et al., ed. Curt F Bühler, Early English Text Society, no. 211 (Oxford, Oxford University Press, 1941)

Don Pero Niño, *The Unconquered Knight: A Chronicle of the Deeds of Don Pero Niño*, trans. and selected by Joan Evans (Kessinger Reprints; New York, Harcourt, Brace & Co., 1928)

Duparc, Pierre (ed.), *Procès en Nullité de la Condamnation de Jeanne d'Arc*, 5 vols (Paris, 1977)

English Suits Before the Parlement of Paris 1420–1436, ed. C T Allmand and C A J Armstrong, Camden Fourth Series 26 (London, 1982)

Expeditions to Prussia and the Holy Land made by Henry Earl of Derby in the Years 1390–1391 and 1392–1393, ed. L Toulmin Smith, Camden Society, vol. 52 (London, 1894)

Fauquembergue, Clément de, *Journal de Clément de Fauquembergue, Greffier du Parlement de Paris, 1417–35*, 3 vols (Paris, 1909)

The First Life of Henry V, written in 1513 by an anonymous author commonly known as The Translator of Livius, ed. C L Kingsford (Oxford, 1911)

Fortescue, Sir John, *De Laudibus Legum Angliae*, ed. and trans. S B Chrimes, (Cambridge University Press, 1942)

——, *On the Laws and Governance of England*, ed. Shelley Lockwood (Cambridge University Press, 1997)

Froissart, Sir John, *Chronicles of England, France, Spain and the Adjoining Countries from the Latter Part of the Reign of Edward II to the Coronotion of Henry IV*, trans. Thomas Johnes,2 vols (London, 1848)

Gairdner, James (ed.), *The Paston Letters* (Edinburgh, 1910)

Gesta Henrici Quinti: The Deeds of Henry V, trans. and ed. Frank Taylor and John S Roskell (Oxford, Clarendon Press, 1975)

Holinshed, Raphael, *Holinshed's Chronicles of England, Scotland and Ireland*, vol. 3 (London, [1587] 1808)

The Hundred Tales (Les Cent Nouvelles Nouvelles), trans. Rossell Hope Robbins (New York, Bonanza, 1960)

Jessopp, A (ed.), *Visitations of the Diocese of Norwich (1492–1532)*, Camden New Series, 43 (London, 1888)

John Page's Siege of Rouen, ed. Herbert Huscher (Leipzig, 1927)

Journal d'un bourgeois de Paris ed. C Beaune, (Paris, Librairie Générale Française, 1990)

Juvénal des Ursins, Jean, *Histoire de Charles VI* in *Nouvelle Collection des Mémoires pour servir à l'histoire de France*, ed. J F Michaud and J J F Poujoulat (Paris 1836)

le Cacheux, Paul (ed.), *Rouen au temps de Jeanne d'Arc* (Paris and Rouen, 1891)

Longnon, A, *Paris sous la domination anglaise* (Paris, Champion, 1878)

Malory, Sir Thomas, *Le Morte d'Arthur* (London, Everyman's Library, 1961)

Le Mistère du siège d'Orléans: Collection des documents inédits sur l'histoire de France (Paris, 1862)

Monstrelet, *The Chronicles of Enguerrand de Monstrelet*, trans. Thomas Johnes, 2 vols (London, 1845)

The Norman Rolls (Rotuli Normanniae), vol. 1, ed. T D Hardy (London, 1835)

Nouvelle Collection des Mémoires pour servir à l'histoire de France, ed. J F Michaud and J J F Poujoulat, vol. 3 (Paris, 1837)

The Parliament Rolls of Medieval England 1275–1504, ed. Chris Given-Wilson (Woodbridge, Boydell Press, 2005)

Proceedings and Ordinances of the Privy Council of England, ed. Sir Harris Nicolas (1834)

Records of the Guild of St George, Norwich, ed. Mary Grace (Norfolk Record Society, vol. 9, 1937)

Registres de la Jurade, 1414–1416 et 1420–22 (Bordeaux, 1883)

Rotuli Parliamentorum (The Rolls of Parliament), ed. John Strachey (London, 1767–77)

Rymer, Thomas, *Foedera* (2nd edition; London, J Tonson, 1729)

Stevenson, Reverend Joseph, *Letters and Papers Illustrative of the Wars of the English in France During the Reign of Henry VI King of England*, 3 vols (London, Longman, Green & Co., 1861–4; reproduced by Elibron Classics, 2007)

Strecche, John, *The Chronicle of John Strecche for the Reign of Henry V*, ed. Frank Taylor (Manchester University Press, 1932)

Vegetius, *Epitome of Military Science*, ed. N P Milner (Liverpool University Press, 2001)

Waurin, Jehan de, *Recueil des Croniques et Anciennes Istories de la Grant Bretagne à préesent nommé Engleterre*, ed. William Hardy (London, Longman, 1864–79)

Worcester, William, *The Boke of Noblesse*, ed. J G Nichols (London, Roxburghe Club, 1860)

——, *Itineraries*, ed. John H Harvey (Oxford, 1969)

Secondary Sources

Allmand, Christopher, 'The *De Re Militari* of Vegetius', *History Today* (June 2004)

Allmand, C T, *Henry V* (London, Methuen, 1992)

——, *The Hundred Years' War: England and France at War c.1300–c.1450* (Cambridge University Press, 1989)

——, *Lancastrian Normandy 1415–1450: The History of a Medieval Occupation* (Oxford, Clarendon Press, 1983)

—— (ed.), *War, Literature and Politics in the Late Middle Ages* (New York, Barnes & Noble, 1976)

Allmand, Christopher and Maurice Keen, 'History and the literature of war: the "Boke of Noblesse" of William Worcester', in Christopher Allmand (ed.), *War, Government and Power in Late Medieval France* (Liverpool University Press, 2000)

Amyot, Thomas, 'Transcript of two rolls, containing an inventory of effects formerly belonging to Sir John Fastolf', *Archaeologia*, 21 (1827)

Anstis, John (ed.), *The Register of the Most Noble Order of the Garter, called The Black Book* (1724)

Archer, Rowena E (ed.), *Crown, Government and People in the Fifteenth Century* (Stroud, Alan Sutton, 1995)

Archer, Rowena E, 'The Mowbrays, Earls of Nottingham and Dukes of Norfolk, to 1432' (unpublished PhD thesis, Oxford, 1984)

—— and Simon Walker (eds), *Rulers and Ruled in Late Medieval England* (London, Hambledon Press, 1995)

Armstrong, C A J, 'Politics and the Battle of St Albans', *Bulletin of the Institute of Historical Research*, 33: 98 (May 1960)

——, 'Sir John Fastolf and the law of arms', in Allmand (ed.), *War Literature and Politics*

Asklund, Jacques, *Histoire des rues de Beaugency* (Beaugency, 1984)

Backhouse, Janet, *The Bedford Hours* (British Library, 1990)

Barker, Juliet, *Agincourt: The King, the Campaign, the Battle* (Abacus, 2006)

Barron, Caroline and Nigel Saul (eds), *England and the Low Countries in the Late Middle Ages* (Sutton Publishing, 1995)

Beadle, Richard, 'Sir John Fastolf's French books', in Denis Renevey and Graham D Caie (eds), *Medieval Texts in Context* (Routledge, 2008)

Bennett, H S, 'Sir John Fastolf', in idem, *Six Medieval Men and Women* (Cambridge University Press, 1955)

Bennett, Matthew, 'The development of battle tactics in the Hundred Years War', www.deremilitari.org/resources/articles/bennett2.htm

Biographia Britannica (2nd edition; London, John Nichols, 1793), vol. 5

Bryson, Bill, *Shakespeare* (HarperPress, 2007)

Burne, Lt-Colonel Alfred H, *The Agincourt War* (Eyre & Spottiswoode, 1956)

Butler, Raymond Reagan, *Is Paris Lost? The English Occupation 1422–1436* (Spellmount, 2003)

Carlin, Martha, 'Sir John Fastolf's Place, Southwark: the home of the Duke of York's family 1460', *The Ricardian*, 5 (1981)

——, *Medieval Southwark* (London, Hambledon Press, 1996)

Carpenter, David, *The Struggle for Mastery: Britain, 1066–1284*, The Penguin History of Britain (Penguin, 2004)

Carus-Wilson, E M, 'Evidences of industrial growth of some fifteenth-century manors', *Economic History Review* (1959)

Castor, Helen, *Blood and Roses* (Faber & Faber, 2005)

——, 'The Duchy of Lancaster and the rule of East Anglia, 1399–1400: a prologue to the Paston Letters', in R E Archer (ed.), *Crown, Government and People in the Fifteenth Century*

——, *The King, the Crown and the Duchy of Lancaster* (Oxford University Press, 2000)

Clark, Linda (ed.), *The Fifteenth Century*, vol. 5: *Of Mice and Men: Image, Belief and Regulation in Late Medieval England* (Woodbridge, Boydell Press, 2005)

—— (ed.), *The Fifteenth Century*, vol. 8: *Rule, Redemption and Representations in Late Medieval England and France* (Woodbridge, Boydell Press, 2008)

Collins, Hugh, 'Sir John Fastolf, John Lord Talbot and the dispute over Patay: ambition and chivalry in the fifteenth century', in Diana Dunn (ed.), *War and Society in Early Modern Britain* (Liverpool University Press, 2000)

——, *The Order of the Garter 1348–1461: Chivalry and Politics in Late Medieval England* (Oxford, 2000)

Contamine, Philippe, *War in the Middle Ages*, trans. Michael Jones (Oxford, Blackwell, 1992)

Cosgrove, Art (ed.), *A New History of Ireland*, vol. 2: *Medieval Ireland* (Oxford University Press, 1987)

Coss, Peter, *The Origins of the English Gentry* (Cambridge University Press, 2003)

Coss, Peter and Christopher Tyerman (eds), *Soldiers, Nobles and Gentlemen: Essays in Honour of Maurice Keen* (Woodbridge, Boydell Press, 2009)

Crosland, Jessie, *Sir John Fastolfe: A Medieval 'Man of Property'* (London, Peter Owen, 1970)

Curry, Anne, *Agincourt: A New History* (Tempus, 2006)

——, 'The first English standing army? Military organisation in Lancastrian Normandy 1420–50', in Charles Ross (ed.), *Patronage, Pedigree and Power in Later Medieval England*

——, *The Hundred Years' War* (Osprey, 2002)

——, 'The military ordinances of Henry V: texts and contexts', in C Given-Wilson et al. (eds), *War, Government and Aristocracy in the British Isles, c.1150–1500: Essays in Honour of Michael Prestwich* (Woodbridge, Boydell Press, 2008)

——, 'Sex and the soldier in Lancastrian Normandy, 1415–1450', www.deremilitari.org/resources/pdfs/curry2.pdf

Curtis, Edmund, *A History of Medieval Ireland* (Methuen, 1923)

Cuttler, S H, 'A report to Sir John Fastolf on the trial of Jean, duke of Alençon', *English Historical Review* (1981)

Deedes, Cecil (ed.), 'Original letters of Sir John Fastolf', *Notes & Queries*, 12 (1909)

Dickinson, J G, *The Congress of Arras 1435* (New York, 1972)

Ditcham, B H, 'The Employment of Foreign Mercenary Troops in the French Royal Armies, 1415–1470' (PhD thesis, University of Edinburgh, 1978): www.deremilitari.org/resources/articles/ditcham1.htm

Dockray, Keith, *Warrior King: The Life of Henry V* (Tempus, 2007)

—— and Peter Fleming (eds), *People, Places and Perspectives: Essays on Later Medieval and Early Tudor England in honour of Ralph A. Griffiths* (Stroud, Nonsuch, 2005)

Doig, James A, 'Propaganda, public opinion and the siege of Calais in 1436', in R E Archer (ed.), *Crown, Government and People in the Fifteenth Century*

Dunn, Diana, 'Margaret of Anjou, Chivalry and the Order of the Garter', in Colin Richmond and Eileen Scarff (eds), *St George's Chapel, Windsor, in the Late Middle Ages*, Historical Monographs concerning the Chapel, 17 (Windsor, 2001)

——, 'Margaret of Anjou, Queen Consort of Henry VI: a reassessment of her role,

1445–53', in R E Archer (ed.), *Crown, Government and People in the Fifteenth Century*

——, 'The Queen at war: the role of Margaret of Anjou in the Wars of the Roses', in Diana Dunn (ed.), *War and Society in Early Modern Britain*

Duthie, D W, *The Case of Sir John Fastolf* (London, Smith, Elder & Co., 1907)

Fortescue, The Rt Hon J W, *A History of the British Army*, vol. 1 (The Naval & Military Press, 2004)

Fowler, Kenneth, *Plantagenet and Valois* (Elek Books, 1967)

Girault, Pierre-Gilles, *Jeanne d'Arc* (éditions Jean-Paul Gisserot, 2003)

Goodman, Anthony, *The Wars of the Roses* (Tempus, 2005)

Gransden, Antonia, *Historical Writing in England*, vol. 2 (Routledge & Kegan Paul, 1982)

Greenblatt, Stephen, *Will in the World* (Pimlico, 2005)

Griffiths, R A, *The Reign of Henry VI* (Sutton, 2004)

——, 'The sense of dynasty in the reign of Henry VI', in Charles Ross (ed.), *Patronage, Pedigree and Power in Later Medieval England*

Hall, Edward, *The Union of the Two Noble and Illustre [sic] Families of Lancaster & York* (London, [1548] 1808)

Harcourt, L W V, 'The two John Fastolfs', *Transactions of the Royal Historical Society*, 3rd series, 4 (1910)

Harper-Bill, Christopher (ed.), *Medieval East Anglia* (Woodbridge, Boydell Press, 2005)

Harriss, Gerald, *Shaping the Nation: England 1360–1461*, The New Oxford History of England (Oxford, 2005)

Harvey, I M W, *Jack Cade's Rebellion of 1450* (Oxford, Clarendon Press, 1991)

Haward, Winifred I, 'Economic aspects of the Wars of the Roses in East Anglia', *English Historical Review*, (1926)

Hawkyard, Alasdair, 'Sir John Fastolf's "Gret Mansion by me Late Edified": Caister Castle, Norfolk', in Linda Clark (ed.), *The Fifteenth Century*, vol. 5

Hill, P R, *The Story of Caister Castle and Car Collection* (a guide to Caister by the owner)

Hilton, R H, 'The content and sources of English agrarian history before 1500', *Agricultural History Review*, 3 (1955)

Hughes, Jonathan, 'Stephen Scrope and the circle of Sir John Fastolf: moral and intellectual outlooks', in *Medieval Knighthood IV: Papers from the fifth Strawberry Hill Conference, 1990* (Woodbridge, Boydell Press, 1992)

Jacob, E F, *The Fifteenth Century*, Oxford History of England (Oxford, 1961, 1997)

Jefferson, Linda, 'MS Arundel 48 and the earliest statutes of the Order of the Garter', *English Historical Review* (1994)

Johnson, P A, *Richard Duke of York 1411–1460* (Oxford, Clarendon Press, 1988)

Jones, Michael, 'John Beaufort, Duke of Somerset and the expedition of 1443', in R A Griffiths (ed.), *Patronage, the Crown and the Provinces in Later Medieval England* (Gloucester, Sutton, 1981)

Jones, Michael K, *Agincourt 1415* (Barnsley, Pen & Sword, 2005)

——, 'The Battle of Verneuil: towards a history of courage', *War in History*, 9 (2002)

——, 'Somerset, York and the Wars of the Roses', *English Historical Review* (1989)

Keen, Maurice, *Chivalry* (Yale University Press, 1984)

——, *England in the Later Middle Ages* (2nd edition; Routledge, 2003)

——, *English Society in the Later Middle Ages* (Penguin, 1990)

——, *The Laws of War in the Late Middle Ages* (Gregg Revivals, 1993)

—— (ed.), *Medieval Warfare: A History* (Oxford, 1999)

——, *Nobles, Knights and Men-at-Arms in the Middle Ages* (London, Hambledon Press, 1996)

——, *Origins of the English Gentleman* (Tempus, 2002)

Keen, M H and M J Daniel, 'English diplomacy and the sack of Fougères', *History* (1974)

Kekewich, Margaret L, *The Good King René of Anjou and Fifteenth Century Europe* (Palgrave Macmillan, 2008)

Kekewich, Margaret L and Susan Rose, *Britain, France and the Empire 1350–1500* (Palgrave Macmillan, 2005)

Lewis, P S, 'Sir John Fastolf's lawsuit over Titchwell, 1448–55', *Historical Journal*, 1: 1 (1958)

Lloyd, Alan, *The Hundred Years' War* (Book Club Associates, 1977)

London, H S, 'Badges of Sir John Fastolf and John, Lord Wenlock', *Notes & Queries*, 193 (1948)

Marin, Jean-Yves (ed.), *La Normandie dans la guerre de Cent Ans 1346–1450: Textes réunis par Jean-Yves Marin* (Caen, Musée de Normandie et Rouen, Musée départemental, 1999–2000)

Mason, R Hindry, *The History of Norfolk* (London, 1884)

Massey, Robert, 'The land settlement in Lancastrian Normandy', in A J Pollard (ed.), *Property and Politics: Essays in Later Medieval English History* (Palgrave Macmillan, 1984)

McFarlane, K B, *England in the Fifteenth Century* (London, Hambledon Press, 1981)

——, 'The investment of Sir John Fastolf's profits of war', in *England in the Fifteenth Century*

——, *Lancastrian Kings and Lollard Knights*, Academic Monograph Reprints (Oxford University Press, 1972)

——, *Letters to Friends, 1940–1966*, ed. Gerald Harriss (Magdalen College, Oxford, 1997)

——, *The Nobility of Later Medieval England* (Oxford, 1973)

Mercer, Malcolm, *Henry V: The Rebirth of Chivalry* (The National Archives, 2004)

Meron, Theodor, *Bloody Constraint: War and Chivalry in Shakespeare* (Oxford University Press, 1998)

Mortimer, Ian, *The Fears of Henry IV* (Jonathan Cape, 2007)

Newhall, R A, 'Bedford's ordinances on the watch of September 1428', *English Historical Review* (1935)

——, *The English Conquest of Normandy 1416–24* (New Haven, 1924)

——, *Muster and Review: A Problem of English Military Administration 1420–40* (Yale, 1940)

Nichols, J G, 'The appointment of Sir John Fastolf as Keeper of the Bastille of St Anthony at Paris', *Archaeologia*, 44: 1 (1873)

Oman, Sir Charles, *A History of the Art of War in the Middle Ages*, vol. 2: *1278–1485* (Greenhill Books, 1991)

Oxford Dictionary of National Biography (2nd edition; Oxford University Press, 2004)

Pernoud, Régine, *The Retrial of Joan of Arc: The Evidence for her Vindication* (San Francisco, Ignatius Press, 2007)

——, *Trente Journées qui ont fait la France* (Gallimard, 1969)

Perroy, Édouard, *The Hundred Years War* (London, Eyre & Spottiswoode, 1965)

Pestell, Tim, *St Benet's Abbey* (Norfolk Archaeological Trust, 1988)

Pettifer, Adrian, *English Castles: A Guide by Counties* (Woodbridge, Boydell Press, 1995)

Pollard, A J, *Sir John Talbot and the War in France 1427–1453* (Barnsley, Pen & Sword, 2005)

Puiseux, Léon, *Siège et prise de Caen par les anglais* (Caen, 1858)

——, *Siège et prise de Rouen par les anglais* (Caen, 1867)

Rawcliffe, C and R Wilson (eds), *Medieval Norwich* (Hambledon and London, 2004)

Reboul, Col. F, *Des Croisades à la Revolution*, in *Histoire de la Nation Française* (ed. G Hanotaux), Tome VII, vol. 1 (Paris, 1925)

Reid, Peter, *Medieval Warfare: The Rise and Fall of English Supremacy at Arms 1314–1485* (London, Robinson, 2008)

Renouard, Yves, *Bordeaux sous les rois d'Angleterre* (Bordeaux, 1965)

Rhymer, Lucy, 'Humphrey, Duke of Gloucester and the City of London', in Linda Clark (ed.), *The Fifteenth Century*, vol. 8

Richey, Stephen W, 'Joan of Arc: a military appreciation', www.stjoan-center.com/military/stephenr.html

Richmond, Colin, 'East Anglian politics and society in the fifteenth century, reflections 1956–2003', in Harper-Bill (ed.), *Medieval East Anglia*

——, 'Once again: Fastolf's will', in Dockray and Fleming (eds), *People, Places and Perspectives*

——, *The Paston Family in the Fifteenth Century: Fastolf's Will* (Cambridge University Press, 2002)

——, 'Sir John Fastolf, the Duke of Suffolk, and the Pastons', in Linda Clark (ed.), *The Fifteenth Century*, vol. 8.

Rodger, N A M, *The Safeguard of the Sea: A Naval History of Britain*, vol. 1 (HarperCollins, 1997)

Rose, Jonathan, 'Fastolf and the founding of Magdalen College', *Magdalen College Record* (2003)

——, 'Litigation and conflict in fifteenth-century East Anglia: conspiracy and attaint actions and Sir John Fastolf', *Journal of Legal History*, 27 (2006)

Rose, Susan, *Calais: An English Town in France 1347–1558* (Woodbridge, Boydell Press, 2008)

Ross, Charles, *Edward IV* (Yale, 1997)

—— (ed.), *Patronage, Pedigree and Power in Later Medieval England* (Gloucester, Alan Sutton, 1979)

Rowe, B J H, 'A contemporary account of the Hundred Years' War from 1415–27', *English Historical Review* (1926)

——, 'Discipline in the Norman garrisons under Bedford, 1422–35', *English Historical Review* (1931)

——, 'The estates of Normandy under the Duke of Bedford, 1422–35', *English Historical Review* (1931)

——, 'The Grand Conseil under the Duke of Bedford, 1422–35', in *Oxford Essays in Medieval History (presented to E. H. Salter)* (Oxford, Clarendon Press, 1934)

——, 'John Duke of Bedford and the Norman brigands', *English Historical Review* (1932)

Rowse, A L, *Historians I Have Known* (Duckworth, 1995)

Saccio, Peter, *Shakespeare's English Kings: History, Chronicle and Drama* (Oxford University Press, 1977)

Salih, Sarah, 'Two travellers' tales', in Harper-Bill (ed.), *Medieval East Anglia*

Scattergood, V J and J W Sherborne (eds), *English Court Culture in the Later Middle Ages* (New York, St Martin's Press, 1983)

Schama, Simon, *A History of Britain*, vol. 1: At the Edge of the World (BBC, 2000)

Scrope, Sir G Poulett, *History of the Manor and Ancient Barony of Castle Combe* (privately printed, 1852)

Seward, Desmond, *The Hundred Years War* (Constable, 1996)

Simpson, Martin, 'The campaign of Verneuil', *English Historical Review* (1934)

Slater, Stephen, *The Illustrated Book of Heraldry* (Hermes House, 2006)

Smith, Anthony Robert, 'Aspects of the Career of Sir John Fastolf (1380–1459)' (unpublished PhD thesis, Oxford, 1982)

——, 'The greatest man of that age: the acquisition of Sir John Fastolf's East Anglian estates', in Archer and Walker (eds), *Rulers and Ruled in Late Medieval England*

Smith, Anthony, 'Litigation and politics: Sir John Fastolf's defence of his English property', in A J Pollard (ed.), *Property and Politics: Essays in Later Medieval English History* (Palgrave Macmillan, 1984)

——, ' "My Confessors have exorted me gretely ther too": Sir John Fastolf's dispute with Hickling Priory', in Colin Richmond and Eileen Scarff (eds), *St George's Chapel, Windsor, in the Late Middle Ages*, Historical Monographs concerning the Chapel, vol. 17 (Windsor, 2001)

Sot, Michel, Jean-Patrice Boudet and Anita Guerreau-Jalabert, *Le moyen âge: histoire culturelle de la France*, vol. 1 (éditions du Seuil, 1997)

Spufford, Peter, *Power and Profit: The Merchant in Medieval Europe* (London, Thames & Hudson, 2002)

Stratford, Jenny, *The Bedford Inventories* (London, Society of Antiquaries, 1993)

Strickland, Matthew and Robert Hardy, *The Great Warbow* (Sutton Publishing, 2005)

Sweetman, David, *Medieval Castles of Ireland* (Cork, Collins Press, 1999)

Talbot, Hugh, *The English Achilles* (Chatto & Windus, 1981)

Taylor, Craig, 'English writings on chivalry and warfare during the Hundred Years War', in Coss and Tyerman (eds), *Soldiers, Nobles and Gentlemen*

Thompson, Guy Llewelyn, *Paris and Its People under English Rule: The Anglo–Burgundian Regime 1420–1436* (Oxford, Clarendon Press, 1991)

Tout, T F, *Chapters in Administrative History* (Manchester, 1928–37)

Tuck, Anthony, 'Why men fought in the 100 Years War', *History Today*, 33: 4 (April 1983)

Turner, Dawson, *Sketch of the History of Caister Castle* (London, 1842)

Urban, William, *Medieval Mercenaries: The Business of War* (London, Greenhill Books, 2006)

Vale, M G A, *The Ancient Enemy* (Continuum, 2007)

——, *Charles VII* (University of California, 1974)

——, *English Gascony 1399–1453* (Oxford University Press, 1970)

——, 'New techniques and old ideals: the impact of artillery on war and chivalry at the end of the Hundred Years' War', in Allmand (ed.), *War, Literature and Politics in the Late Middle Ages*

——, 'Sir John Fastolf's report of 1435: a new interpretation reconsidered', *Nottingham Medieval Studies*, 17 (1953)

Vaughan, Richard, *Philip the Good* (Woodbridge, Boydell Press, 2002)

Wakelin, Daniel, *Humanism, Reading and English Literature 1430–1530* (Oxford, 2007)

Watts, John, *Henry VI and the Politics of Kingship* (Cambridge, 1999)

Williams, E Carleton, *My Lord of Bedford, 1389–1435* (Longmans, 1963)

Wilson, H A, *Magdalen College*, University of Oxford College Histories (London, Robinson, 1899)

Wilson, J Dover, *The Fortunes of Falstaff* (Cambridge, 1961)

Wolffe, Bertram, *Henry VI* (Yale, 2001)

Wylie, J H, *The Reign of Henry V, 1415–16* (Cambridge University Press, 1919)

Some Websites

www.boltoncastle.co.uk

www.british-history.ac.uk

www.deremilitari.org

www.fr.wikipedia.org (in French)

www.hearthstone.co.uk

www.histoire-genealogie.com (in French)

www.history.ac.uk/makinghistory

www.historytoday.com

www.h-net.org/reviews

www.library.phila.gov/medieval/propaganda.htm

www.magd.ox.ac.uk/history

www.medievalsoldier.org

www.nationalarchives.gov.uk

www.norfarchtrust.org.uk/stbenets

www.richardiii.net

www.wikipedia.org

Index